The Bleak Political Implications of Socratic Religion

Also by Shadia B. Drury

Aquinas and Modernity: The Lost Promise of Natural Law (2008)
The Political Ideas of Leo Strauss (Updated Edition, 2005)
Terror and Civilization: Christianity, Politics and the Western Psyche (2004)
Leo Strauss and the American Right (1998)
Kojève and the Roots of Postmodern Politics (1994)
Chauvinism of the West (in progress)

Shadia B. Drury

The Bleak Political Implications of Socratic Religion

Shadia B. Drury
Department of Philosophy & Classics and Department of Politics
and International Studies
University of Regina
Regina, Saskatchewan, Canada

ISBN 978-3-319-85393-2   ISBN 978-3-319-54442-7 (eBook)
DOI 10.1007/978-3-319-54442-7

© The Editor(s) (if applicable) and The Author(s) 2017
Softcover reprint of the hardcover 1st edition 2017
This work is subject to copyright. All rights are solely and exclusively licensed by the Publisher, whether the whole or part of the material is concerned, specifically the rights of translation, reprinting, reuse of illustrations, recitation, broadcasting, reproduction on microfilms or in any other physical way, and transmission or information storage and retrieval, electronic adaptation, computer software, or by similar or dissimilar methodology now known or hereafter developed.
The use of general descriptive names, registered names, trademarks, service marks, etc. in this publication does not imply, even in the absence of a specific statement, that such names are exempt from the relevant protective laws and regulations and therefore free for general use.
The publisher, the authors and the editors are safe to assume that the advice and information in this book are believed to be true and accurate at the date of publication. Neither the publisher nor the authors or the editors give a warranty, express or implied, with respect to the material contained herein or for any errors or omissions that may have been made. The publisher remains neutral with regard to jurisdictional claims in published maps and institutional affiliations.

Cover illustration © iStock / Getty Images Plus

Printed on acid-free paper

This Palgrave Macmillan imprint is published by Springer Nature
The registered company is Springer International Publishing AG
The registered company address is: Gewerbestrasse 11, 6330 Cham, Switzerland

*In memory of my beloved
J. Dennis Drury*

Preface

Ever since his death by hemlock in 399 BCE, Socrates has been lionized as a fount of wisdom, virtue, and intellectual freedom—a whirlwind of insight whose philosophical prodding thrust humanity to unprecedented intellectual heights as well as spiritual depths. By subjecting conventional opinions to the tribunal of reason, he forced the West to transcend the puerile polytheism of Homer in favor of a moral vision that was loftier, more advanced, and more sublime. In the most shameful and cowardly act imaginable, Socrates was unjustly condemned to death by an ignorant Athenian mob, harboring a venomous aversion to his genius and his goodness. The death of Socrates was a backlash against the Greek Enlightenment by men who were eager to preserve the childish myths and superstitions of their society. However, they miscalculated, and lived to regret their dastardly deed: Socrates died a martyr for truth, reason, and morality. With the indispensable help of Plato, he bequeathed to the West a new and more responsible conception of the self, a new and more sophisticated conception of the good, and a new and more "advanced" conception of the divine. So the story goes. This is the legend of Socrates, created by Plato (and echoed through the ages) that this book sets out to challenge.

Those who follow Plato in valorizing Socrates have never explained the supreme historical enigma that is concealed by the legend. How can a sage who was pious and good be so closely associated with a treasonous opportunist such as Alcibiades who betrayed his city and contributed to her defeat in the Peloponnesian War? How can a sage who preached the supreme value of the moral life, and the importance of caring for the soul, have among his most intimate students and friends the likes of Critias and Charmides, the bloodthirsty leaders of the Thirty Tyrants who launched a reign of terror in Athens after her defeat in the Peloponnesian War? How can these criminal thugs (both relatives of Plato) appear in the dialogues without a word about the dastardly role they played in the history of Athens?

It cannot be irrelevant to discover that the closest associates of a man who dedicated his life to the moral improvement of the soul were guilty of criminal treachery and wickedness on a grand scale. It is not simply the case that some of the students of Socrates suffered from the vices that afflict ordinary mortals. No. Men such as Alcibiades surpassed ordinary humanity in ambition, cunning, lust, and self-absorption. Men such as Critias and Charmides surpassed all tyrants known to ancient historians in cruelty, violence, and murderous brutality. So, it is not simply that Socrates failed to teach virtue. The source of the mystery is that he failed so spectacularly. Anyone who is willing to attend to the historical facts of the case will soon realize that Plato's legend cannot begin to explain this enigma. On the contrary, Plato's dialogues unwittingly legitimize the case for the prosecution. When the religious and political ideas that Plato attributes to Socrates are taken together, it is easy to see how they could inspire political extremism.

The purpose of this book is twofold. First, to make sense of the case for the prosecution by showing that Plato's legend is divorced from the historical events surrounding the trial. The incriminating evidence—political as well as religious is overwhelming, and Plato's defense is inadequate. Indeed, Plato's own dialogues legitimize the case for the prosecution, because the totalitarian ideas of Plato's later dialogues cannot be separated from the ideas attributed to Socrates in the early dialogues—for they are the logical consequences of Socratic ideas. It is not difficult to see how the ardor, intolerance, and intemperance of these ideas could incite political violence and extremism.

The second objective of this book is to tackle Plato's defense on its own terms. Plato's defense of Socrates fails to address the issues head on. Instead, Plato turns the trial into a contest of ideas. He defends Socrates by arguing that the wisdom of Socrates was infinitely superior to the political naiveté and religious puerility of his contemporaries. I will argue that Plato's critique of Homer and the tragic poets is untenable. Their religious, moral, and political perspectives contain a degree of sobriety and moderation that have been eclipsed by Socratic innovations. It is my contention that the legend that Plato has created around Socrates has succeeded only because the ideas that Plato attributes to Socrates have triumphed in the history of the West. The point of this book is to argue that this triumph has been unfortunate and deleterious.

Section 1, "The Political Case Against Socrates," examines the historical context in which Socrates is tried and convicted. Socrates was not prosecuted because he disagreed with the democratic principles of the regime. He was not killed by the envy and resentment of the democratic mob. He was prosecuted because he was the teacher of Alcibiades, Critias, and Charmides. Three men who played leading roles in the defeat of Athens in the Peloponnesian War, the oligarchic coup of 404 BCE, and the reign of terror that followed. The prosecution was not motivated so much by revenge, as by fear for the future of Athens, in view of his radicalizing influence and its potentially calamitous results.

Section 2, "The Religious Case Against Socrates," examines the charge of impiety in the context of Greek civil religion. Impiety is generally connected to actions, and is therefore distinct from both atheism and heresy. Were it not for the fact that members of his inner circle were accused and convicted of disfiguring the Herms (statues of the god Hermes) and profaning the Eleusinian Mysteries in 415 BCE, the religious innovations of Socrates might have been treated with neglect. However, in view of what has transpired, the suspicion that his religious teaching incited the violence and treachery of the notorious members of the Socratic circle was only natural. The key to understanding the religious ideas of Socrates is Plato's *Euthyphro*, where the radically subversive Socratic conception of piety is revealed. Equally important is the influence of Orphism—the earliest of the mystery religions. The fact is that the religious ideas of Socrates have triumphed so completely in the West that it is difficult to see how lethal that triumph has been, and continues to be.

Section 3, "The Defense," focuses on those aspects of Plato and Xenophon's defense of Socrates that are relevant to the historical circumstances of the trial: the edict of the Thirty Tyrants, the case of Leon of Salamis, the case of the generals in the battle of Arginusae, Socrates' refusal to escape, and more. Despite the inadequacy of Plato's *Apology*, the legend of Socrates has not diminished thanks to the beguiling tropes that Plato has used to cement the legend of the innocent sage persecuted by the mob—the parable of the ship, the medical analogy, the care of the soul, the Socratic paradox—are all seriously flawed.

Section 4, "How Plato Legitimizes the Case for the Prosecution," explains how reading Plato's dialogues—especially the *Symposium, Protagoras,* and *Laws*—in light of the historical facts, allows us to see the legitimacy of the case for the prosecution. Scholars have long assumed that there is a dichotomy between the early dialogues influenced by Socrates, and the later dialogues in which Plato expresses his own ideas—ideas that are supposedly at odds with Socrates. It follows that the early dialogues provide a portrait of the historical Socrates, while the late dialogues indicate that Plato's ideas have parted company with the teacher of his youth. Contrary to this view, I hope to show that there is a seamless fit between the early and later dialogues. The repressive authoritarianism of Plato in the *Laws* follows logically from the ideas of Socrates as presented in the early dialogues. Far from being a betrayal of the Socratic spirit, as some have maintained, Plato's repressive authoritarianism is a logical consequence of the wedding of Socratic religion and politics. After all, it was the religion of Socrates that was made mandatory on pain of death in the *Laws*.

Section 5, "Plato's Critique of Homer Repudiated," challenges what is perhaps Plato's most powerful defense of Socrates—the defense that has had the greatest impact on posterity. According to Plato, Socrates was the best and wisest man of his time, and silencing him was silencing the true and the good. Even if Socrates rejected the gods of the city, so what? These Homeric gods were puerile and contemptible—based on lies that had morally deleterious effects. This chapter highlights the merits of Homeric religion that were eclipsed by the historical triumph of Socratic ideas. I argue that the myths of Homer are superior to the Orphic myths to which Socrates and Plato were committed.

Section 6, "The Tragic Poets Defended," recognizes that the Socratic objection to the tragic poets is philosophical. I reject the Hegelian view of tragedy as a conflict between equally valid moral claims. I also reject the related claim that Socrates is a tragic figure. Instead, I defend the view of tragedy as innocent suffering against the Socratic contention that no harm can come to a just man. Using Sophocles' *Philoctetes*, I illustrate why the portrait of the just man provided by Sophocles is both morally and intellectually superior to the Platonic ideal in which Socrates is the paradigm of the just man.

In Section 7, "Socratic Mischief," I catalogue the detrimental effects of Socratic religion analyzed in the book—the morally destructive burden of guilt, the repressive authoritarianism, the eclipse of pluralism, the alliance of religion and morality, the transformation of *hubris* into piety, and the fanaticism, zealotry, dualism, and nihilism that are unleashed as a result. Far from bequeathing to the West a more "advanced" conception of the divine as scholars from Hegel to Gregory Vlastos have argued, Socratic religion anticipated the conceits of monotheism, the intolerance of Christianity, the cruelty of priestly rule, the appetite for martyrdom, the criminalization of thought, and even the nihilism of postmodernity.

Finally, it is worth noting that this book is not a work of classical scholarship. Socrates cannot be confined to the classics because his influence has penetrated every field of study in the West. As a political philosopher concerned with the intersection of religion and politics, I believe that understanding the prodigious role played by Socrates in the history of the West is not merely an academic exercise. There is a sense in which Socrates is a microcosm of "the West." Like Socrates, the West claims to have a special access to a single universal truth, applicable to all humanity. Like Socrates, the West has been extravagant in its vanity, arrogance, and self-importance. Like Socrates, the West has a habit of disregarding its critics and refusing to tame its *hubris*.

Acknowledgments

Ever since I wrote my Master's thesis on Albert Camus with J. A. W. Gunn at Queen's university, I have admired the tragic perspective as more compatible with lived experience than the puerility of the Christian faith in cosmic justice. During my doctoral work at York University, I was fortunate to be the teaching assistant in a course on Plato and Aristotle, taught by Alan Cobb, who has remained my model of teaching excellence. The course I took in Greek language with Dr. Martin Cropp at the University of Calgary has been equally invaluable. Most of all, I wish to thank my colleagues at the University of Regina for a stimulating intellectual climate. I have fond memories of the evening discussions of Plato's *Laws* and other texts, led by George Marshall, in which Phillip Hansen, David Elliott, Eldon Soifer, and others participated. The endless postmodern challenges posed by Lynn Wells, Nicole Coté, and Carlos Londono helped me to recognize the arrogance of my unrepentant rationalism. I owe special thanks to Annabel Robinson, who read sizable parts of the manuscript, and taught me how to appreciate Achilles. I am beholden to Nils Claussen, who is the inspiration behind my comparison of tragedy as a popular genre with crime fiction. Even though he was disturbed by my views of his beloved Socrates, Béla Szabados encouraged me to pursue this project. My greatest debt is to Ken Leyton-Brown—without whose support I might not have embarked on this book. He allowed me to attend his lectures on the history of Greece, read parts of my manuscript, made excellent suggestions, and was totally unstinting with his time and knowledge. Earlier versions of some of these chapters were presented at the University of Maryland in D.C., Oakland University in Detroit, and Whitmore College in Walla Walla, Washington. My thanks to Jeanne Morefield of Whitmore College, the late Richard Burke, Mark Rigstad, and Elysa-Koppleman-White of Oakland University, and Fred Alford and James Glass of the University of Maryland. I am grateful to Ron Dart, John Dennis Verney, Carol Prager, and especially my daughter Kelly and son-in-law Gary Fewer, for their support in the absence of the one who gave meaning to my endeavors. I would also like to thank the anonymous reviewers at Palgrave Macmillan for their constructive criticism. I am indebted to the Canada Research Chairs program for providing the funding that made it possible to dedicate my time to research.

Contents

1 The Political Case Against Socrates   1
  1 Alcibiades and the Defeat of Athens   3
  2 Critias and the Thirty Tyrants   8
  3 The Amnesty   11
  4 Oligarchic Radicals   13
  5 Socrates and Plato   21
  6 Socrates and Critias   23
  7 The Gadfly of Athens   27
  Notes   27

2 The Religious Case Against Socrates   35
  1 Greek Civil Religion   36
  2 Mutilating the Hermae   42
  3 Defeating Euthyphro   44
  4 Moralizing the Gods   47
  5 Perverting Piety   52
  6 Aristophanes: The Atheism of Socrates   55
  7 The Orphism of Socrates   57
  Notes   63

3 The Defense   71
  1 Xenophon's Denial   72
  2 Edict of the Thirty Tyrants   74
  3 The Case of Leon of Salamis   74

4	The Case of the Generals at Arginusae	76
5	Unwillingness to Escape	77
6	Plato's Legend	80
7	Tropes in Plato's Defense of Socrates	82
8	Socrates and Jesus	88
9	Verdict of the Ages	90
10	Socrates and Heidegger	96
	Notes	97

4 How Plato Legitimizes the Case for the Prosecution — 103
  1 The Socratic Paradox — 104
  2 Resolving the Paradox I: Divine Inspiration — 107
  3 Resolving the Paradox II: Statesmanship — 112
  4 The Sunny Side of Plato's Politics — 114
  5 The Dark Side of Plato's Politics — 116
  Notes — 126

5 Plato's Critique of Homer Repudiated — 131
  1 Religion Without Lies — 132
  2 Religion Without Asceticism — 136
  3 Religion Without Dualism — 137
  4 Religion Without Cosmic Justice — 143
  5 The Hubris of Emulating the Gods — 149
  6 Accepting Responsibility — 153
  7 The Manly Virtues — 159
  8 Savage Moralism Averted — 163
  Notes — 164

6 The Tragic Poets Defended — 171
  1 Tragedy as Innocent Suffering — 173
  2 Hegel: Was Socrates a Tragic Figure? — 178
  3 Sophocles: Why True Nobility is not Socratic — 180
  4 Nietzsche: Did Socrates Defeat Tragedy? — 187
  5 Tragedy, the Bible, and Crime Fiction — 190
  Notes — 193

7	**Socratic Mischief**	197
	1 The Burden of Guilt	198
	2 Authoritarianism Unhinged	200
	3 Turning Hubris into Piety	202
	4 Socrates, Enlightenment, and Imperialism	203
	5 Postmodern Nihilism	205
	6 Debunking the Socratic Legend	211
	Notes	214

Annotated Bibliography   217

Index   265

CHAPTER 1

The Political Case Against Socrates

The persecution of Socrates has often been understood as a precursor to the persecution of Christians in Rome during the first three centuries of the Common Era. In both cases, we have people who are singled out for persecution in societies where religious persecution was relatively unknown. What inspired these dreadful persecutions? How could it happen in a world without dogmas, scriptures, or priestly rule? How could it happen in a place where the concept of heresy was unknown? How could it happen in a society where an obscene institution such as the Inquisition would have been unthinkable? And yet, it happened.

In 399 BCE, Socrates was charged with impiety—a crime against religion.[1] The official charge was:

1. Not recognizing the gods of the state
2. Introducing new divinities
3. Corrupting the young.[2]

The penalty demanded was death. Socrates was prosecuted by Meletus, Anytus, and Lycon. He was found guilty, and condemned by a majority of a jury of 501 Athenian citizens. Why?

There are at least three interpretations of the trial: the intellectual, the political, and the religious. The *intellectual* interpretation regards the trial as a case of the persecution of ideas: Socrates was killed by a society that was intolerant of his critique of its dominant political and religious ideas—

the view of Plato, which I will take issue with. The *political* interpretation regards the charge of impiety as a ruse—a pretext to conceal the real charge against Socrates, which was political.³ However, this is no reason for thinking that the religious charges were simply a ruse. The *religious* interpretation regards the novel religious ideas of Socrates as a threat to Greek civil religion (i.e., the religion of the state); it follows that in the context of Greek civil religion, the religious and political dimensions of the trial cannot be separated.⁴ Nevertheless, the two are distinct.

Even though Plato thought that the conflict between Socrates and Athens was intellectual, he did not neglect the political elements of the trial entirely. Both Plato and Xenophon believed that Socrates was found guilty by association. The lost pamphlet of Polycrates, *Accusation of Socrates* (393 BCE), declares that the case against Socrates had everything to do with his close association with Alcibiades, Critias, and Charmides: three men who played a significant role in the demise of Athens during, as well as after, the Peloponnesian War—men who were responsible for the bloodiest chapter in the history of ancient Athens.⁵ In so far as these three men were considered the fruits of Socratic teaching, the latter was rightly suspect. Half a century later, Aeschines said that the Athenian people "put Socrates to death because he was shown to have educated Critias."⁶

As Xenophon explains:

> The accusers claim that he [Socrates] led his associates to treat the established constitution with contempt, declaring that it was folly to appoint the rulers of the city by lot, when no one would be willing to employ a navigator or builder or other technician who had been selected in this way, although the mistakes of such people would have far less disastrous consequences than political mistakes. Arguments like these, the accuser claimed, incited young men to despise the established political order and turned them into violent revolutionaries.⁷

In defending Socrates, Xenophon tries to distance him from these violent revolutionaries. Interestingly, Plato does not. As Plato's dialogues confirm, these men were very close friends and associates of Socrates. These three characters appear in Plato's dialogues—some dialogues even bear their names (*Alcibiades, Critias,* and *Charmides*).⁸ Critias appears in Plato's *Protagoras, Timaeus,* and *Charmides.* Alcibiades appears in the *Protagoras,* the *Gorgias,* and the *Symposium.* They were not adversarial interlocutors, but part of the Socratic entourage. However, not a word is said about the treacherous role they played in the history of Athens, or the reign of terror that they inflicted on their fellow citizens.[9]

Unwilling or unable to face the political charges head-on, Plato has spawned the legend that Socrates was persecuted for having unorthodox ideas—ideas that, in Plato's estimation, bring humanity face to face with the true, the good, and the beautiful. Plato's strategy for the defense is heroic—he goes on the offensive. He impugns the motives of the prosecutors and the jury; he claims that they were motivated by ignorance and resentment to banish a divinely inspired man from their midst. In silencing Socrates, they have silenced the truth, and turned their back on the good. This is the legend that Plato has bequeathed to the ages. The objective of this book is to challenge Plato's assumption that the triumph of the ideas of Socrates—a triumph that his martyrdom facilitated—brought humanity closer to either truth or goodness. The legend of Plato succeeds only in the absence of the historical events that make sense of the case for the prosecution. The purpose of this chapter is to examine these historical events.

1   ALCIBIADES AND THE DEFEAT OF ATHENS

As told by Thucydides in the *History of the Peloponnesian War,* the demise of Athens was both tragic and self-inflicted. What made her defeat tragic is that she was the victim of forces beyond her control. The first was a terrible plague, and the second was the hostility of Sparta—a city characterized by militancy and anathema to philosophy, culture, and democracy. Fearing the power and influence of Athens led Sparta to start the war.[10] The Spartans sent Athens an ultimatum—either you comply with the following demands or we will attack you.[11] Under the leadership of Pericles, the Athenians refused either to be bullied or to declare war. Instead, they appealed to the peace treaty with Sparta, which required that conflicts be resolved through arbitration. They asked the Spartans to submit their complaint to arbitration, and pledged to comply with the outcome, whatever it may be.[12] But the hawks among the Spartans, like hawks everywhere, maintained that the legal route would take time and would allow Athens to become even more powerful, better prepared, and more lethal and intimidating than she was already; enemies must be destroyed *before* they get powerful; survival in a dangerous world requires quick action and unwavering resolve, not legal proceedings, debate, and indecisiveness.[13] So, Sparta decided to declare war instead of submitting to arbitration.

Thucydides intimates that the very greatness, power, and wealth of Athens somehow "compelled" Sparta to declare war.[14] Scholars do not agree on what Thucydides meant.[15] However, it could not be taken to mean that the Athenians are to blame for starting the hostilities—except indirectly, for being so powerful and magnificent. Thucydides believes that the causes of war in general are "fear, honor, and self-interest."[16] In this case, it seems that the Spartans acted mainly out of fear—fear of the growth and influence of the Athenian Empire and the spread of her democratic values throughout the Greek world—values that were altogether antithetical to the Spartan way of life.

When the Spartans marched into Attica (the Athenian territory), the Athenians retreated inside their walls and allowed the Spartans to ravage their farms and vineyards. This was the strategy of Pericles, who refused to fight the Spartans on land. One year after the start of the war, having retreated behind their walls, the Athenians found themselves—suddenly and inexplicably—the victims of a gruesome and deadly plague, which took the lives of many Athenians, including Pericles.

What made the plague so shocking and so horrible was not simply that it came without warning, but that it was undeserved. The plague attacked only the Athenians—both at home and on the battlefield. The Peloponnesians were totally unaffected by it. The Athenians attributed it to the gods—not as a deserved punishment but as an effort on the part of Apollo to keep his promise to the Spartans.[17] When they decided to embark on the war, the Spartans consulted Apollo, and he promised to help them despite the fact that they refused to submit their complaint to arbitration and started the war. As Pericles tells his fellow Athenians: "what heaven sends, we must bear with a sense of necessity."[18] He does not tell them that they must bear it because it is the just punishment of the gods or that the gods are our benefactors, so it must be for the good in the end. The Athenians were not under the illusion that Athens was the darling of the gods or that the gods were on her side in this war. Nor did they have any illusions about the justice of the gods; they never pretended that the gods reward virtue and punish vice. If the gods had any regard for justice, the Spartans would have suffered the effects of the plague.

Some modern commentators cannot accept the totally arbitrary nature of the plague and its tragic consequences. They prefer to moralize it, claiming that the plague must have been a divine punishment visited on Athens for her imperialism.[19] But this amounts to superimposing a

Christian mentality on pagans who do not see the world in terms of cosmic justice. Socrates and Plato anticipate this Christian moralism, but there is precious little evidence that non-Socratic Greeks believed anything of the sort. Besides, this moralism has the effect of undermining the tragic element in the demise of Athens, which is highlighted by Thucydides.

As told by Thucydides, the demise of Athens was also self-inflicted. In the first half of the Peloponnesian War,[20] the Athenians stuck to the policy of Pericles—they conceded the land to Sparta, and Sparta conceded the sea to Athens. Thucydides has a great deal of praise for the personal integrity, incorruptibility, skill, and intelligence of Pericles.[21] He tells us that Pericles led the people rather than being led by them.[22] The Athenians also admired Pericles, since they elected him as a general again and again for three solid decades (461–29 BCE). Despite the plague (430 BCE) and the death of Pericles (429 BCE), the Athenians were somewhat victorious in the first half of the war. However, the political leaders and generals who followed Pericles were inferior and unwise, so things began to unravel. It follows that Athens was not simply destroyed by the caprice of the gods. Thucydides blamed the leaders who succeeded Pericles—especially Cleon and Alcibiades—because they lacked judgment, and were extremely rash and bellicose. In other words, the demise of Athens cannot be understood simply in terms of tragedy, but also in terms of *hubris*, which manifested itself in the radical, reckless, treasonous, and hawkish policies of Cleon and Alcibiades.

Alcibiades was responsible for planning the disastrous Sicilian invasion (known as the Sicilian Expedition) of 415 BCE. Even though the war in Greece was still going on, Alcibiades managed to convince the Athenian Assembly that they should send an expedition to conquer Sicily—starting with Syracuse (the most powerful city), then proceed to take over the rest of the island, then all of Italy, and then Carthage. The fact is that Syracuse posed no threat to Athens. Syracuse was a democracy that was interested in extending its hegemony over Sicily, which was its own natural sphere of influence. The Athenians had no business meddling in Sicilian affairs, but such facts are not relevant to the likes of Alcibiades and other imperialistic hawks. Alcibiades used the testimony of some exiles from Sicily who were badly treated by Syracuse as an excuse for his imperial dreams. Alcibiades told the Athenians that if we do not rule over others, they will rule over us; so, we cannot sit around and wait to be attacked before defending ourselves. No, we must take preemptive action—we must "take measures in advance to prevent the attack materializing."[23] If we hope to maintain the empire that our ancestors left us, we have to be active, not passive. An empire must be continually on the offensive; it must keep its enemies busy fighting to defend their home turf, which leaves them neither the time nor the opportunity to attack the empire's homeland. In other words, we must fight them over there so we do not have to fight them over here—a familiar refrain. Alcibiades maintained that an empire that is not perpetually active and expanding is bound to become soft and decadent.[24] Besides, Alcibiades argued that there is nothing to fear from Syracuse; it has a rag-rag population that is hardly capable of sticking to a consistent policy, let alone acting together in concert.[25] In this way, Alcibiades convinced the Athenians that the whole affair was bound to be a slam-dunk.[26]

The Athenians were totally sold on the Sicilian Expedition. So much so, that they completely ignored the warnings of Nicias—the sober and moderate general, who argued against the Sicilian Expedition on the grounds that (1) it is foolhardy to expand the empire when we are still having trouble defending the homeland from attacks by the Peloponnesians. (2) Syracuse is already democratic, so we Athenians will not have the opportunity to present ourselves as liberators and help them establish a democracy. (3) We cannot depend on the exaggerated claims of exiles, who have nothing to lose; and if we fail, we will lose our reputation, our perceived power, our men, and more. (4) We should not be overconfident, especially in a strange, far away land that will be difficult to rule, even if we are successful.

Athens ignored this sober advice. There is something timeless about the debate between the cautious Nicias and the reckless Alcibiades. As things turned out, Athens met a colossal defeat. Suddenly, the Athenians who were accustomed to having the upper hand, found themselves defeated in a foreign land without ships, supplies, or their usual grandeur—just dead bodies, wounded men, and desperate survivors at the mercy of their enemies. Families throughout Athens were devastated. According to some estimates, forty thousand soldiers and two hundred and forty ships—cavalrymen, hoplites, and rowers in the triremes—all men of military age who could not be replaced any time soon.[27] On the financial level, the cost of the expedition was also staggering; the treasury was almost bankrupt and the Athenian ability to get money from allies was slim. Many of the allied cities took the weakness of Athens as an opportunity to revolt. The Athenian

Empire was crumbling. The debacle set the stage for the oligarchic coup of 411, the eventual triumph of Sparta in the Peloponnesian War in 404, and the reign of terror that followed.

Thucydides tells us that the treachery of Alcibiades was at the heart of this colossal disaster.[28] He adds that when democracies find themselves in dire straits, they are willing to give up their freedom and self-government and put their fate in the hands of a competent few. In this condition of fear and panic, a handful of oligarchs managed to convince the Athenian *demos* to surrender its power to a group of Four Hundred who would have absolute power to govern as they saw fit; that was supposed to be a temporary measure to deal with the crisis. As it turned out, this was a lie to win over the people. In reality, power was concentrated in the hands of a small group of conspirators.[29] The Assembly of the Four Hundred continued to meet, but all the speakers were members of the small revolutionary group; and nothing was ever said, nor was any proposal made, that was not already approved by the conspirators. Anyone who dared to speak in opposition to them was secretly killed, imprisoned, or exiled—as was anyone they suspected might cause trouble. When rough work needed to be done, the conspirators made use of 120 "Hellenic youth."[30] These thugs terrified the people so that they did not dare oppose the oligarchs. The revolutionaries murdered Androcles, the chief leader of the popular party who was responsible for the banishment of Alcibiades. Desperate and afraid, the people of Athens were more concerned about their survival than about their constitution.

In the meantime, Alcibiades—notorious for his good looks and sexual escapades—was kicked out of Sparta when he was caught seducing the wife of the Spartan King. Abandoned by the Spartans, he decided to ally himself with the Persians. He tried to use his close relationship with Tissaphernes, the Persian satrap, to get the Persian King to support Athens against Sparta. In this way, he hoped to be recalled back to Athens and regain his position of prominence within the democracy. So, after destroying Athens, he tried to pose as her savior, saying that he could rescue her with Persian gold—only on the condition that an oligarchy was established.[31] Despite his efforts, Alcibiades could not bring the Persians to support Athens; nevertheless, he pretended that he could. Naturally, his scheme was appealing to the oligarchs who were in control of the city. By murdering Androcles and turning Athens into an oligarchy, the conspirators thought that they could bring Alcibiades out of exile and win the financial backing of Persia. But it was not to be. The Persians backed Sparta. So, in 410, almost a year after the coup, the democracy was restored and the oligarchs were exiled. Immediately after,

Andocides tells us that a law was passed requiring every Athenian to swear an oath as follows:

> I shall kill by word and deed, by vote and by my own hand, if I can, anyone who subverts the democracy at Athens, and anyone who, when the democracy has been subverted, holds any office thereafter, and anyone who sets himself up to be tyrant or helps to set up the tyrant.[32]

However, when Athens was defeated by Sparta, and the exiles were allowed to return to Athens, she suffered another oligarchic coup in 404 by the friends of Socrates, whose reign was the bloodiest in Athenian history. So, the Athenians could hardly afford to keep Socrates on the loose without tempting fate. Socrates could have been charged under this law of treason if the case against him had been exclusively political, but it was not, as we shall see in the next chapter. Clearly, being an intellectual critic of democracy was no crime, but aiding and abetting the overthrow of the democratic regime was another matter.

In the minds of the Athenians at the trial of Socrates, Alcibiades played a pivotal role in the demise of Athens. He was associated with a hawkish foreign policy, military adventurism, imperial hubris, self-serving antics, treason, impiety, and the lawlessness of the radical oligarchs who masterminded the coup of 411 BCE, the eventual triumph of Sparta in the Peloponnesian War in 404, and the reign of terror by Critias, Charmides, and the Thirty Tyrants that followed. The historical evidence provided by Thucydides and Xenophon reveals that these associations were legitimate.[33]

In my view, it is unlikely that Socrates was a co-conspirator in the shenanigans of Alcibiades. Nevertheless, a fair-minded jurist had every reason to wonder if Alcibiades was the sort of radical oligarch that Socrates cultivated and inspired; and may continue to inspire.

2 Critias and the Thirty Tyrants

Thucydides' *History* breaks off just before the final defeat of Athens at the hands Sparta in 404 BCE.[34] In his *Hellenica*, Xenophon continues the history of the Peloponnesian War where Thucydides broke off. With the help of Persian gold and the former allies of Athens, the Spartans built a navy and continued the war against Athens. In 404 BCE, Athens was besieged and forced to surrender unconditionally. After the fall of Athens,

Lysander, the victorious Spartan general, appointed a group of thirty to draft a new constitution for the defeated city (an oligarchic constitution that would bring an end to the democracy). Instead, this group of thirty became the infamous Thirty Tyrants led by Critias and Charmides—two close relatives of Plato, and students of Socrates. Critias was the cousin of Plato's mother (Perictione, who traced her lineage to Solon), and Charmides was Plato's uncle (Perictione's brother).[35] This means that Critias and Charmides were cousins.[36] Together, Critias and Charmides were responsible for the oligarchic terror in which, according to Aristotle, at least fifteen hundred residents of Athens were executed without charge or trial (404–403 BCE).[37] Critias was considered "the worst of all the men who have gained a reputation for wickedness," and in "cruelty and blood-thirstiness outdid the Thirty."[38]

This was not the first oligarchic coup in which Critias was involved. He played a part in the coup of 411 BCE—he was the leader of the pro-Spartan wing of the oligarchic government. In that position, he made every effort to bring Alcibiades back to Athens. Phrynichus, the oligarchic leader who was murdered in 411 BCE, was opposed to bringing Alcibiades back.[39] Critias had such a savagely murderous quality that he was not satisfied to defeat his political opponents; he had to annihilate them. Sometimes death was not enough where his political opponents were concerned. In his vengefulness, Critias insisted that the corpse of Phrynichus be tried for treason, and if condemned, the corpse was to be treated with indignity.[40]

In 407 BCE, Critias was banished on the ground of being lawless. He went to Thessaly, where he was involved in unspecified political intrigues, but returned to Athens after her defeat in 404 BCE at the hands of Lysander, the Spartan general. Being a well-known champion of Sparta, earned Critias the most prominent role in the Spartan backed government as leader of the Thirty. This was regime-change Spartan style. Once in power, Critias gave vent to his violently anti-democratic inclinations. He abolished the popular assembly, and the people's courts. Fearing an uprising, he asked Lysander for a garrison commander akin to those that Sparta had installed in all the states it had "liberated" from Athenian hegemony. Critias and the Thirty Tyrants also surrounded themselves with three hundred "whip-bearers" to protect them, as they continued the systematic extermination of their enemies.[41] Those who were not co-operative with the regime were arrested on trumped up charges and became victims of extra-judicial killing. At first, the victims were mostly democrats or sympathizers with the democracy. But as the terror intensified, moderate oligarchs were also exiled or killed, and their property confiscated.[42] No one was safe. In this way, a free a city that had prided itself on the fact that the lowliest citizen can get justice in the courts and can speak his mind in the Assembly, was now gripped by fear, mutual suspicion, terror, and tyranny.

Theramenes, one of the somewhat moderate members of the Thirty, protested the lack of due process. He was opposed to Critias' demand for wholesale executions, and denounced him before the council or *boulē*.[43] So, Critias agreed to establish a "citizen role of three thousand" whose members would be entitled to a trial by the *boulē*. In democratic Athens, the *boulē* was made up of five hundred male citizens chosen by lot, whose task was mainly to prepare the business of the assembly. However, Critias had appointed a new *boulē* of five hundred anti-democrats. The concession to Theramenes made matters worse. It meant that everyone not protected by the citizen role of three thousand was fair game. The result was a bloodbath that included wealthy metics (resident aliens) whose property was confiscated by the Thirty.[44]

Fearing that Theramenes might organize a revolt, Critias and the Thirty summoned him to a trial by the *boulē*. Apparently, he made a brilliant and impassioned speech in favor of moderate government. When it seemed that he might sway the *boulē*, Critias struck his name off the citizen role and had him dragged off to prison without a trial. Forced to drink hemlock, Theramenes ironically toasted to the health of Critias.[45] With Theramenes out of the way, Critias had complete domination of public affairs and Athens was plunged into a dark period of tyranny, lawlessness, and bloodshed.[46]

All the while, Sparta supported this brutal regime. She tried to prevent exiles pouring out of Athens from finding refuge in neighboring cities by prohibiting any neighboring states from accepting refugees from Athens. Luckily, the rule was defied by Thebes and Megara. The excesses of the regime in Athens were so shocking that even Spartans became alarmed. Eventually, seven hundred of the exiled citizens of Athens, led by Thrasybulus, marched on the Piraeus. In an effort to defeat his political opponents, Critias (along with Charmides and seventy of their followers) was killed in 403 BCE.[47]

The oligarchs refused Thrasybulus' call for peace and reconciliation because they expected the continued support of Sparta. In a surprising move, the Spartan King (Pausanias) sidelined his general (Lysander) because the brutality of the Thirty was too ugly to bear. The King decided to settle the rift between the two Athenian parties. He allowed the democratic rebels to march to the Acropolis, sacrifice to Athena, and re-establish the democracy, on the condition that they respect the Amnesty that would end the bloodshed and the cycle of revenge and recrimination.[48]

Socrates was tried by the newly established democracy in 399 BCE, only four years after the overthrow of the Thirty Tyrants. He was associated in the minds of his fellow Athenians with the treachery of Alcibiades, and the crimes of Critias and Charmides. This bloody chapter in Athenian history was fresh in the minds of members of the jury whose friends and relatives were killed or brutalized by the students of Socrates. The puppets of Socrates are dead, but "the contriver of all harms,"[49] the wily puppeteer, lives on and is still surrounded by young men from wealthy families with staunch oligarchic sympathies. It would be the height of political naiveté to allow him to poison the minds of the young once more with his rabid anti-democratic ideas.

3 The Amnesty

The Amnesty was an Act of Oblivion arranged by the Spartan King (Pausanias) that made it unlawful for ordinary citizens to be prosecuted simply for going along with the Thirty Tyrants and their reign of terror. The point of the Amnesty was to prevent an endless cycle of retribution between the oligarchic and the democratic factions, fan the flames of partisanship, and destroy the mutual trust necessary for democratic citizenship.

Some scholars are under the impression that the Amnesty made it difficult for Meletus to spell out the political case against Socrates unambiguously, hence the charge of impiety and the vague language about "corrupting the young."[50] This means that Meletus was rather handicapped, and that is one reason, besides his lack of experience, that allowed Socrates to get the better of him—assuming that Plato is more or less accurately reporting what happened at the trial.

It is important to point out that the Amnesty was for ordinary citizens, not members of the Thirty, their officers, or close associates. The latter could be brought to justice for crimes committed against the state.[51] In other words, there was no reason to grant amnesty to those who plotted against the state, or those who mentored them. Besides, the Amnesty would only have prevented the prosecution from charging Socrates with spreading anti-democratic sentiments prior to 403, but it could not prevent them from being concerned about the corruption of the present generation.[52] So, the prosecution of Socrates need not involve bending the conditions of the Amnesty. In fact, Anytus, who initiated the charges against Socrates, was the leading advocate of the Amnesty, so he would have had no reason for going against it. As A. E. Taylor rightly explains:

> The motives for the prosecution are unintelligible unless it is understood that Anytus honestly held Socrates and his teaching responsible for the mischief done to Athens by the man who had taught the enemy where to strike the deadly blow at her [i.e., Alcibiades, who gave Athenian secrets to Sparta], and the man who had been the leader in the Terror which followed her downfall [i.e., Critias].[53]

According to Taylor, Anytus had no unworthy motive.[54] Anytus had no desire to shed blood.[55] The trial of Socrates was never supposed to have happened.[56] By bringing charges against Socrates, Anytus hoped that this pesky political agitator would go into voluntary exile; and even the sentence of death was designed to make him suggest banishment.[57] This is an important point because Plato's defense rests on impugning the motives of the prosecution.

At the time of the trial, both Alcibiades and Critias were dead. Alcibiades was murdered in 404 BCE: Plutarch thinks it was either by Lysander's orders acting on behalf of King Agis of Sparta (whose wife Alcibiades had seduced) or by the insulted and enraged relatives of his noble mistress (Timandra) whose relatives thought that Alcibiades had dishonored her with his debauchery.[58] As mentioned earlier, Critias was killed in a fight with the exiles returning to reclaim their city under the leadership of Thrasybulus.[59] Since the real culprits were dead, Anytus must have regarded Socrates as an obstacle to the realization of peace and mutual trust between the democratic and the oligarchic parties in the present and future of Athens. It was not a question of revenge; it was fear that the new democracy could be victimized once again by the radicalism of Socrates and his oligarchic friends.

The prosecution was not motivated so much by vengeance as by fear. The opponents of Socrates saw him as the consummate intellectual puppeteer who pulled the strings behind the scene. Leaders of the newly re-established democracy feared his ability to incite another bloody coup. It follows that Socrates was not prosecuted for having unorthodox views, but for his capacity to incite violence and treachery, not only in the past but also in the present and future. In which case, the Athenians had to convict him for their own self-protection.

4 Oligarchic Radicals

There was in the minds of the accusers of Socrates a certain stereotype of the kind of young men, who, thanks to the influence of Socrates, were likely to be subversive of the democracy. No one represented that stereotype better than the anonymous author of *The Constitution of the Athenians*, which, until the twentieth century, scholars believed was the work of Xenophon. It is now believed to have been authored by someone else, and is generally referred to as the work of pseudo-Xenophon or Xenophon the Orator, or the Old Oligarch.

In their introduction to the translation of '*The Old Oligarch*,' J. L. Marr and P. J. Rhodes argue that most scholars do not "*want*" Xenophon to be the author of this work, because it might undermine the esteem in which they hold him and his teacher.[60] However, as Marr and Rhodes rightly point out, there is nothing to prevent the young Xenophon (or any other young Socratic for that matter), from being the author of this treatise. Yet, Marr and Rhodes believe (for all sorts of reasons) that *The Constitution of the Athenians* is the work of a young student of Antiphon, a great speechwriter who played a leading role in the oligarchic coup of 411 BCE.[61] Regardless of who authored this treatise, it is paradigmatic of a dangerously radical and subversive ideology, characterized by a virulent animus toward the Athenian democracy, an absurd partiality to oligarchy, and a love of all things Spartan, with the usual laconizing pretensions. This radical ideology was associated with Socrates and his disciples—with good reason.

In *The Constitution of the Athenians*, the Old Oligarch presents the political alternatives as a stark dichotomy between the rule of the *oligoi* and the rule of *demos*. The *oligoi* are the best men, the men with wealth, education, and refinement; they are the noble and worthy few to which the Old Oligarch clearly belongs. In contrast, the *demos* are the many poor, who are undisciplined, worthless, shameless, and contemptible. Athens is the poster child of bad government in which these worthless people rule. In short, the Athenian constitution is intended to promote the interests of the most worthless people, while keeping the superior people down. These worthless people hate the superior few; they take away their political rights, confiscate their property, exile them, and kill them.[62] They even use the law courts to further the interests of the *demos* and ruin the genuinely valuable people.[63] This echoes Plato's view of the plight of Socrates at the hands of the Athenian *demos*.[64]

The Old Oligarch thinks of democracy as the illegitimate rule of the *demos* or the many poor. However, if the *demos* represents the poor, then it cannot also be identified with the majority. In Athens, the majority of people were peasant farmers, who served as hoplites or heavily armed infantry in war.[65] As Marr and Rhodes point out, the Old Oligarch is reluctant to include peasant farmers in the *demos* because it would make it more difficult to use it in an extremely pejorative sense.[66] Even if the term was used to refer only to the poorest people, it cannot be said that they were not valuable to the city, since they manned the triremes—the ships that made Athens a great naval power. The Old Oligarch was aware of the fact that Athens' reliance on her naval power allowed the plebeians to have a say in the running of their government.[67] And why not? After all, their lives were on the line. Manning these ships in combat was dangerous work; and the glory of Athens depended on it. So, why should these people have no say in the running of their city?

The idea of sharing power with the incompetent many is as absurd for the Old Oligarch as it is for Socrates. Socrates echoes the Old Oligarch in maintaining that the *demos* should have no say in the affairs of the city. Xenophon tells us in the *Memorabilia* that it was common knowledge that Socrates' favorite topic was the utter absurdity of allowing ordinary people, who have no special expertise in political affairs, to rule. Plato also portrayed Socrates making the same arguments—comparing political rule with the expertise of cobblers, shipbuilders, captains, doctors, and metal workers.[68] The implication is that putting power in the hands of ordinary people is as reckless as allowing any hack to operate on a seriously ill patient. Ordinary people must be prevented from "meddling" in politics.[69]

The Old Oligarch considered Athenian democracy as mob rule. Socrates and Plato echoed the same view. This was a jaundiced outlook that was at odds with reality. There is evidence that Athenian democracy was much more moderate and stable than the denunciations of Socrates, Plato, and the Old Oligarch would lead us to believe. The radical conception of democracy as the attempt by the common people to keep the rich, wellborn, and well educated out of government, was not accurate. The Athenians elected leaders and generals from the aristocratic elite in recognition of their education, merit, and skill. Cimon, Pericles, Alcibiades, and

Nicias were all elected by the *demos* for their merits. It follows that Athens was not as hostile to the superior few as the radical anti-democrats claimed. On the contrary, it granted them power, honor, and glory, in accordance with their merits.

Athenian democracy recognized that there is a case to be made on behalf of the aristocratic few—a case that does not get a fair hearing in our current democratic stupor.[70] After all, the aristocratic few have some legitimate claims in thinking that they are fit to rule—the claims of wealth, education, and the traditions that go along with them, including a code of conduct that is passed from one generation to the next. Conservatives have made this argument from Aristotle to Edmund Burke. This claim has some validity, but it is important to point out that it also has limits. Just because an aristocratic father has the wisdom and temperament needed for statesmanship, it does not follow that his offspring will have the same abilities—despite having the same education and upbringing.[71]

Nevertheless, those with the privileges of wealth and education have a claim. It is not a claim of birth, strictly speaking, but of the merit that is derived from the opportunity to develop natural talents. So, neither birth nor wealth as such can be the basis of any claim to rule. Like Socrates, the Old Oligarch is fully cognizant of this fact. Like Socrates, he makes his claim on the basis of merit—the merits that he assumes the rich and wellborn automatically possess. But that is the question: Do the wealthy and wellborn automatically possess these virtues? Socrates did not think so. He thought they needed to be educated by someone with special knowledge—and he was busy doing just that—educating the sons of the wealthy. However, he was not educating them so that they could participate in the democracy as leaders and generals.

Like the Old Oligarch, Socrates did not think that the noble ones should participate in the democracy, because such participation is demeaning, since it involves service to the interests of the inferior many. At his trial, Socrates made a point of saying that he never took part in the politics of Athens and never held office except for a single occasion in his long life.[72] Alcibiades describes how Socrates made him feel a deep sense of shame for seeking power and glory in the context of the Athenian democracy. In Plato's *Symposium*, Alcibiades tells us that his love of politics led him to "seek the favor of the mob."[73] This is Socratic lingo for partaking in the Athenian democratic process and being elected as a general. By participating in the democracy, and winning the favor of the *demos*, Alcibiades was made to feel like a traitor, not only to Socrates, but also to his higher self. Alcibiades adds that his experiences with "this satyr," as he calls Socrates fondly, are not peculiar to him, and that the others know what he is talking about since he has inspired the same feelings of shame in others.[74]

In *Alcibiades I*, we get another glimpse of the shame that Alcibiades felt for partaking in the democracy. In that dialogue, the sycophantic element of the relationship between Socrates and Alcibiades is even more evident. Alcibiades is encouraged to become more servile and dependent on Socrates.[75] He is made to admit his ignorance of statesmanship, which he can transcend only by the help of god and Socrates.[76] In both dialogues, Alcibiades is torn between his love of Socrates and his love of the honor and glory that Athens offered him.

In both the *Symposium* and *Alcibiades I*, Alcibiades is made to feel as if he is groveling, or pandering to the mob. By all accounts, Alcibiades is not capable of groveling. He is too arrogant for that. He was elected on the basis of his merit, his skill, and his success in Olympic competitions. After all, only the richest elite in society can afford to be part of the cavalry.[77] Alcibiades had the skills that only those with wealth, opportunity, and inclination, could cultivate. This was clearly recognized by the people of Athens, and it led them to elect him again and again, not because they were fond of him, or because he pandered to them, but for his accomplishments. Yet, Socrates made him feel that he betrayed his mentor as well as his better self. The upshot of the matter is that it was impossible to be true to Socrates without repudiating the Athenian democracy as unequivocally as the Old Oligarch.

If all participation in the democracy is shameful, then what are the superior few supposed to do if they find themselves living in a democracy? There seems to be three alternatives: (1) withdraw from the life of politics and action altogether and live a reclusive ascetic life free from the pollution of the mob; (2) embark on an effort to reform the democracy; (3) overthrow the democratic regime by any means. The defenders of Socrates through the ages have assumed that Socrates opted for the reclusive life of reflection and "care of the soul."[78]

The second option—reforming the democracy is out of the question. For Socrates and other radical anti-democrats, democracy is irredeemable —it is impossible to reform it.[79] They could not imagine anything like Aristotle's mixed regime—a sharing of power between the *oligoi* and the *demos*. It follows that if a regime cannot be reformed or improved, then it must be overthrown. That is the only option left to those (such as Alcibiades) who are not enamored by the reclusive life.

The Old Oligarch is overt about choosing subversive or seditious action. He explains that the noble ones have no choice except to break the law if they are to serve the higher good. They must be "unjust" in a world where justice is defined as the interest of the *demos*. This is what the Old Oligarch means when he says:

> whoever is not a member of the *demos*, and yet has chosen to have a political life in a democratic city rather than an oligarchic one, has deliberately set himself to act unjustly.[80]

So, if they partake in the political life of the democracy, the superior people must use their power to subvert it.

When he escaped to Sparta, Alcibiades gave a speech before the Spartan Assembly in which he reminded the Spartans of his own aristocratic pedigree (he came from the same family as Pericles). He told them that they should trust him because he is one of them and has bona fide philo-Laconian sentiments. He assured them that he shared their aversion to democracy because anyone with any sense knows that democracy is an utterly foolish form of government. Then he proceeded to tell them exactly how to defeat Athens.[81] He did not worry about being a traitor. On the contrary, understood from his Socratic perspective, Alcibiades' subversive activities were redemptive. By betraying Athens, he redeemed himself because he was no longer pandering to the mob, but was saving Athens from democracy.

Thucydides explains that the evidence against Alcibiades was "found in the unconventional and undemocratic character of his life in general."[82] Alcibiades never made any bones about how splendid and magnificent he was, and how the seven chariots he entered in the Olympic Games defied the imagination; so much so, that he believed the reflected light from such a display of glory, power, and skill, was bound to bring untold honor to Athens.[83] Alcibiades had no desire "to be put on the level with everyone else."[84] He was beyond equality. The only Athens to which he could be loyal was one in which he did not live by the same rules as others.[85] These attitudes made Alcibiades capable of all manner of lawlessness and injustice. So, it is no wonder that the Athenians saw the students of Socrates as dangerous radicals.

In contrast to Socrates and the Old Oligarch, moderate democrats such as Athenagoras, from Syracuse, explained that the democratic laws are not intended to keep the rich, wellborn, and well-educated out of power, they are intended to keep out only those who are unwilling to "live on the same terms as everyone else" because "members of the same State ought, in justice, to enjoy the same rights."[86] Protagoras was in agreement. In contrast, Plato and Socrates thought that a successful democratic leader must be a demagogue who panders to the mob, flatters the people, promises the moon, but never tells them the truth. In Plato's estimation, the truth is anathema to the people; like children, they love the candy-maker but not the cook—and they certainly hate the medicine man.[87]

Socrates denounced the famous Athenian politicians—including Pericles, as flatterers of the mob, charlatans akin to cooks and candy-makers who cater to the desires and pleasures of the people.[88] Socrates regarded the *demos* as a wild beast that must be trained, made docile, subservient, and acquiescent to its superiors. He claimed that instead of taming the *demos*, Pericles and other celebrated Athenian politicians made it wilder. Despite their incompetence, they are venerated for filling the city with "harbors and dockyards and walls and revenues and similar rubbish."[89] The people sing the praises of these charlatans, meanwhile they heap abuse on true statesmen like "*my friend Alcibiades*"[90] who try to introduce discipline, and shape the desires of the people in a better direction.[91] In truth, Alcibiades was known for his lies, deception, treason, and tricks. The idea of holding Alcibiades in higher esteem than Pericles is laughable—if it were not so catastrophic.

Pericles was a popular democratic leader without being a demagogue. His skill as a general was matched by his skill as a public speaker. Pericles did not use the usual democratic tricks of telling the people what they wanted to hear. As Thucydides tells us,

> He would not humor the people in his speeches so as to get power by improper means, but because of their esteem for him he could risk their anger by opposing them. Therefore, whenever he saw them insolently bold and out of season, he would put them into fear with his speeches; and again, when they were afraid without reason, he would raise up their spirits and give them courage.[92]

Nor did Pericles deceive or manipulate the people into supporting his policies. He told them the truth and provided reasons for his policies without pretending that they were foolproof formulas for success. When things did not work out, and the plague made the Athenians desperate, they blamed Pericles. He scolded them saying that they were being irrational in blaming him for what he could not control. Besides, they were the ones who chose these policies and should take responsibility for the outcome. So, it is no wonder that Pericles was elected again and again by the Athenians, because they trusted him to treat them like adults and tell them the truth.

Even though he belonged to an aristocratic family, Pericles was the antithesis of the arrogant, self-absorbed aristocratic young men that Socrates attracted—men like Alcibiades, Critias, and Charmides, who had a Socratic disdain for democracy and who believed that their superiority entitled them to rule single-handedly without reference to law, let alone the consent of the *demos*. In the *Protagoras,* Plato reports that as the guardian of the younger brother of Alcibiades, Pericles was so worried about the corrupting influence of Alcibiades that he sent the boy away for his education.[93] Plato mentions only the corruptive influence of Alcibiades, but he also informs us in the same dialogue that Socrates' favorite pass time was the "pursuit of the captivating Alcibiades."[94] So, it was not just Alcibiades that Pericles was trying to protect the boy from—it was Alcibiades and the rest of the Socratic circle.

At his trial as presented by Plato, Socrates poses as an apolitical sage who was neutral between Athens and Sparta, democracy and oligarchy. If he were indeed above the political fray, then one would expect him to have some democratic students. With the single exception of Chaerephon, all of the students of Socrates came from wealthy aristocratic families.[95] Plato tells us in the *Phaedo* that at the time of his death by hemlock, Socrates' companions were wealthy oligarchs from Thebes, Elis, and Phlius.[96] These were all enemy cities in the Peloponnesian War. Clearly, Socrates was the darling of young oligarchs, and was continuing to work his magic on the youth of the rich and well born, not only those from enemy cities, but also on young Athenians, such as Plato.

What about Chaerephon? He was the one who went to the oracle at Delphi and asked the Pythia if there was any man wiser than Socrates. In an effort to show that he was not a partisan extremist, a party hack, and a political agitator, Socrates, as presented in Plato's *Apology*, mentions Chaerephon as a badge of honor, and reminds his prosecutors that Chaerephon is one of them, belongs to their party, and had to leave the city during the dark days of the Thirty. This tactic backfires because it highlights the fact that Socrates and all his other companions stayed in the city during the terror, which indicates that they had nothing to fear. As I. F. Stone points out, having "stayed in the city" was a mark of dishonor, a social stigma, which even the Amnesty could not erase.[97] In short, Socrates was clearly on the side of the ruling oligarchs.

It may be objected that all the Socratics should not be lumped together with radical oligarchs. After all, Socrates and Plato were aristocratic, not oligarchic. They believed in the rule of the best in the interest of the whole (aristocracy), and not the rule of the rich in their own interest (oligarchy). Plato distrusted wealth and did not think that its claim to rule is as strong as the Old Oligarch assumes. Nevertheless, Plato made it clear that aristocracy is a theoretical ideal that does not and cannot exist in the real world[98]; so, the most that one could hope for is a regime that would come as close as humanly possible to the ideal. For Plato, that regime is oligarchy.

Plato's hierarchical order of regimes in Bk. VIII of the *Republic* starts with aristocracy and ends with tyranny. Oligarchy comes closest to the aristocratic ideal, while democracy is closely related to tyranny. Despite historical evidence to the contrary, Plato held stubbornly to the conviction that democracy leads to tyranny—the worst regime possible. The theory fit Plato's hierarchical scheme of things, but it was at odds with the history of Greece, where tyrants emerged as champions of the people against greedy and exploitative oligarchs. Besides, Plato was not opposed to tyranny in cases where the tyrant listened to the advice of a philosopher.[99] This leaves democracy as the only irredeemable form of government, which means that, when it comes to democracy, Socrates and Plato were just as radical and just as uncompromising as the Old Oligarch.

Needless to say, the enthusiasm of Socrates and his ilk for Spartan oligarchy was misplaced. After winning the Peloponnesian War, and destroying Athens, Sparta was unable to provide Greece with moderation, peace, or stability. Her imperial designs were far more brutal than Athens. She meddled continuously in the internal affairs of states, using force to destabilize existing governments, and replace them with ruthless pro-Spartan regimes. Even her long-time allies, Thebes and Corinth renounced her in an open alliance with Athens after the war. Her victory over Athens would not have been possible without Persian gold. Yet she managed to alienate Persia by sending mercenary troops to fight on behalf of Cyrus the Younger in a contest for the Persian throne against his brother, the Great King, Artaxerxes who succeeded Darius II. One of those who chose to fight for this dubious Persian cause was Xenophon. When Cyrus was killed, thirteen thousand Greek mercenaries found themselves stranded in a hostile territory of a king they were trying to overthrow. Their trek back to the sea and their ships were dramatized in Xenophon's *Anabasis*. Meanwhile, Athens managed to restore her democracy, which displayed an impressive degree of vigor, moderation, and stability in the fourth century. In a stunning reversal of fortune, Persia abandoned Sparta and shifted her financial support to Athens and her allies. In short, Sparta's political ineptitude was staggering.[100]

5 Socrates and Plato

The traditional picture of the relationship of Socrates and Plato needs to be overhauled. Almost every introductory text in philosophy begins with the towering figure of Socrates. According to the traditional view, Socrates is a free spirit, shattering orthodoxy with his rational inquiry and unsurpassed critical acumen. In his early dialogues, Plato provides us with a vivid picture of this indomitable figure—a figure that could only thrive in the freewheeling openness of Athenian culture. However, in Plato's later dialogues, the influence of Socrates seems to fade. Instead, a harsh and rigid authoritarianism takes root. Plato becomes the advocate of the closed society. So much so that in the later dialogues, Socrates is no longer the main speaker. In Plato's *Laws*, the main speaker is an "Athenian Stranger." So, it is no surprise that the political order recommended by Plato in that dialogue is one that would not tolerate the free spirit of Socrates. If Socrates were to appear in that polity, he would be put to death. So the story goes.

Alas, this commonly held view is not substantiated by the texts. I will discuss Plato's dialogues at greater length in Section 4, what is relevant here is the relationship of Plato and Socrates where democracy is concerned. Plato's radical rejection of democracy in his early and middle dialogues is a reflection of Socratic attitudes. It is a clear indication that Plato was one of the young oligarchs radicalized by Socrates—men who posed a threat to Athenian stability in the eyes of the prosecution. As we saw earlier, Plato's treatment of democracy in the *Republic* was uncompromising. Democracy is not only closely allied to tyranny, but it is also the only form of government that is irredeemable—it cannot be improved either by the influence of the wise or by the restraining power of laws.

As Plato got older, and historical events cast a shadow on Sparta, the influence of Socrates waned; as a result, Plato's view of democracy softened.[101] In the *Statesman*, we get a much less rigid view of democracy than we find in the earlier dialogues, when Plato was echoing the Socratic view. In the *Statesman*, Plato entertains the idea that, like all other forms of government, democracy can be improved by being subject to laws.[102] In other words, democracy is not singled out as being the only irredeemable form of government; it is possible to have a moderate democracy governed by laws that limits the power of the *demos*—a position that does not appear in any of the early dialogues, and is flatly rejected in the *Republic*.

In the *Statesman*, the main speaker is a "Stranger" who instructs the "Young Socrates." The tables are turned. It is Plato's turn to instruct Socrates. Interestingly, we get a typology of regimes that is very different from what we encounter in the *Republic*. The Stranger tells the young Socrates that there are *seven* regimes altogether. The rule of one, the few, and the many are each divided into two depending on whether they are governed by law or in the absence of law; and whether they involve rule over willing or unwilling subjects. In the case where the rule of one, rule of the few, and rule of the many are governments subject to law, exercised over willing subjects, then they are monarchy, aristocracy, and *constitutional democracy*, respectively. Of these three, Plato still thinks that democracy is the worst, but it is not a totally lawless regime that inevitably gives way to tyranny.[103] However, when these three types of regimes abandon the rule of law and rule over unwilling subjects by force, then they are called tyranny, oligarchy, and democracy.[104] Ironically, in that scenario, democracy is the best of the lot: "Thus if all constitutions are unprincipled the best thing to do is to live in a democracy."[105] Plato's rationale is that "the rule of the many is the weakest in every way; it is not capable of any real good or any serious evil as compared with the other two."[106] In other words, democracy is better than tyranny and oligarchy! These are somewhat underhanded compliments to democracy, but they are the sorts of compliments that are incompatible with his earlier Socratic views. In the *Laws*, Plato goes even further and insists that the best regime must have elements of democracy, if it hopes to combine wisdom with freedom and friendship.[107] It must have finally dawned on him that what brought Athens down was the distrust between the democrats and the oligarchs—a distrust that was aggravated by the strident nature of the Socratic antipathy to democracy. So, when it comes to democracy, Plato's mature view has evolved into something much less radical than his earlier Socratic position.

In that light, the traditional view of the relationship of Plato to Socrates needs to be modified. Clearly, Socrates was more extreme in his rejection of democracy than the mature Plato. This is not to deny the harsh authoritarian tenor of Plato's philosophical project from his earliest to his latest dialogues. It is merely to highlight the fact that, if the influence of Socrates waned somewhat, it did so in the opposite direction than is generally believed, and mostly because it had to yield to logic—there is no logical reason why a democracy cannot be limited by law.

As a young man, Plato must have been of concern to the prosecution as one of the oligarchic radicals that Socrates mentored. It is to the credit of Athens that she allowed such an uncompromising critic to live and thrive within her walls in the fourth century. Plato's Academy is itself a supreme example of the freedom and tolerance with which Athens treated her Socratic critics. Yet, Plato's students were not satisfied with the freedom of the contemplative life that fourth century Athens provided. They were inclined to be politically active. Werner Jaegar tells us that unlike the graduates of the Isocratic School of rhetoric, who usually became successful lawyers and statesmen, the graduates of Plato's Academy were more likely to become political agitators who ended up in exile.[108] Another student of Plato, Demetrius of Phaleron, became a tyrant of Athens.[109] Others were involved in murderous political intrigues in Syracuse and Heraclea.[110] So, the threat posed by Socrates continued long after his demise.

6 Socrates and Critias

The relationship of Socrates and Critias is puzzling. Was Critias a psychopath who enjoyed killing, torturing, and terrorizing others? Or, was he a murderer out of principle? Was he motivated by some high-minded desire to destroy the democracy and restore the natural order of things? Was he an ideological madman for whom no atrocity was too great a price to pay, if only Athens could be rescued from her democracy, so that the superior could rule over the inferior? Did Socrates radicalize him? Or, did he misunderstand Socrates? How can the crimes of Critias be reconciled with the Socratic preoccupation with the "care of the soul"? How can the callous inhumanity of Critias be squared with the Socratic dictum that the wise man does evil to no one? We cannot know for certain the answers to these questions, but there are some strong clues and probabilities.

What makes Critias too interesting to dismiss as a bloodthirsty tyrant, is not only his association with Socrates, but also the fact that he was by all accounts an intellectual in his own right, and a prolific writer. He wrote political prose on several constitutions; he wrote verse, including elegiacs (one of them for Alcibiades); and he wrote several plays. Other than fragments, most of his work is lost. A long excerpt from *Sisyphus*, one of his satyr-plays, was preserved—Sextus quoted it in full.[111] Sextus describes Critias as the atheist "who held tyrannical power in Athens."[112] In the ancient world, as in the modern one, scholars assume that Sisyphus is the mouthpiece for the bold atheism of Critias.[113] In the play, Sisyphus declares that:

> There was a time when the life of men was uncivilized and bestial and subservient to brute force,... It seems to me that men next set up laws as chastisers,... Should anyone commit an error, he was penalized. Next, since laws hindered them from committing obvious crimes by force, yet they acted secretly;... at this point some clever and wise man... invented fear <of the gods> for mortals, that the wicked might experience fear, even if they act or say or think <something> in secret. As a consequence he introduced the divine: "There is a deity... It will hear all that is said among mortals and will be able to see all that is done. If in silence you plan some evil, this will not escape the notice of the gods...." Making these statements, he introduced the most pleasant of doctrines and with false discourse obscured the truth... With such fears did he encircle men,... and through laws he quelled lawlessness.[114]

In short, a man of genius, intellect, and wisdom, came along and invented gods, who are preoccupied with human conduct and eager to punish the wicked and reward the just, if not in this life, then in the next. These gods were all knowing: no secret could be hidden from them, including human thoughts and desires. This ingenious ploy, this artful fiction, was a boon to humanity.

In my estimation, Critias is not the bold atheist he is reputed to be. It is more accurate to describe Critias as a theocratic opportunist. He regards the invention of moralistic gods, coupled with the immortality of the soul, and the torments of the afterlife, as useful lies. Critias is committed to the political utility of these cunning fabrications. In contrast, a genuine atheist would insist that human beings live without lies. A bold atheist would have nothing but contempt for those who frighten humanity into moral conduct. A bona fide atheist would surmise that propping up morality with fear undermines it. An intelligent atheist would realize that living a life of immorality eventually catches up with you.

Moreover, the story told by Sisyphus in this fragment is disingenuous. The invention of moralistic gods, who punished people in the afterlife, not only for their wicked deeds, but also for their wicked thoughts, was a recent invention. In the fragment, Critias sets the tale in the mists of time, as if suppressing lawlessness has always been the purpose of the gods. Like Socrates and Plato, he co-opts and re-invents the traditional myths to fit the Socratic conception of the divine. As we shall see, the gods of Homer were not in the business of punishing immorality. They punished those who offended them. Otherwise, they would gladly partake in any nefarious plot to help their favorite mortals. Sisyphus was not punished for being wicked; he was punished for his *hubris*—the arrogance toward the gods that led him to think he could trick Death. By using Sisyphus as his mouthpiece, Critias is obscuring the distinction between the gods of Homer and the new religious sensibility adopted by Socrates.

The fragment suggests that Socrates is the cunning philosopher of the lie. The idea that Socrates spread lies about gods that he did not believe in has become very popular in recent years, thanks to Leo Strauss and his minions.[115] If Socrates is a religious trickster as Critias and Strauss maintain, then all of Plato's dialogues, in which Socrates is the main speaker, are a sham—a ruse intended to spin an elaborate lie for its social utility. Was Socrates a fake? Was he pretending to be a theist for the good of mankind? Was he as deceitful as Critias and Strauss suggest? I doubt it.

As we shall see in the next chapter, there is every indication that Socrates was a true believer in moralistic gods, as well as in the rewards and punishments of the afterlife. He was an advocate of ascetic purification as necessary for salvation. Thanks to the influence of the mystery religions, Socrates swore off his passion for boys, and broke the heart of Alcibiades (Section 4.2). Indeed, Socrates was so confident in his purity and the prospect of immortality that he chose death over exile or escape, which were readily available to him. As Søren Kierkegaard has pointed out, Socrates believed in immortality enough to stake his life on it.[116] For Critias, the religion of Socrates was a stroke of political genius. If Socrates and Critias had such different religious sensibilities, what explains their close association? The answer is that what they agreed on was much more substantial than their differences.

There is more to Critias than pathological wickedness. As the fragments of his work indicate, Critias was obsessed with the superiority of the Spartans. He considered their whole way of life infinitely superior to that of the Athenians. He attributed the invention of moderation to a Spartan sage (Chilon) whose dictum "Nothing in Excess" was the quintessential motto of Lacedaemonian life.[117] He admired Spartan cloaks, shoes, and drinking cups. His passion for the Lacedaemonians may well have inspired him to rid Athens of her democracy and to transform her along the Spartan model—a task that was not, in his estimation, or that of his circle, a selfish affair.

Critias may have regarded his crimes as necessary to rescue his beloved city from what the whole Socratic circle believed to be the most dreadful fate that could befall any city—democracy. He would not have been the only member of the Socratic circle to regard the purge during the terror of the Thirty as a necessary means of securing the good of the city. In the *Gorgias*, Socrates talks of killing, banishing, and confiscating the property of people as a "good thing" when it is "accompanied by advantage" as determined by those in possession of the art of politics.[118] Socrates does not say that they are necessary evils, but considers them "just actions," even though the context makes it clear that these are not actions under law. It is far more plausible that Critias and Charmides were inspired by the conceit of Socratic ideas and the superhuman confidence they imparted among those who believed themselves in possession of the "royal art," than by gratuitous wickedness.

I am suggesting that Critias was not merely a manifestation of the gratuitous evil associated with a flawed humanity. It is more likely that his wickedness was intimately connected to his Socratic sensibility. The latter consisted of an exaggeration of the evils of democracy. So much so, that life in a democracy seemed intolerable for the superior few, as if the world was on the verge of imploding, unless it was rescued by some miracle. In the absence of this redemptive intervention, all is lost, the center cannot hold. Yet, the anticipated redemption is not a magical cure—it is more akin to an amputation that is believed (by the redeemer) to be necessary for the salvation of the body politic. The project is not without cost in pain, agony, and great risk for the redeemer, who will naturally be misunderstood by the mob. Nevertheless, it is a price worth paying. I suspect that Critias was a man eager to save his city from what Socrates taught him was a catastrophe akin to being operated on by a hack, or setting out to sea on a ship built by charlatans with drunken sailors at the helm. He was willing to do whatever it took to wrest the ship of state from the drunken sailors and place a competent seaman at the helm— before it was too late. So, it would be no surprise if Critias was a hero among the followers of Socrates.

In honor of Critias, some of his friends erected a monument depicting Oligarchy setting a torch to Democracy. The inscription read: "This is a monument of *good men*, who checked for a time the accursed Athenian democracy from its violence."[119] The Old Oligarch would have enthusiastically endorsed this monument—so would have any number of the members of the Socratic circle. One wonders if Plato's silence on these historical events is not an endorsement of Critias as a heroic warrior against democracy. It is hard not to conclude that Plato must have been among the friends of Critias who erected this monument.

7 The Gadfly of Athens

The evidence against Socrates was considerable. His bad reputation was a function of the criminal conduct of his students and the terrible toll they exacted from their fellow citizens in blood and treasure. Instead of facing the charges forthrightly, Socrates was arrogant and self-righteous at his trial. He compared Athens to a large slumbering horse and himself to a pesky, but ultimately beneficial gadfly: "I believe that I am the gadfly which the god has fastened upon the city."[120] He flattered himself into thinking that he was called to a divine mission: to wake Athens from her moral slumber. To those who acquitted him, he must have seemed to be a totally deluded man, who was divorced from reality. Others disagreed.

In hindsight, the metaphor of the gadfly and the horse may have been very appropriate. Plato assumed that a gadfly is a little irritant that is ultimately beneficial to the large animal it pesters. Modern scientists know better. In reality, a gadfly secretes a sticky and irritating substance that it deposits on the skin of its host—normally horses and livestock. When the animal licks off the irritating substance, the larvae are ingested into the stomach of the animal where they live and feed. Eventually, they weaken the animal and ultimately kill it. If Athens was the horse and Socrates was the gadfly, then his students must have been the larvae that fed on Athens until they killed it. This is a more realistic analogy, which sums up the political case for the prosecution.

Notes

1. The charge of impiety in Athenian law was undefined, and could cover a variety of offenses: Douglas M. MacDowell, *The Law in Classical Athens* (Ithaca, New York: Cornell University Press, 1978), pp. 197–200.
2. *Apology*, 24 b–c. It is worth noting that "apology" is not a translation of the Greek *apologia*, which means defense. What Plato tells us about the indictment is confirmed by Xenophon, *Memorabilia*, I.i.1., and by Diogenes Laertius, *The Lives and Opinions of Eminent Philosophers* (London: G. Bell

and Sons, Ltd., 1915), Bk. II, sec. XIX. The modernized English as quoted by W. K. C. Guthrie, *Socrates* (London: Cambridge University Press, 1971) p. 62, runs as follows:

"This indictment is entered on affidavit by Meletus son of Meletus of the deme Pitthus against Socrates son of Sophroniscus of Alopeke. Socrates is guilty of refusing to recognize the gods recognized by the state and introducing other, new divinities. He is also guilty of corrupting the youth. The penalty demanded is death." Xenophon follows the same order as the official indictment. Plato places the corruption of the young first, then the religious charges. The difference between the two versions raises the question regarding which is more fundamental: corrupting the young or not recognizing the gods? For historical details on the trial, see Thomas C. Brickhouse and Nicholas D. Smith, *Socrates on Trial* (Princeton, N.J.: Princeton University Press, 1989).

3. I. F. Stone, *The Trial of Socrates* (Toronto: Little, Brown & Co., 1988), is an example of this view of the trial. See Bibliography for more details.
4. A. E. Taylor, *Varia Socratica* (Oxford: James Parker & Co., 1911) represents that view. See also Robert Parker, *Athenian Religion: A History* (New York: Oxford University Press, 1996), p. 202. See Bibliography for more details.
5. W. K. C. Guthrie, *Socrates* (London: Cambridge University Press, 1971), p. 11, tells us that Isocrates and several other later writers mentioned the lost work by Polycrates. He also suspects Plato's *Gorgias* and other dialogues were written in response to Polycrates.
6. Taylor, *Varia Socratica*, p. 4 n.1; Parker, *Athenian Religion*, p. 201.
7. Xenophon, *Memorabilia*, I.ii.9. Quoted in Guthrie, *Socrates*, p. 91. Some scholars believe that the "accuser" referred to by Xenophon is Polycrates, others believe that it is Meletus.
8. It may be that the Critias who appears in Plato's *Timaeus* was Plato's maternal great-grandfather, who was also Critias' grandfather since the Critias in question was the cousin of Plato's mother. See A. E. Taylor, *Socrates*, p. 35.
9. Stone rightly thinks this is very telling, Stone, *The Trial of Socrates*, pp. 64–65. See Thomas C. Brickhouse and Nicholas D. Smith *Plato's Socrates* (New York: Oxford University Press, 1994), pp. 171 ff. argue that Socrates sought them out in order to improve them.
10. Thucydides, *History of the Peloponnesian War*, I.23, I.88.
11. The Spartans wanted the Athenians to rescind the Megarian Decree, which was a trade embargo on Megara for her anti-Athenian activities. Other immediate causes of the war included the Athenian siege of Potidaea, and the Athenian decision to help the island of Corcyra against Corinth, an ally of Sparta. Thucydides, *History of the Peloponnesian War*, I.39.
12. Ibid, I.78, I.144.
13. Ibid, I.86.

14. Ibid, I.23 and I.76.
15. Martin Ostwald, *ANAΓKH in Thucydides* (Atlanta Georgia: Scholars Press, 1988). See also Adam Milman Parry, *Logos and Ergon in Thucydides* (Salem, New Hampshire: The Ayer Company, 1981).
16. Thucydides, *History of the Peloponnesian War*, I.75.
17. Ibid, II.54.
18. Ibid, II.64.
19. This is the view of Paul Woodruff in his commentary on Thucydides in *On Justice, Power and Human Nature: Selections from the History of the Peloponnesian War* (Indianapolis: Hackett Publishing Company, 1993), p. 48, note 116.
20. The first half of the Peloponnesian War is often referred to as the Archidamian War, in contrast to the second half, which is referred to as the Decelean or Ionian War.
21. Malcolm F. McGregor, "The Politics of the Historian Thucydides," *Phoenix*, Vol. 10, No. 3 (Fall 1956), pp. 93–102. Provides details of the aristocratic lineage of Thucydides and speculates on the significance of his admiration of Pericles.
22. Thucydides, *History of the Peloponnesian War*, II.65. The contrast with the democratic leaders of our day, who are afraid of offending people with the truth, could not be starker.
23. Ibid, VI.18.
24. Ibid, VI.18.
25. Ibid, VI.17.
26. On the similarities with the foreign policy of George W. Bush, see "Thucydides and the Neoconservatives," in my forthcoming work, *Chauvinism of the West*.
27. Thucydides, *History of the Peloponnesian War*, VII.1. These estimates come from Isocrates through Woodruff, *On Justice, Power, and Human* Nature, p. 153, note 161.
28. Thucydides, *History of the Peloponnesian War*, VIII.45–56, VIII.65–68.
29. Ibid, VIII.66.
30. Ibid, VIII. 69. The similarity with the Nazi "Brown shirts" is uncanny.
31. Ibid, VIII.53–56, VIII.65-69.
32. Andocides, *On the Mysteries*, I.96–7, quoted in McDowell, *The Laws in Classical Athens*, p. 175.
33. Leo Strauss, *City and Man* (Chicago: Rand McNally, 1964), pp. 199, 235: defends Alcibiades saying that becoming a tyrant of Athens was the only way to save the city; and that the wise man, when forced to operate in a democracy, cannot benefit his city without deceiving it.
34. It is worth noting that Sparta's glory, as the sole superpower of the Hellenic world, was short lived. After breaking with the Persian King and provoking

the hostility of her allies, Thebes and Corinth, she was conquered by the Thebans, and was not a force in Greek politics. Even though Athens was utterly defeated, she was not destroyed. In the fourth century, Athenian culture flourished; and under the leadership of Demosthenes, Athens did what she could to defend Greek freedom against the expansion of the Macedonian Empire—until that was no longer possible. See A. H. M. Jones, *Athenian Democracy* (Oxford: Basil Blackwell, 1957), p. 63.

35. Stone says that Critias was Plato's cousin: I. F. Stone, *The Trial of Socrates*, p. 64. In view of the fact that Plato was approximately 43 years younger than Socrates, it is not likely that Critias was his cousin, although he could have been his mother's cousin, as indicated in the *Charmides* 154b, where Critias tells Socrates that he is Charmides' cousin. Since Charmides is the brother of Plato's mother, it follows that Critias must also be her cousin. Taylor says that there is also a Critias who was Plato's maternal great-grandfather, who appears in the *Timaeus*. See Taylor, *Socrates*, p. 35.
36. *Charmides*, 154b.
37. Aristotle, *Constitution of Athens*, transl. by Kurt von Fritz and Ernst Kapp (New York: Hafner Publishing Company, 1950), sec. 35; Winspear and Silverberg, *Who Was Socrates?* (New Jersey: The Cordon Company, 1939), p. 76; Stone, *The Trial of Socrates*, p. 158.
38. Philostratus, *Lives of the Sophists*, I.16, available in Rosamond Kent Sprague (ed.), *The Older Sophists* (Columbia, South Carolina: University of South Carolina Press, 1972), pp. 242 ff.
39. Kathleen Freeman, *The Pre-Socratic Philosophers* (Cambridge, Massachusetts: Harvard University Press, 1959), pp. 406–07.
40. Ibid, p. 406.
41. Stone, *The Trial of Socrates*, p. 359.
42. Xenophon, *Hellenica*, II. iii. 21.
43. Freeman, *The Pre-Socratic Philosophers*, p. 407.
44. Sarah B. Pomeroy, et al., *Ancient Greece*, (New York: Oxford University Press, 2012), p. 359.
45. Ibid, p. 359.
46. Freeman, *The Pre-Socratic Philosophers*, 407.
47. Ibid, p. 407. Freeman thinks that the fact that Critias appears in so many dialogues is an indication that there is no basis for the hostility to Socrates that Xenophon maintains. Even though Freeman has all the facts regarding the brutality of the tyranny led by Critias, she contradicts them by saying that he could not have been such a dreadful tyrant if Plato included him in so many dialogues, p. 408.
48. Pomeroy, *Ancient Greece*, p. 360, claims that it was the first amnesty in history.

49. Taylor, *Varia Socratica*, p. 12.
50. Taylor, *Socrates*, p.110–112; Parker, *Athenian Religion*, p. 209; Pomeroy, et al., *Ancient Greece*, p. 360; Stone, *The Trial of Socrates*, p. 146.
51. Jones, *Athenian Democracy*, p. 54. See also Emily Wilson, *The Death of Socrates: Hero, Villain, Chatterbox, Saint* (London: Profile Books, 2007), p. 54.
52. Parker, *Athenian Religion*, p. 207.
53. Taylor, *Socrates*, p. 114. Despite the brilliance of Taylor's path-breaking work, he nevertheless clings to the illusion that Socrates was innocent. In his view, the fact that Socrates was a friend of Alcibiades, Critias, and Charmides, was his "misfortune," pp. 100, 115.
54. Taylor, *Socrates*, p. 102.
55. Taylor, *Socrates*, p. 102: on the contrary, he defended Andocides, who was also on trial for impiety on account of the profanation of the Mysteries, to be discussed in the next chapter.
56. Ibid.
57. Ibid, pp. 54, 109.
58. Plutarch. *Lives*. 4 Vols. Translated by Aubrey Stewart and George Long (London: G. Bell and Sons, Ltd., 1910), "Life of Alkibiades," Vol. I, sec, XXXIX. Plutarch claims that Timandra showed his corpse all the honor and respect she could muster.
59. Sarah B. Pomeroy, et al., *Ancient Greece*, p. 360.
60. '*The Old Oligarch*' or *The Constitution of the Athenians Attributed to Xenophon*, trans. by J. L. Marr and P. J. Rhodes (Oxford: Oxbow Books, 2008), pp. 7 ff.
61. Ibid, p. 16. Antiphon was tried and convicted for treason. At his trial, he gave a brilliant speech that has been compared to that of Socrates. Like Socrates, Antiphon was about seventy years old, he did not flee as did the other oligarchs, and he refused to appeal to the sympathy of the jurors with supplications. Antiphon argued that bringing down the democracy would be contrary to his own interests since his rhetorical skills would not benefit him in an oligarchy. See Antiphon, *The Speeches*, edited by Michael Gagarin (New York: Cambridge University Press, 1997), pp. 247 ff.
62. Marr and Rhodes, '*The Old Oligarch*,' 1.14.
63. Ibid, 1.16.
64. This is best represented in Plato's famous allegory of the ship, *Republic*, 488a.
65. *History of the Peloponnesian War*, II.13–16.
66. Marr and Rhodes, '*The Old Oligarch*,' Introduction, pp. 20–21.
67. Ibid, 1.2.
68. Plato, *Republic*, 342e; Xenophon, *Memorabilia*, II. ii.37.

69. Gregory Vlastos makes a sharp distinction between the Socrates of Plato and the Socrates of Xenophon. He denies that Plato's Socrates was oligarchic. See "The Historical Socrates and Athenian Democracy," *Political Theory*, Vol. 11, No. 4 (Nov., 1983), pp. 495–516. See also the definitive refutation of this argument by Ellen Meiksins Wood and Neal Wood, "Socrates and Democracy: A Reply to Gregory Vlastos," *Political Theory*, Vol. 13, No. 1 (Feb., 1986), pp. 55–82. See Bibliography for details.
70. A. G. Woodhead makes this point in *Thucydides on the Nature of Power* (Cambridge, Massachusetts: Harvard University Press, 1970), pp. 63–67.
71. That is the reason that Thomas Hobbes preferred a tyrant to a monarch—the tyrant can choose a competent successor, whereas the monarch is bound by the traditional rules of succession.
72. Socrates was a member of the Council when the Athenians decided to put the Generals on trial for failing to pick up the surviving sailors after their defeat at the battle of Arginusae.
73. *Symposium*, 216b.
74. Ibid, 216c.
75. *Alcibiades I*, 135c, in Vol. I of *The Dialogues of Plato*, translated by B. Jowett (London: Oxford University Press, 1931) in 4 vols. On the authenticity of the dialogue, see footnote on p. 601, and the introduction to the dialogue on pp. 627–28. It is important to note that regardless of the authenticity of the dialogue, the relationship between Socrates and Alcibiades presented here is not inconsistent with the *Symposium*.
76. Ibid, 118a–b.
77. "The Life of Alcibiades," in Vol. I of Plutarch's *Lives* (4 Vols.), transl. by Aubrey Stewart and George Long (London: G. Bell and Sons, Ltd., 1910).
78. I will argue in Section 4 that the Socratic pre-occupation with "the care of the soul" has a more political and less reclusive dimension than is generally believed.
79. For the Old Oligarch, every regime serves the interests of those who rule, and democracy is no exception. It is natural and inevitable for those who rule to make laws that promote their own interests. So, the perversity of democracy is integral to its very nature. The political assumptions of the Old Oligarch appear similar to the assumptions made by Thrasymachus as presented in the first book of Plato's *Republic*. Those who rule make laws in their own interests—whether it is a democracy, an oligarchy, or a tyranny. In each case, the interest of the stronger (i.e., the ruling party) defines what is just and legal. So, justice is a matter of obedience to the laws that are intended to serve the interests of the ruling party—i.e., justice is the "interest of the stronger." However, this resemblance is superficial. It is a mistake to associate the Old Oligarch with the iconoclastic view of the Sophists. The Old Oligarch is a true believer; he thinks that the interests of the *oligoi* (the

noble and worthy) are worth promoting and a city that promotes the interests of the valuable people is a better city than one that promotes the interests of the good-for-nothings.
80. 'The Old Oligarch,' 2.20.
81. Thucydides, *History of the Peloponnesian War*, VI. 38–39.
82. Ibid, VI.28.
83. Ibid, VI.16.
84. Ibid, VI.16.
85. Leo Strauss, guru of the American neoconservatives, shares the attitudes of Alcibiades and the Old Oligarch. But in America, he and his disciples are hailed as patriots, not accused of treason. See *Liberalism Ancient and Modern* (New York: Cornell University Press, 1968), chapter 2, "Liberal Education and Responsibility," a rare occasion where Strauss speaks in his own name.
86. Thucydides, *History of the Peloponnesian War*, VI. 38–39.
87. *Gorgias*, 522a.
88. Ibid, 503c.
89. Ibid, 519a.
90. Ibid, 519a–b. My italics.
91. Ibid, 517b.
92. Thucydides, *History of the Peloponnesian War*, II. 65.
93. *Protagoras*, 320a.
94. Ibid, 309a.
95. *Apology*, 21a.
96. Taylor, *Socrates*, p. 76. There was Phaedo of Elis, Simmias and Cebes (the two Pythagoreans) from Phlius, and the two Eleatics from Megara. Taylor notes this but does not seem to notice that these facts undermine Socrates' claim that his life would be utterly meaningless were he to leave his beloved city. Apparently, Plato was not present because of illness, and Xenophon left Athens in 401 BCE to join the expedition of Cyrus in his effort to seize the Persian throne. According to Taylor, there is no evidence that Xenophon visited Athens between that time and when he was banished in 394 BCE.
97. Stone, *The Trial of Socrates*, p. 153.
98. *Republic*, 472c–e.
99. The same can be said for Xenophon, since *On Tyranny* is an effort by the wise man to influence the tyrant and transform the regime.
100. Pomeroy, *Ancient Greece*, pp. 372 ff.
101. Taylor, *Socrates*, p. 150, makes a similar observation, but it does it lead him to any significant conclusions.
102. *Statesman*, 302d–e.
103. Ibid, 303a–b.

104. That gives us six regimes. The seventh is the only true constitution governed by the true or god-like statesman—a regime that is exalted above all others, and to which we will return in the next section.
105. *Statesman*, 303b.
106. Ibid, 303a.
107. *Laws*, 693 d-e.
108. Werner Jaeger, *Paideia: the Ideals of Greek Culture*, Vol. III: *The Conflict of Cultural Ideals in the Age of Plato* (New York: Oxford University Press, 1944), p. 137.
109. Pomeroy, *Ancient Greece*, pp. 398–99.
110. Popper, *The Open Society and Its Enemies*, Vol. 1, *The Spell of Plato* (Princeton, N.J.: Princeton University Press, 1966), p. 136.
111. Kathleen Freeman, *The Pre-Socratic Philosophers* (Cambridge, Massachusetts: Harvard University Press, 1959), explains why this satyr-play should be attributed to Critias, p. 411.
112. Ibid.
113. Some scholars believe that the play might belong to Euripides, but most scholars attribute the play to Critias. This fragment is the only surviving piece of a work that is of interest because it is alleged to be one of the earliest expressions of atheism in the ancient world; see James H. Dee, "Critias of Athens," *Free Inquiry*, Vol. 32, No. 2 (February/March 2012), pp. 48–49.
114. Sextus, *Against the Schoolmasters*, IX.54, in Sprague, *The Older Sophists*, pp. 259–60.
115. See my *Political Ideas of Leo Strauss, Updated Edition*.
116. Søren Kierkegaard, *Concluding Scientific Postscript* (1835), in Louis P. Pojman, *Classics of Philosophy, Vol. II: Modern and Contemporary* (Oxford University Press, 1997), p. 167.
117. Sprague, *The Older Sophists*, p. 252. I doubt that the Helots (serfs of the Spartan state) found the brutality they endured to be the epitome of moderation. In any case, Critias' enthusiasm for moderation was for others, not for himself.
118. *Gorgias*, 470a–b.
119. Freeman, *The Pre-Socratic Philosophers*, pp. 407–08. My italics.
120. *Apology* 30c–31a.

CHAPTER 2

The Religious Case Against Socrates

In this chapter, I will examine the charge of impiety in the context in which it was made. We cannot fully understand the trial if we do not take the religious charges seriously, as having a validity distinct from the political dimensions of the trial.[1] Plato's *Euthyphro* makes it clear that Socrates despised the traditional conception of piety and of the gods. Socrates was known to associate with Pythagoreans and shared their Orphic ideas—ideas that were foreign to the Athenian religion. Socrates did indeed "invent new gods" in the sense of endorsing a conception of the divine that was at odds with the traditional gods of the city.[2] In that light, it is difficult to avoid the conclusion that Socrates was guilty as charged—guilty of not recognizing the gods of the city and introducing novel divinities.[3]

Interestingly, Plato never defends Socrates against the charge of impiety. Clearly, he does not regard it as a "crime" that deserves to be taken seriously. On the contrary, he thinks that the Socratic view of the gods and of piety is infinitely superior to the traditional view. Indeed, he regards these Socratic ideas as a gift to humanity—and the verdict of the ages seems to agree. Thanks to the success of Christianity, the religious ideas of Socrates have triumphed historically. But the triumphant ideas are not necessarily the best. By lionizing the innovations of Socrates, we congratulate ourselves, and the Christian tradition to which we belong. However, if we abandon our Christianizing lenses, it will be clear that the ideas introduced by Socrates may not be as innocuous as they seem.

To grasp what is at issue, we must refrain from confusing impiety with a more familiar concept—namely, heresy. The religious case against Socrates is not separate from the political one, because Greek religion was a civil religion, which is to say that it was a state religion. In other words, religion and politics were not separate. In what follows, I hope to show that the charge of impiety is logically connected to the political charge of "corrupting the young." In contrast to Plato and his admirers, I believe that the Socratic conception of piety, as presented in Plato's *Euthyphro*, is not only a startling innovation, but also a destabilizing political concept that invites political violence and extremism. This leads me to conclude that the religious ideas of Socrates are linked to the political violence and extremism displayed by his students.

1   GREEK CIVIL RELIGION

Greek religion was a civil religion—which is to say that it was an affair of the state. The gods of the city were a unifying symbol around which the city was constituted.[4] Religion was a civic duty; one's religious duties were part of one's duties as a citizen. Religion was not separate from politics; it was a matter of political allegiance. Honoring the gods of the city by participating in the feasts, festivals, and sacrifices ordained by the city was part of being a citizen. It follows that respect for the gods of the city was identical with respect for the city and its welfare. By the same token, offending the gods of the city was a transgression against the city. So closely intertwined were the city and its gods that there was a single law in Athens that applied to traitors and temple robbers—exile, confiscation of property, and even death were the penalties.[5]

All the temples, statues, and altars, all the feasts, festivals, singing, dancing, libations, rituals, and sacrifices, were intended to please the gods in the hope of eliciting their favors. These activities wedded the community together in a shared fate, citizenship, and allegiance. On the other hand, offending the gods might lead them to withdraw their protection and allow the city to suffer misfortunes that their guardianship might have averted. In the absence of divine protection, the city might be vulnerable to the destructive forces of nature or the aggression of other cities. So understood, religion was a function of survival in a dangerous world. Like politics, it was intended to enhance human prosperity and success *in this world*—the only world we know. Herodotus tells us that Athens was deemed to be important and prosperous because it was endowed with "useful gods."[6]

The gods did not only account for the city's prosperity, they were also useful in upholding its laws. The gods were invoked to inflict harm on traitors, thieves, swindlers, and those who break their oaths and contracts. When citizens swear by the gods to uphold contracts or to tell the truth in court, they are risking divine retribution if they break their agreements or fail to keep their word. The Athenian Assembly "included curses threatening utter destruction against any who might speak out of bribery or with the intent to deceive."[7] The gods cannot perform this function if they are moralistic gods who refrain from inflicting *any* harm; and are believed to be only the source of good in human life, and never the source of mischief. In other words, impeccable moral credentials can make the gods less useful to the state. Moreover, gods that can be harnessed in service to the state cannot be gods who represent immutable and eternal justice that transcends the justice of the city. They must be the sorts of gods who are willing to retaliate against those who break the laws of the city. In other words, the gods of the city must be partial to the city. As we shall see, Socrates insists on moralizing the gods, making them the custodians of a transcendent justice independent of the city, and hence, useless to the city, if not also threatening.

The alliance of politics and religion meant that new gods could not be introduced without the approval of the state.[8] In Athens, it was against the law to introduce foreign gods not authorized by the state, especially if a shrine for the new gods was to be built on Attic soil.[9] However, there was no blanket rejection of new or foreign gods. Athens was famous for its generosity to foreign gods—witness Pan, Bendis, and others. Paganism had a collector's mentality when it came to gods. Pagan gods were not jealous gods. They did not deny the existence of other gods; and it was common to have more than one god in the same sanctuary. In a polytheistic world, every city had its patron god or goddess, but other gods or godesses were also worshipped. The plurality of gods ensured an acceptance of plurality in the human world. It meant a plurality of purposes, projects, points of view, and religious practices. Religious diversity was a function of human and political diversity. At the same time, freedom of religion was not recognized *in principle*, it depended on the sanction of the city and the practices involved.[10]

The role played by the gods in the city may be compared to the role played by Queen Elizabeth II in the United Kingdom. The Queen has no political power; she is a figurehead. Nevertheless, any effort to replace her would be an act of sabotage against the constitution. She is the symbol around which the state is established; to change the symbol is to change the nature of the constitution over which she presides. Honoring the Queen is the same as accepting the constitution of the state. It means accepting the rules with which a civilized society replaces force: the rules that determine how decisions are made, how power is allocated, and how commerce is conducted. Defacing her portraits all over the kingdom would be an act of political sabotage—a rejection of the constitution of the state. Something very similar is at stake in dishonoring the gods of the city. So understood, religious piety was respect for the patron gods of the city. Understood as an integral element of the state, religion was a pragmatic affair. By the same token, impiety was a public display of disrespect of sufficient gravity that a jury might regard it as dangerous to the continued existence of the city and its safety.

Pagan religion had no scriptures, creeds, orthodoxies, doctrines, or dogmas. It had no theologians to spin the most preposterous ideas into a wellspring of profundity. Nor was there any need for a priestly caste or an organized priesthood with a stranglehold on education and political power, as was the case in ancient Egypt, Medieval Europe, Tibet (until the Chinese expelled the Dalai Lama in 1950), and the French Canadian province of Quebec under Maurice Duplessis (until the Quiet Revolution of the 1960s). In ancient Greece, serving as a priest or priestess at a sacrifice was a civic honor, not a life-long career. The rituals were easy to learn. Sacrifices were feasts—occasions to get dressed up, sing, dance, and eat lots of meat.[11] The sacrificial animal was adorned before being marched to the altar for the slaughter. Then someone responsible for carrying water, sprinkled it on the hapless creature, so it would nod its head in assent to the sacrifice; then another person, usually a pretty maiden, carried a basket with a knife concealed by grains of barley that were thrown over the victim; the throat was cut, the animal was dismembered, the meat was cooked, and the feasting began. Only the most inedible parts—the bones and the fat—were offered to the gods.[12] A priest presided over these proceedings. It was not a difficult job. It required no professional training. It was an honor reserved for citizens, not foreigners, slaves, or resident aliens.

Even though pagan religion had no professional priesthood, it had seers and exegetes who were employed by the state to interpret omens, signs, and oracles. As told by Herodotus, no military strategy was ever decided without a seer to make sure that the omens were favorable.[13] Seers had to interpret the flight of birds, or examine the condition of the entrails of victims after a sacrifice, in search of auspicious omens; otherwise the army could not march. Their function was to predict if a military strategy will or will not be successful. In other words, they had to foretell the future—like reading tealeaves. It was a very dangerous profession for those who were unlucky enough to make the wrong predictions.[14] They could be arrested and condemned to death, if the army suffered too many reverses on their account.[15] Some seers were very famous, such as Lampon, who was a friend of Pericles, and helped in the founding of colonies by deciding on the best site for the towns. It was the sort of job that anyone with commonsense could do. Nevertheless, Lampon was believed to have a special relationship with the gods.[16] But on the whole, seers were considered charlatans. Even the famous Pythia at Delphi was criticized for giving improper responses.[17] Not surprisingly, seers were the butt of many jokes by Aristophanes. The notorious Diopeithes was depicted in Aristophanes' *Birds* as a madman. The gods were themselves the butt of jokes. Laughing at the seers and at the gods was not impiety. Nor was it impious to deny the very existence of the gods. It was just talk and good fun. Otherwise, Aristophanes would have been prosecuted. Impiety was an *act* of desecration, defilement, or vandalism directed at religious sanctuaries, temples, or statues, as symbols of the state.

The cornerstone of Greek religion was ritual, not faith.[18] Most scholars agree that intellectual dissent alone was not sufficient to convict anyone of impiety. In other words, impiety was not a *purely intellectual* form of disloyalty; it had to manifest itself in *conduct* that was overtly disrespectful of the gods as patrons of the city. We cannot understand the charge of impiety through our Christianizing lenses. The latter lead us to conflate impiety with heresy. Even scholars, who are extremely scrupulous in avoiding Christianizing lenses, provide baffling accounts of the concept of impiety. On one hand, they rightly point out that Greek religion had neither church nor dogma, and therefore, "heresy and religious persecution were in principle impossible."[19] Yet, when it comes to discussing impiety, they claim that impiety (*asebeia*) involves not believing in the gods, or holding wrong opinions about them—a definition that is refuted by their own analysis.[20] Heresy makes sense only in a religion of dogmas. In the absence of any compulsory beliefs, it is impossible to be guilty of heresy, which is having wrong beliefs. To undermine the gods of the city by a public display of contempt was both politically treasonous and an act of impiety.

However, some scholars wonder if this state of affairs did not begin to change in the second half of the fifth century.[21] They surmise that impiety was no longer confined to irreligious *deeds*, but began to include also irreligious *words*. Supposedly, expressions of atheism—not believing in the existence of the gods or being skeptical about the gods—came to be seen as a threat. In legal terms, this development is associated with a decree introduced by Diopeithes, just before the Peloponnesian War of 431 BCE. The decree required that those who did not believe in the gods, and provided scientific accounts of the heavens, should be prosecuted.[22] Despite admittedly scanty evidence, it is believed that there was a backlash against intellectuals in the second half of the fifth century.[23] Anaxagoras was supposedly charged with impiety just for claiming that the sun was a hot stone. Aspasia, the brilliant companion and common-law wife of Pericles was supposedly charged with impiety for her unorthodox ideas. Protagoras supposedly fled from Athens after being charged with impiety.[24] Then there were the trials of Phryne, Alcibiades, Diagoras, and Socrates. It follows that Socrates is simply the most famous individual to be caught up in these events.

The only evidence for the decree by Diopeithes is in Plutarch, who wrote five hundred years after Socrates.[25] There is nothing in Plato, Xenophon, or Thucydides about this significant development. Even though Diopeithes appears in more than one play by Aristophanes, his decree is not mentioned in any of them.[26] We know that Anaxagoras was attracted to Athens for its intellectually exciting atmosphere, and that he became a good friend and mentor to Pericles.[27] Scholars who believe that Anaxagoras and Aspasia were charged with impiety suspect that the motive was political—an effort by the enemies of Pericles to undermine him by showing that his closest associates were foreigners who were not committed to the welfare of Athens.[28] However, as I. F. Stone has argued, if these events had happened, they would have been significant enough to be mentioned by Thucydides.[29] After all, Thucydides was an admirer of Pericles, and the latter played a central role in the historian's account of the Peloponnesian War.

The same is true for Protagoras. We know that Protagoras was agnostic about the gods; he thought that nothing could be known about them with any certainty. This observation is hard to refute. The rumor that Protagoras was charged with impiety is just that. He was a figure of great admiration and respect throughout his life. Pericles asked him to draft laws for an Athenian colony in Thurii in 444 BCE.[30] It was the sort of honor that Socrates would have never been accorded, despite his claims to political expertise. Protagoras was respected in the way that Socrates was not. In Plato's *Meno*, Socrates claimed that Protagoras corrupted everyone, but died with his reputation undiminished.[31] Clearly, the Athenians disagreed about who was busy corrupting the young.

Prosecuting people for *holding* heterodox religious views makes no sense in the context of a religion with no creed. To resolve this problem, Gregory Vlastos suggested that Socrates was not prosecuted simply for not believing in the Greek gods. His crime was *teaching* these ideas to others.[32] However, this claim does not resolve the difficulty. Even if Socrates taught his students not to believe in the gods, it would not explain the charge of impiety. The private disbelief of these students would not qualify as impiety. Impiety must be displayed in some sort of *conduct* that is insulting to the gods and threatening to the community. We are not dealing with a religion (such as Christianity) that is obsessed with what is in our hearts or minds. We are dealing with a religion that combines superstition with pragmatism. Superstition is rooted in fear of the precariousness of existence, the fickleness of fate, and the terrors of the unknown—all of which are represented by the capriciousness of the gods. At the same time, a pragmatic approach to new forms of worship meant that they were accepted or rejected depending on what the worship involved, or what conduct it inspired.[33]

Nevertheless, the claim that there was a backlash against intellectuals persists. This picture is appealing because it fits the legend of Socrates as a martyr for truth. According to Dodds, the Greek Enlightenment threatened the diviners, who saw their prestige and livelihood fading. Socrates was unlucky enough to be caught up in the backlash against reason.[34] However, a man who receives private messages from a daemon, a god or otherworldly spirit, belongs with the diviners, and can hardly be at the forefront of the Greek Enlightenment. Dodds tells us that the failure of Greek rationalism led to the augmentation of superstition and unreason, which paved the way for the triumph of Christianity. I would not deny that Christianity triumphs best in an atmosphere of ignorance, superstition, and irrationality.

However, Socrates was not a model of Greek rationalism; he was an advocate of a new conception of the divine, an Orphic conception that opened the door to Christian monotheism, to the rewards and punishments of the afterlife, to a savage asceticism, and to all the terror and irrationality that is integral to Christianity.

The problem is that impiety (*asebeia*) was never clearly defined. So, the definition depended on the jury—they knew it when they saw it.[35] This is not to deny that there were clear cases of impiety. Phryne, a courtesan and self-proclaimed priestess, was prosecuted for introducing new gods that were unauthorized by the city. She was the leader of marauding bands of men and women, who were a threat to law and order.[36] There is a resemblance between the lawlessness of Phryne's bands of revelers and the lawlessness of the young oligarchic radicals who followed Socrates and who were charged with impiety for mutilating the Hermae or Herms—the stone statues of the god Hermes. However it was understood, impiety involved some destructive or threatening conduct beyond mere thought. In truth, the first person to criminalize thought was Plato.

2 Mutilating the Hermae

When the gods are capricious and mischievous, then each city must do its best to flatter its own gods in the hope that they might protect it against misfortune. In such a world, every city is entitled to have its own gods—its own protection against the slings and arrows of outrageous fortune. In this way, the gods that people worship have nothing to do with whether they are good or bad people. In such a world, those who do not bother to worship and sacrifice may be considered reckless (taking unnecessary risks), but there is no reason to assume that they will be unjust in their dealings with others—including foreigners. The same is true for those who deny the existence of the gods. Those who publicly insult the gods with acts of vandalism are another matter—they threaten the safety of the community. Defacing the Herms was a case in point.

On the eve of the fateful Athenian invasion of Syracuse (415 BCE), the stone statues of the god Hermes were mutilated throughout Athens. These stone statues with bearded faces, a rectangular stone body, and an erect phallus, were first used as territorial demarcations throughout Attica to mark the midway points between Attic villages and the Athenian agora. Later, every neighborhood in Athens had its Herms, where private sacrifices and feasts often took place.[37] The Herms became so popular that they adorned entrances to public buildings, including the agora; and were also found at the entrance of many private homes throughout the city. The Herms were believed to bring good luck and protection from danger.[38] So, when they were found with their noses chopped off, and on some accounts, their erect genitals severed, the city was gripped with a sense of foreboding.

Thucydides tells us that when it was discovered that these sacrilegious *acts*, had been committed the Athenians were alarmed; they were afraid that the expedition would fail.[39] After all, Hermes was the messenger of Zeus and the god of voyages. The scale of the destruction indicated that the mutilation of the *Hermae* was an organized and concerted effort, and not just the result of a haphazard drunken brawl. As Emily Kearns explains, the message was not simply, "we insult the gods" because we are rich and drunk and were on our way home from a *Symposium* (i.e., a drinking party for aristocratic young men), but rather, "we insult the gods of the Athenian democracy" because we are sober, organized, and know exactly what we are doing with the symbolism of this terrorist attack.[40] It was a clear rejection of the established order. It was an indication that a revolution was immanent. Moreover, the suspicion that the gods would be offended by the impious conduct of Alcibiades and other members of the Socratic circle seemed to be confirmed by the fact that the Athenian invasion of Sicily was a catastrophe—the loss in blood and treasure for Athens was unprecedented. Families were stricken with grief at the loss of sons, husbands, and fathers. Five of the people convicted were associates of Socrates—the charge was impiety.[41] Alcibiades was suspected of plotting to overthrow the democracy. So, shortly after the start of the Sicilian expedition, he was recalled to Athens to face charges, but he escaped and went to Sparta.[42]

Adding to the fury was a rumor that a mocking version of the Mystery rites at Eleusis was staged to profane the gods. The Eleusinian Mysteries were rites of a harvest festival devoted to Demeter and her daughter (Persephone) at Eleusis. It started as a "secret" cult that was forbidden to unauthorized persons. But when Eleusis was united with Athens (some time in the seventh century) then it became an official cult of Athens, directed by the government.[43] Once Athens became the center of Greek life (around the 440 s), all of Greece became interested in this festival. It was open to everyone who was not accused of shedding blood—which was true for all religious ceremonies of the state. In this way, it became a symbol of the openness and generosity of the Athenian democracy.[44] It was sacred to the Athenians, who considered it a symbol of their wealth, power, and well-being.[45] Participation in the Eleusinian Mysteries inspired unusual hope in the minds of the participants who thought they would be blessed with riches in this world and a better fate in Hades.[46] This aspect of the cult has led some scholars to associate it with the mystery religions of the Orphic variety.[47] However, others believe that this is too radical a departure from the "path of logic and lucidity" that characterizes the state religion. Besides, Hades remains what it has traditionally been—an unhappy place without either bliss or torment. The "secret" of the Mysteries was not a dogma but a dramatic performance or "religious pantomime," probably representing the rape of Persephone, the wandering of Demeter in search of her daughter, and their eventual reunion.[48]

Alcibiades was suspected of orchestrating the destruction and leading the mockery, because, as Thucydides informs us, he was notorious for his lawlessness and anti-democratic proclivities. Also prosecuted were four other members of the Socratic circle: Axiochus, Alcibiades' uncle, and two other people who appear in Plato's *Symposium*—Phaedrus, Eryximachus, as well as Acumenus, the father of Eryximachus.[49] Diagoras of Melos was also prosecuted for mocking the Mysteries shortly after. Needless to say, memories of all these events were still fresh for members of the jury at the trial of Socrates—and that did not auger well for him. Socrates was suspected of inspiring these lawless acts of impiety, which grew out of a profound contempt for the democratic city and its symbols.

The mutilation of the Hermae was a clear example of impiety, understood as an affront to the constitution, safety, and well-being of the city. Plato believed that the charge of impiety was a trumped up accusation without foundation.[50] He denied that the ideas of Socrates could possibly incite this sort of conduct. Is this credible? Is there nothing about the religion of Socratic that could lead to the desecration of the statues of the god and the mockery of the rituals of the state? Plato's *Euthyphro* provides the best insights into the religion of Socrates.

3 Defeating Euthyphro

Plato's *Euthyphro* is much more ambitious than it appears. It is certainly not the "most disappointing thing in Plato."[51] Nor is the dialogue simply a display of the Socratic *elenchus,* or dialectical refutation, which is destructive rather than constructive. It does not simply destroy the definitions of piety that Euthyphro, his interlocutor, concocts, without providing us with a constructive account of the Socratic view of piety.[52] In other words, it is not just an example of Socrates displaying his virtuosity by revealing the muddle-headedness of others. On the contrary, Plato's *Euthyphro* tells us a great deal about the Socratic conception of piety and of the divine.[53] Even though the dialogue dismisses the theory of morality as adherence to divine commands, the gods are not left out of the moral picture altogether.[54] On the contrary, they are integral to the Socratic morality. The dialogue is also the cornerstone of Plato's all-out offensive against Homer, the Greek gods, and traditional Greek religion in general. The dialogue tries to use Euthyphro's nuttiness as an illustration of the shortcomings of Homer and traditional Greek religion. However, it does not succeed, because, among other things, Euthyphro is not a representative of traditional or Homeric religion, as I hope to show.[55]

Plato's *Euthyphro* is the key to understanding how Socrates turned Homeric ideas about the gods and about piety on their head. The dialogue is nothing short of a watershed in the history of the West. It explains why Socrates set out to replace the old gods of Homer, and why Plato followed in his footsteps by banishing the old gods in favor of the new gods invented by Socrates, both in the *Republic* and the *Laws*. The question is: Are the new gods superior to the old? Did the old gods deserve to be banished?

In the dialogue, Socrates meets Euthyphro outside the courthouse while he is waiting for his trial. When Euthyphro hears about the charges against Socrates, he is extremely sympathetic, since he assumes that Socrates is a man after his own heart; he regards himself and Socrates as birds of a feather—subtle theologians exposed to the wrath and misunderstanding of the vulgar masses, *hoi polloi* who do not appreciate lofty insights. Euthyphro is appearing in court to prosecute his father for murder. This was not a fictional case. Apparently, one of the servants of Euthyphro's father got drunk and knifed and killed one of the household slaves. So, Euthyphro's father had him bound and kept in a ditch and sent someone to the authorities to inquire what should be done with the drunken murderer. Meanwhile, the murderer died in the ditch, likely from cold and hunger, before the messenger came back. Euthyphro blamed his father and decided to prosecute him for murder. Family and friends were appalled at Euthyphro's conduct. The general attitude is that prosecuting one's father is an outrage. Besides, the father did not kill the servant, nor did he intend to kill him; moreover, the man was a killer who hardly deserved a thought.[56] That was the common sense view of the matter. But Euthyphro considered himself an expert on moral as well as religious matters, and did not agree with the common view. He thought that the guilty must be punished no matter who they were. Euthyphro's self-righteousness was encouraged by Zeus's treatment of his father—Zeus bound and banished his father for his injustice, which included swallowing his children. In punishing the injustice of his father, Euthyphro had the nerve to model himself after Zeus.[57]

From the conventional point of view, Euthyphro is guilty of *hubris*. The gods were not role models for human beings to emulate. In the Homeric scheme of things, different standards apply to mortals and immortals. The gulf between the human and the divine ought not to be bridged. Even though in Greek mythology mortal women bore children that were fathered by gods, and goddesses bore children that were fathered by mortal men, the demarcation between the mortals and the immortals was nevertheless stark. The close connection of the heroes to the divine was a way of explaining their achievements. The immortals had everlasting life, but the mortals were like the leaves—creatures of a season, here today and gone tomorrow. Apollo describes them as "wretched creatures who, like the leaves, flourish in fiery brilliance for a little while on the bounty of the earth, then in a moment, droop and fade away."[58] Mortals were inconsequential, ephemeral nothings in the scheme of things, and should therefore know their place and act accordingly.[59] It follows that the gods are not models for human emulation. The idea that human beings should emulate the gods is *hubris*.[60] The latter is the opposite of piety, which requires humility—not to be confused with false modesty. The Greek injunction, "know thyself" is not so much an endorsement of introspection, but a reminder of the fact that we are not gods. As Walter F. Otto explains, the injunction of the Delphic temple "does not imply examination of conscience or confession of sins," but simply a recognition of the limitations of humanity."[61] In short, the vice of *hubris* is oblivion to the gulf between mortals and immortals. Who does Euthyphro think he is? Is he comparing himself to Zeus? How laughable. Does he think he is being pious? How ridiculous. The arrogance of acting like a god is *hubris*. Warring against the father can be accomplished without self-destruction—only by a god. So, we should not assume, as Plato would like us to assume, that a victory over Euthyphro is a victory over Homer, or traditional Greek religion for that matter. Euthyphro is not an ordinary fellow, nor does his view of religion represent the conventional Greek view, as is often believed.[62] Euthyphro is not a poster child for the Homeric religion; he has one foot in the traditional religion and the other in the newfangled ideas that influenced Socrates. This is why Socrates easily entraps him in a contradiction.

Far from being irrelevant to the trial, as I. F. Stone maintains, the *Euthyphro* is an integral part of Plato's apology for Socrates.[63] We are supposed to be appalled that the Athenians dare to accuse Socrates of impiety when their own sordid view of the gods leads the most ardent members of their society astray. The conventional reading of the dialogue, the one that Plato hoped to convey, is that Socrates was justified in trying to overhaul the old religion of Homer. The dialogue is intended to acknowledge that Socrates did indeed invent new gods—but under the circumstances, who can blame him? He was doing the Greeks a favor, but they were too dim-witted to realize it. That is the crux of Plato's response to the charge of impiety. In short, the dialogue is integral to Plato's offensive strategy for the defense. But, we should not be fooled.

Plato's argument is not as successful as it appears. It succeeds only by a sleight of hand. It succeeds only because the triumph over Euthyphro is mistaken for a triumph over Homer. It succeeds only if Euthyphro's conduct is regarded as the kind of error that Homeric religion invites—but this is not the case. The message, which Plato will deliver again and again in other dialogues, is that Homer's gods set a bad example that leads even the most ardently pious people astray. Euthyphro was just imitating the bad old gods. New gods are needed if pious men, such as Euthyphro, are not to be corrupted. This is why the traditional view of the gods must be over-hauled by inventing new gods—virtuous gods who can serve as models to be emulated by human beings. It follows that piety can only be a virtue if the old gods are rehabilitated. The moralistic gods of Socrates are intended to do just that. It follows that Socrates does not believe in the bad old gods of Homer or the city, but is devoted to new gods.

4   Moralizing the Gods

Adopting his most ironic and self-effacing posture, Socrates begs Euthyphro to explain what piety is so that he can defend himself against the charge of impiety. Euthyphro tells Socrates that the pious is what the gods love. Socrates and Euthyphro agree that the gods love justice and goodness; it follows that pious acts are a subset of just acts—i.e., whatever is pious is also just. These assumptions make religion part of morality. Homer would not have so casually accepted this claim—but Socrates and Euthyphro are in total agreement on this matter.

Having established that piety is part of justice, and that justice is beloved by the gods, Socrates asks Euthyphro if the gods always agree, or do they disagree and quarrel? Euthyphro instinctively falls back on Homer's stories and says that the gods disagree and quarrel.[64] Then he is sunk. If they disagree, then the same thing will be loved by some of the gods and hated by others. This means that the same thing will be simultaneously just and unjust, pious and impious.[65]

To escape logical contradiction, Euthyphro is forced to concede that the gods never disagree about the pious, the right, and the good—they are invariably unanimous. In this way, a new conception of the divine is born. The plurality and diversity of the gods gives way to oneness and unity, which is the pre-requisites of monotheism. This is why the dialogue is a watershed in the religious history of the West. The transition from plurality to unity and oneness where the divine is concerned is momentous.

Socrates wonders whether something is pious or righteous simply because it is loved by the gods, or whether it is loved by the gods because it is already (on independent rational grounds) just and good.[66] The relation between goodness and approval is a perfectly valid moral question that is independent of theological concerns. One need not believe in god or gods to be uneasy about the relation between goodness and approval. A totally secular version of the question is: What do we mean when we describe something as good or just? Does it mean that we approve of it and hope that others will approve of it also? Or, is casting goodness and justice in terms of approval a matter of putting the cart before the horse? If things can be made good and just simply by our approval, then we can go about approving all sorts of sordid things, and in so doing, make them good. If goodness were the same as approval, then, when Dostoevsky describes prisoners in Siberia approving and enjoying the torture of others, we must understand him to be saying that torture is right because the people involved approve of it. Of course, that would be missing the point of the story—which is meant to illustrate just how morally depraved people can be, especially when incarcerated in squalid prisons.

Socrates is quite right in wanting to separate justice from mere approval—of human beings, governments, figures of authority, and even the gods. The dialogue succeeds in showing how hopeless and confusing the world would be if we were to reduce the meaning of the just, the right, and the good to approval. However, having established that piety is a subset of justice, Socrates wonders if it can be independent of the approval of the gods. If piety can be defined independently from the gods, then it is not distinct from justice, so we might as well forget about piety and simply focus on justice. However, having been accused of impiety, Socrates is particularly eager to understand what it is. So, he asks Euthyphro to explain what kind of acts are pious and how they differ from just acts in general.[67]

When prodded, Euthyphro falls back on the traditional view. He defines pious acts such as prayer and sacrifice as necessary to "preserve both private houses and public affairs of state."[68] Piety is giving honor and reverence to the gods in the hope that they will benefit us. Put bluntly, human beings flatter the gods to satisfy the latter's desire for self-aggrandizement; in exchange, the gods bestow their favors. Piety emerges as an exchange between men and gods for mutual advantage. In this traditional view, piety and morality are distinct. Piety is about the relation of human beings (individually or collectively) with the world and the inscrutable powers that operate in it—represented by the gods. Morality is about the relation of human beings with one another. In other words, serving the gods (piety) and being good to our fellow human beings (morality) are two different things. The gods reward people for serving them, not for serving other human beings. Xenophon tells us that in speaking to Heracles, Virtue tells him that

> if you want the favor of the gods, you must worship the gods: if you desire the love of friends, you must do good to your friends: if you covet honor from a city, you must aid that city....[69]

To flourish (individually or collectively), you must worship, flatter, and serve the gods in exchange for their gifts—good fortune or success in your ventures. Of course, this was wishful thinking. This conception of piety cannot be confused with barter or commerce, because there is nothing secure or reliable about it. There is no guarantee that the gods will reciprocate.

In the Homeric world, no great feat is ever accomplished without the assistance of some god or goddess. Any impressive achievement is assumed to have the hand of a god in it. Almost all the feats of Odysseus were accomplished by the assistance Athena, whose love for him is the mystery at the heart of the tale. Success in *any* project, no matter what its moral merits or lack thereof, is attributed to the gods. This did not stop people from appealing to the gods in the name of justice, as the Melians did when besieged by the Athenians. Threatened with destruction (unless they give up their independence and agree to be ruled by Athens), the Melians put their trust in the gods and in the Lacedaemonians (i.e., Spartans) to whom they appealed for help. The Melians believed that the gods were on their side and will bless them with good fortune because they are innocent in the face of Athenian brutality. However, the gods took no notice; and the Spartans failed to arrive before the Athenians slaughtered them and destroyed their city.[70]

The traditional gods were not particularly moved by considerations of justice. When the Athenians suffered a colossal defeat in their effort to conquer Sicily, Nicias, the Athenian general was determined to inspire his defeated army to muster enough courage to make a dangerous and daring escape from the clutches of the enemy. He did not have a single ship left, his men lay dead or dying, he was himself terribly ill, and they were almost out of provisions. But he comforted the living men by saying that there was still reason for hope because in their utterly wretched condition, the gods are likely to feel pity for them rather than jealousy.[71] So, the gods were moved by all kinds of considerations—pity, anger, jealousy, or justice. The latter was not the only, or even the primary, motivation of the gods. For example, in *Prometheus Bound*, Aeschylus portrays Zeus as a tyrant, who rules according to his own arbitrary whims, and subverts whatever traditions of law and justice existed before he came to power. Prometheus is an idealist and a philanthropist who is disappointed with the revolution in the heavens that was led by Zeus. He does not consider Zeus an improvement over his predecessor. Prometheus is a benefactor of mankind. He brings man gifts (including the technical skills represented by fire), which allow humanity to survive.[72] Zeus punishes Prometheus for daring to give man divine gifts that Zeus believes were totally inappropriate for this "creature of a day."[73] For his love for humanity, the tyrant of the gods orders Prometheus nailed to a rock out in the sea where a vulture feeds on his liver daily. In this version of the story, Prometheus is the victim of innocent suffering that is imposed by Zeus.

Socrates and Plato reject the traditional view of the gods. They insist on moralizing them. They think that the gods are concerned with justice above all else. They are motivated *only* by concerns for justice or righteousness, and have no other motive. Moreover, being supremely just, they are the source of all good things in human life, and never the source of evil. In the *Protagoras,* Plato re-invents the myth of Prometheus. He tells us that when the gods were ready to bring the creatures out of the bowels of the earth, they gave Prometheus and his brother Epimetheus the task of distributing to them all the available powers. Epimetheus begged Prometheus to let him do the job and Prometheus agreed. Epimetheus gave some creatures furs, other features; to some, he gave speed; to others, strength. To those who had neither speed nor strength, Epimetheus gave them fertility. However, Epimetheus distributed all the powers at his disposal and forgot all about mankind. As a result, human beings emerged "naked, unshod, unbedded, and unarmed."[74] Without furs, feathers, speed, strength, or fertility, man is at the mercy of the elements, is threatened by wild beasts, and is on the brink of annihilation. So Prometheus tries to fix the mess by giving man fire—but this only makes things worse. Technical skill allows human beings to survive for a while, but in time, they turn these weapons against each other. So, Zeus steps in and rescues humanity with an invaluable gift—the art of politics and the knowledge of justice, without which all the technical skill is a hazard to human survival.[75] In keeping with the Socratic moralization of the gods, Plato makes Zeus the true benefactor of mankind.

The moralization of the gods was not new or unique to Socrates. In Hesiod's famous fable of the hawk and the nightingale, the hawk tells the nightingale he is clutching in his talons high above the clouds, to stop squealing because he will do with her as he pleases, and there is no sense in struggling against the law of the stronger. However, Hesiod thinks that the law of nature that applies to the hawk and the nightingale does not apply to humanity because mankind knows that "Right," will always get "the upper hand over violence in the end."[76] Righteous communities flourish: the earth bears them plenty of food, and their sheep are laden down with wool. In contrast, Zeus punishes unrighteous communities—sometimes the entire community is punished for the evil of one man.[77] Punishing a whole community for the unrighteousness of the few is patently unjust. Nevertheless, Hesiod provides the first steps in the moralization of the gods. However, by taking the moralization of the gods to new heights, Socrates makes the gods the source of good only, and never of any harm. It follows that they cannot threaten unjust cities with divine retribution.

When the gods are moralized, piety is no longer a set of rituals believed to help the city by enhancing its chances at success and prosperity. Religion is no longer a unifying force for the city that reminds citizens that their individual fate is linked to that of the collective. Instead, those who claim to be divinely inspired, such as Socrates, set themselves above the state. They declare that allegiance to the true gods and to one's own salvation trumps allegiance to the state.

So what? One may well ask. Why should the city not be accountable to a moral standard independent of itself? The answer is that the city has always been subject to a moral standard, which is not of its own making. However, it was a standard grounded in human rationality, and therefore capable of being used to persuade fellow citizens. It was a standard to which human beings could appeal without relying on mysterious authorities communing with the divine. By making morality a function of religion, Socrates makes it otherworldly and mysterious; he withdraws it from the public realm—the realm of reason and persuasion. He sets himself up as an authority transcending not only the city, but also reason. His authority must be obeyed because of his special relation to the divine, and not because of what he says.

Far from supporting morality, the alliance of religion and morality has contributed to immorality on a grand scale. There has been a plethora of moral monstrosities committed in the name of the Abrahamic God, directed at those who do not believe in Him, or his Son, or his Prophet. Despite the atrocities that they inspire, we continue to think of the monotheistic religions as an indispensable support for morality. We worry that in the absence of these religions, morality will be left without foundation. Yet, no one can imagine the mass murder (e.g., the *auto-da-fé* of the Spanish Inquisition) of those who do not believe in Zeus or his clan. The simple reason for this is that believing or not believing in Zeus is not connected to one's morality. By moralizing the gods, Socrates weds morality and religion, and in so doing, invites the criminalization of religious ideas.

5 Perverting Piety

Once the new rehabilitated gods are in place, then piety can be redefined. The new gods are not going to be satisfied with rituals, sacrifices, and libations.[78] None of this empty flattery can be of any interest to the new gods. So, when Euthyphro hits on the idea that piety must be "care for the gods," Socrates is intrigued, because his conception of justice and piety is intimately connected with "care" (especially of the soul). Socrates tells Euthyphro that care is the antithesis of harm: care makes a thing better, while harm makes a thing worse.[79] So, when Socrates says in the *Republic* that the just man should not harm anyone, he means that he should not make anyone worse.[80] Socrates associates care (and justice) with occupations, such as dog breeding, horse breeding, and cattle breeding. All these activities are intended to benefit or improve the thing that is cared for. The view of justice as care for the soul looms large in Plato's *Laws,* and as we shall see, it is not as benign as it appears. So, even though Socrates is happy with the connection that Euthyphro makes between justice and care where human beings are concerned, the idea of piety as care for the gods does not sit well with him. Since the new gods are models of perfect goodness, it makes no sense for human beings to "care" for them. How could human beings improve the gods the way that cattle breeders improve cattle?

Euthyphro reconsiders and then hits on the idea that piety is perhaps "service to the gods." This is a promising idea—indeed, it is the crux of the Socratic conception of piety. It is the furthest thing from the trivial flattery of the gods. After all, the new gods are serious gods who have work to do. So, the best way for human beings to benefit them is to be of service to them by helping them in their endeavors. Socrates compares the service we could render the gods to service one might render a shipbuilder, a house builder, a general, or a farmer. Then, Socrates asks Euthyphro the penultimate question: "what is that excellent aim that the gods achieve, using us as their servants?"[81] And just when we are about find out what kind of objective or activity occupies the gods, the dialogue comes to a crashing halt. Euthyphro brushes him off saying that the gods do "many fine things," and when pressed by Socrates, he falls back on the familiar conception of piety as making the necessary prayers and sacrifices to make sure the gods protect our homes and our city.

Needless to say, Socrates expresses terrible disappointment, saying he was just on the verge of knowing what piety is when Euthyphro turned away.[82] Euthyphro is blamed for not revealing the distinctive work, activity, or endeavor of the gods. Despite the abrupt interruption, the dialogue succeeds in establishing (1) that piety is a subset of morality; (2) that the right and the good is not merely a function of command or approval of either gods or men; and (3) that piety is a partaking with the gods in their distinctive activity, *whatever that may be*. Scholars who recognize that the dialogue provides us with the distinctively Socratic conception of piety nevertheless complain that "the specific product of piety is never revealed and thus the definition is left incomplete."[83] In my view, the ambiguity is the key to the allure of this new concept of piety. By leaving the majestic work of the gods undefined, it allows those who imagine themselves the agents of the divine to fill in the blank. The answer can be easily fabricated by men who claim to know the mystery of existence; men who believe in the transfiguration of the world; men with the mystique of Socrates, Jesus, Muhammad, or Marx. Such men appeal to those who dream of doing something that would transform reality.

The Socratic conception of piety as serving the gods and furthering their great and glorious work, whatever that might be, is not as modest as it appears.[84] It is a boon to those with grandiose projects that they would like to impose on humanity. It allows them to present their ambitious schemes in the humble guise of serving the gods—and there is no shortage of such pretenders. The ploy is particularly useful when there is a great deal of opposition to their endeavors. The idea is a precursor to the understanding of piety as *jihad*—a concept at the heart of the Crusades, the English Revolution of Oliver Cromwell and the Puritans (also known as the "Revolution of the Saints"), the Exceptionalism of the American juggernaut, Al Qaeda, the "Islamic State," and Hezbollah (the Palestinian militia fighting Israel in Lebanon), to name a few. All these warriors regard themselves as servants of the divine, dedicated to furthering the deity's great and glorious work in the world.

The idea presupposes the sort of exclusive intimacy with the deity embraced by Socrates, but is altogether hubristic from a Homeric point of view. In Homer, mortals ask the gods to help them with *their* projects, and not the other way around. In the *Odyssey*, Odysseus killed all the suitors with the help of Athena. It was *his* project. He did not pretend that in killing all the suitors, he was bringing Athena's justice to the world. He was not helping Athena with *her* project. Mortals did not attribute their projects to the gods, even though they doubted that success was possible without divine assistance. Mortals *owned* their projects, which is to say, they took responsibility for their endeavors—for good or ill.

In contrast to Socratic innovation, the Homeric conception of piety is the recognition of the subordinate place of humanity in the scheme of things. As we shall see (Section 5.6), the traditional understanding of piety is the opposite of *hubris*. So understood, piety inspired modesty and moderation; it was contemptuous of human beings who attributed their projects to the gods, imitated the gods, and behaved like gods among men. The strict demarcation between mortals and immortals meant that mortals are in no position to claim that they are acting on behalf of the gods, doing the bidding of the gods, or furthering their great and glorious projects in the world. Moreover, since there is a plurality of gods with diverse and conflicting goals, projects, and aspirations, furthering the objectives of one god may elicit the ire of another. The endeavor is decidedly perilous. Moralizing the gods, and replacing their plurality with unity, allows Socrates to claim that the gods are united in a purpose that is morally beyond reproach. It follows that acting on behalf of the divine, or furthering the projects of the deity (whatever we imagine them to be) become the hallmarks of piety *and* justice. In this way, the limits invoked by the concept of *hubris* are undermined.

The Socratic understanding of piety turns the conventional view on its head—it turns *hubris* into piety. The Socratic conception of piety lends itself to the fatuous delusions of political actors who regard their crimes as integral to the realization of the grandiose projects of the deity. Unfortunately, Socratic ideas have triumphed so completely in the world in which we live, that it is difficult to see how destructive that triumph has been and continues to be. It is my contention that the hubristic conception of piety advocated by Socrates is a recipe for political disaster. Since the gods are deemed to be supremely good, their projects are beyond reproach.[85] It is easy to see how that attitude cripples responsibility, as well as the capacity for self-criticism. In so far as he regarded his philosophical activity as a mission "in service of the god,"[86] Socrates was unable to take responsibility for his abysmal influence on his students, or to turn his critical powers on himself and his teaching.

6 Aristophanes: The Atheism of Socrates

In his *Apology*, Plato makes no effort to defend Socrates against the charge of impiety. He makes no effort to show that the religious ideas of Socrates are not a threat to the city. Instead, he transforms the charge of impiety into a charge of atheism. In Plato's account of the proceeding, Socrates leads the befuddled Meletus to accuse him of atheism, and in so doing, introduces a totally new and perplexing dimension to the trial. Atheism was no part of the indictment, nor is there any reason to think it was an indictable offense. This allows Socrates to get the better of Meletus, since the charge of atheism contradicts the official charge of inventing new gods. In this way, the bewildered Meletus is caught in the contradiction of saying that Socrates does and does not believe in gods.[87] In a sarcastic and triumphal tone, Socrates asks his prosecutor, "My dear Meletus, do you think that you are prosecuting Anaxagoras?"[88] In other words, do you think you are prosecuting an atheist?

The charge of atheism was patently absurd—Socrates was no atheist. Socrates was a divinely inspired man with a celestial mission. He received guidance from a personal deity, and was known to stand in a trance for hours on end while receiving these supernatural messages.[89] Clearly, atheism was not the issue. Socrates makes it the issue at the trial in order to confuse Meletus, and make a mockery of the proceedings. By confusing the charge of impiety with atheism, Plato succeeds in giving the impression that the trial was about ideas, and that Socrates was prosecuted for having unorthodox *beliefs*.[90]

According to Plato's version of the trial, the charges brought against Socrates by Anytus and Meletus reflect hostility toward him in the community that has its source in long-standing slanderous lies that have their origin in Aristophanes' comedy, the *Clouds*, written twenty-four years before the trial. He therefore sets out to address—not Anytus or Meletus or the actual charges against him—but Aristophanes or his "first accusers."[91] In the *Clouds*, Aristophanes represented Socrates as one of the Ionian scientists—a buffoon with atheistic proclivities. As a scientist, Socrates explained thunder in terms of the combustion of gases, without reference to Zeus. In the play, Socrates teaches his students how to make the worse argument appear the better, so they can take advantage of others. He also teaches them contempt for their fathers and other figures of authority. At the end of the play, the think tank blows up, much to the delight of the audience. Plato claims that this portrait contributed to Socrates' bad reputation as an atheist, and a threat to traditional beliefs.

There is every indication that the portrait of Socrates presented by Aristophanes was not a total fabrication. Plato provides evidence in two of his dialogues that what Aristophanes was saying was true of the young Socrates. In the *Phaedo*, Socrates provides an autobiographical note, saying:

> When I was a young man I was wonderfully keen on that wisdom they call natural science, for I thought it splendid to know the causes of everything, why it comes to be, why it perishes, and why it exists... finally I became convinced that I have no natural aptitude at all for that kind of investigation.[92]

The same autobiographical information is repeated at the beginning of the *Parmenides*. So, Aristophanes was not making things up. Socrates was impressed with Anaxagoras' idea that mind is the source of the order of the universe.[93] But he was disappointed when he realized that Anaxagoras used Mind only as the "initial impetus" of the universal order, but did not assume any "intelligent plan."[94] The shift in the ideas of Socrates explains why Plato presents Socrates and Aristophanes on very friendly terms in the *Symposium*. It was likely that the shift in philosophical perspective was also a shift in political perspective—away from the Sophists or freethinkers who were associated with democracy and toward the more conservative and aristocratic ideas of Aristophanes—which means that the two men came to share the same antipathy to democracy.[95]

Blaming the tarnished reputation of Socrates on a twenty-four-year-old play was a brilliant ruse that transformed the charge of impiety into a charge of atheism. The point of the *Apology* is to show how absurd this charge was by showing that Socrates was neither an atheist nor a moral relativist—and that his ideas were the epitome of a wisdom, morality, and piety that were manifestly superior to the dominant views of his time. It follows that his ideas could not have corrupted anyone. Contemporary apologists for Socrates agree.[96]

7   The Orphism of Socrates

A. E. Taylor has argued that the impiety of Socrates had nothing to do with atheism. It had everything to do with his allegiance to Orphic religious ideas—foreign gods that were not ratified by the state.[97] After all, as the dialogues of Plato confirm, Socrates was known to consort with religious ascetics and mystics of the Orphic variety, including the Pythagoreans. Indeed, Orphic myths appear in the *Phaedo, Gorgias, Symposium, Meno, Phaedrus,* and *Republic*.[98] Even if Socrates and Plato did not believe in the literal reality of these myths, they nevertheless treated them with sympathy as containing deep truths that are altogether lacking in the myths of Homer. The question is: What are these Orphic beliefs, and could they be a threat to the community of sufficient gravity to bring about a charge of impiety, even in the absence of the mutilation of the Hermae and the profanation of the mysteries?

Orphic religious ideas were totally outside the horizon of traditional Greek religion. Orphism was not a state religion but an "international" church,[99] made up of a society of believers. Instead of focusing on collective and individual well-being in this world, the Orphics were concerned with the salvation of the soul in the beyond. Nevertheless, they managed to co-op aspects of the Olympian pantheon for their own purposes. Orpheus was a man who went to Hades to retrieve his beloved wife, Eurydice, who died of a poisonous snake bite. With his lyre, a gift from Apollo, he bewitched Hades, Persephone, Cerberus, the Furies, and even stones! As a result, he was allowed to lead Eurydice out of Hades, as long as he did not look back at her before they reached the sunlight. Needless to say, he looked back, and lost Eurydice forever. The message is that the greatest love cannot overcome death. Having lost the companion whose presence gave his life meaning, Orpheus rejected all other women.[100] This familiar tale was transformed by Orphic zealots into an ascetic doctrine whereby sexual abstinence was an asset in attaining salvation. Orpheus became a man who was in possession of an esoteric doctrine that allowed him to triumph over death—and a whole body of Orphic literature was attributed to him.

By appropriating and distorting the *Theogony* of Hesiod, Orphic literature provided a grand narrative explaining how the world came to be, what it all means, and the place of humanity in the scheme of things. Despite variations, the grand narrative goes something like this.[101] Zeus is a deity who comes at the end of a series of divine powers, each one usurping the one before it in an effort to build an organized world "animated with one spirit and, with all its infinite variety, a unity."[102] So, instead of being the head of an unwieldy family of diverse and feuding gods, as Homer presents him, Zeus becomes a symbol of divine oneness and unity pointing to monotheism—one god, one truth, one path!

For some reason, Zeus entrusts Dionysus to rule the world on his behalf. The Titans, assumed to be the primordial source of evil, are defeated by Zeus and banished to the fiery Tartarus beneath the earth in the deepest recesses of Hades. They manage to escape by distracting Dionysus with gifts, including a mirror, and when he was looking at his own image, they tried to kill him. He eludes them by transforming himself into all sorts of different creatures. Eventually, he takes the form of a bull; but he is captured, ripped apart, and devoured by the Titans. Somehow, Athena succeeds in saving his heart, which she returns to Zeus. With the help of Semele, Zeus insures that Dionysus is reborn, and the Titans are zapped to ashes by Zeus' formidable lightening rod. Out of the ashes, man is created. This explains the dual nature of humanity—simultaneously good and evil—with a wicked, mortal, and corporeal body (from the Titans) on one hand, and a divine soul (from the spirit of Dionysus) on the other.[103] This accounts for the inner struggle between the promptings of the body and those of the soul—the central theme of Plato's psychology, where morality is understood as the triumph of the divine part of the soul over the appetites of the body.

For Socrates and the Orphics, the human drama is all about the entrapment of the divine soul in the corporeal body. The goal is to purify the soul, so that it can escape from the defilements of the body. To that end, an ascetic life of prohibitions, initiations, liturgies, and incantations, is necessary. Those who live a pure life will be rewarded in the beyond, whereas those who live an impure life will end up in Tartarus.[104] In this way, Orphism weds morality with religious worship. The Pythagoreans, including those who were part of the Socratic circle, shared these Orphic beliefs, and spread them throughout Greece.

Needless to say, the purification and liberation of the soul is no simple process. The soul must die, suffer punishment in the underworld, and be reborn again in a diversity of creatures—horses, dogs, sheep, birds, and serpents.[105] The process of purification may take several rounds of birth and rebirth, punishment, and purgation. At the end of the process, the triumphant soul is finally released from its corporeal incarceration and ascends to the light and is united with the divine to which it belongs. This final release from the cycle of birth and rebirth requires the active pursuit of a life of asceticism. The latter is not to be understood as the cultivation of the classic moral virtues. It is a quest to sever oneself from the world.[106] It presupposes the centrality of the concept of sin. The latter is not vice, or even crime; it is an abhorrence of the corporeal self, with its natural passions and pleasures. Salvation also requires initiation, liturgies, rituals, and magical incantations. It is no wonder that Orphism deteriorated into pardons, the selling of indulgences, and other schemes to ameliorate one's destiny or that of one's family in the beyond.[107]

In contrast to Homer's myths, Plato's myths were notoriously Orphic. In *Alcibiades I*, Socrates unravels the Homeric worldview by claiming that the human soul resembles the divine. He posits a dualism between body and soul, in which the latter is superior to the former because it is akin to the divine. Socrates compares the relation between body and soul with the relation between the harp and the harpist, or the shoemaker and his tools: whereas one is an agent, the other is merely its instrument.[108] It is clear which is superior and which is inferior. The soul is not only superior to the body, it also rules over it. This ruling principle is the true self, whereas the body is the instrument that the soul uses for its ends.

In the *Phaedo*, Socrates declares that the soul is akin to the immortal and divine, while the body is a mass of evil that introduces so much turmoil and confusion into the world that it hinders the soul from seeing the truth.[109] In this way, the soul is declared a prisoner of the body.[110] The goal of life is the release of the soul from her imprisonment, which can only happen in death; only then can the soul dwell alone, without the body in a state of blessedness, in the presence of the divine element to which she truly belongs. However, not every soul will dwell in the company of the divine. Only the soul that purifies herself from the confused and dizzying pollution of the body, only the soul that makes the body her enemy can succeed in releasing herself from the corporeal prison. The project of purification requires practice. Philosophy, properly understood, is recommended as the practice that is required to release the soul from the body—the practice of dying.[111] For only a soul that is no longer bewitched by the pleasures of the body, only a soul that lives an ascetic life in this world, only a soul that is purified can be freed from the prison of the body and become united with the divine element that defines her true nature.[112] Accordingly, Socrates redefines injustice to include gluttony, and drunkenness—vices that generally do not injure other people. In other words, he redefines justice as an inner condition of the self—the relation between body and soul—not a relation between human beings.[113]

In line with Orphic strategies of co-opting traditional myths, Socrates transforms Hades into a benevolent god, ruling over a heavenly place where only the pure are welcome. The rest are re-incarnated into wasps, bees, wolves, hawks, or donkeys.[114] In the *Gorgias,* Plato tells us that the souls of the wicked are destined for Tartarus, a place of eternal punishment. Meanwhile, the souls of the righteous are ushered to the "Isle of the Blessed" where they experience the bliss they deserve.[115] Socrates presents all these farfetched ideas to a gullible and sycophantic audience as if they were deep philosophical insights. For the sober, clear-eyed Homer, Hades represented the inevitability of death. The underworld was neither heaven nor hell; it was not reserved for those who lived a pure life that was unpolluted by the pleasures and concerns of the body; it was a place where everyone eventually ended up. It was a place devoid of the vigor and vitality of a life lived basking in the sunshine; it was not intended to punish the wicked or reward the good.[116]

A. E. Taylor has argued that the impiety of Socrates was in belonging to a foreign and secret cult that was not approved by the state, and that was totally removed from the world of Athens and her Ionian connections.[117] He was guilty of "irregular religious practices" that were not sanctioned by the state.[118] Moreover, Orphism was associated with the Pythagoreans from "enemy cities" of northern and central Greece in the Peloponnesian War.[119] These sects turned the Greek world upside down. They placed the hereafter ahead of the here and now. They made serving one's own soul more important than serving the state and its gods.[120] The threat that these Orphic beliefs posed to the religion of the state is real enough. After all, they co-opted religion from the domain of the state to that of the individual's cosmic drama. However, it is not clear to me that the threat would have been recognized in the absence of acts of desecration.

Taylor begs to differ. He thinks that a secret cult about the soul is a matter that "no ancient *polis* could be expected to treat lightly."[121] He thinks that these cults were "obnoxious to the Athenian democracy."[122] He considers Euripides' Hippolytus, in the play by the same name, as an indication of the contempt with which Orphic saints, such as Hippolytus, were regarded.[123] There is indeed a similarity between Hippolytus and the legendary singing Orpheus. The latter met a violent death at the hands of women—depicted on vases clobbering him with stones and other weapons—but even after his death, his severed head was still singing—a testament to the tenacity of these mystery religions.[124] Hippolytus also suffered a dreadful fate at the hands of Aphrodite and his stepmother (Phaedrus). While their asceticism inspired contempt, it did not constitute a political threat in and of itself.

Taylor is right in thinking that Orphism turned Greek religion on its head. The idea of sin was foreign to Greek religion. The hatred of life in this world was antithetical to the *joie de vivre* that came naturally to the Athenians. The pretentions of ascetics are contemptible; those who address each other as "the Pure" are invariably suspected of being licentious hypocrites. Moreover, the idea that the human soul is divine is *hubris*, which is the opposite of piety. Furthermore, the rewards and punishments of the soul in the afterlife assert a level of cosmic justice that was not part of the traditional religion.

Nevertheless, it is not clear that living an ascetic life, caring for one's soul and its salvation, while minding one's own business, would have necessarily been perceived as a threat. It would be a threat if this "society of believers" made a point of refusing to participate in the religious festivals of the state—perhaps because they refused to kill animals or eat their meat. These believers would be an even greater threat if they mocked the state religion for its banality, puerility, lack of depth, and spirituality—just what the profanation of the mysteries must have done. Worst of all, this society of believers would be even more threatening if it got hold of political power and set out to create a political order designed with the salvation of citizens in mind. It happened in Southern Italy, in Croton, which was the center of the Pythagorean order. When they "secured sovereign power," their reign was "intolerable."[125] A revolution followed, and civil order was restored (450 BCE). Scholars have compared it to the reign of the Calvinists in Geneva.[126] So, there is no denying that the religion of Socrates was a threat to the well-being of the state—any state.

In contrast to the focus of pagan religion on the here and now, otherworldly religions threaten the only world we know. In our time, there is a plethora of terrorists posing both domestic and international threats in the name of a divine power believed to have moral authority that trumps the security and survival of human beings in this world. The claim that these terrorist acts are not products of true religion is not credible.[127] Ideas cannot be severed from the conduct they inspire. The genocidal slaughter of the Philistines in the Old Testament, the damnation of unbelievers to eternal hell-fire in the New Testament, and the jihad against infidels in the Qur'an are the vicious manifestations of the monotheistic legacy, whose war against the worldly ends of the state has not abated. So, it is not a question of the persecution of ideas, but the legitimate censure of *conduct* that is a palpable threat to the only world we know. In the case of Socrates as well as the early Christians, the new religious ideas would not likely have elicited the ire of the community if they had not been affiliated with *deeds* that threaten the well-being of the state. There is no indication that skeptical beliefs were prosecuted.[128] Nor is there any indication that a concerted effort was ever made to clamp down on unorthodox beliefs—not because the Athenians were champions of liberty of thought, but simply because they had no sacred texts and no ecclesiastical authorities.[129]

In conclusion, Plato believed that Socratic religion would improve morals.[130] With the benefit of more than twenty five hundred years of hindsight, we can safely say that Plato was wrong—not just because these mystery religions inspire violence in the most passionately devout, but also because they breed a callous indifference to human suffering in this world.[131] Plato is a classic case in point. He censured the tragic poets for their pre-occupation with human suffering. He declared that "no human experience is worth taking very seriously," and even great misfortunes should be accepted stoically "because it is not clear whether such events are good or bad" in the grand scheme of things.[132] When human suffering in this world is insignificant, then snuffing out the lives of fifteen hundred men in a space of a few months to save Athens from democracy (as Critias did) may not have been regarded as such a terrible deed by members of the Socratic circle.

Notes

1. Taylor in *Varia Socratica* (Oxford: James Parker & Co. 1911), p. 3.
2. Gregory Vlastos, *Socrates: Ironist and Moral Philosopher* (New York: Cornell University Press, 1991), p. 166. See also, F. M. Burnyeat, "The Impiety of Socrates." In Thomas C. Brickhouse and Nicholas D. Smith (eds.), *The Trial and Execution of Socrates: Sources and Controversies* (New York: Oxford University Press, 2002), originally in *Ancient Philosophy*, Vol. 17 (1997), pp. 1–12. Mark L. McPherran, *The Religion of Socrates* (University Park, Pennsylvania: Pennsylvania State University Press, 1996), rejects this view, pp. 149ff. He thinks that Socrates might accept the gods of the city as long as the sacrifice had an "internal, nonmercantile dimension" that did not emphasize the materiality of the sacrifice, and does not involve asking the gods to retaliate against others, which would contravene the principles of justice of not returning evil for evil.
3. Taylor, *Varia Socratica*, pp. 9, 30.
4. I owe this understanding to my colleague, historian Ken-Leyton-Brown.
5. Xenophon, *Hellenica*, 1.7.22–23: If tried and found guilty, traitors and temple robbers will have their property confiscated, and will not be allowed burial in Attica.
6. Herodotus, *The Histories*, 8.111.
7. McPherran, *The Religion of Socrates*, p. 23. Despite pointing this out, McPherran does not think that the Socratic moralization of the gods threatens the city. Thomas C. Brickhouse and Nicholas D. Smith, *Plato's Socrates* (Oxford University Press, 1994), p. 183: also think that no matter how revolutionary the Socratic moralization of the gods may seem to us, there is no evidence that Socrates' contemporaries were troubled by it. There is some truth to this. In a society eager to curry favor with the gods, praising the gods and saying that they are the sources of all good things need not arouse any hostility or anxiety. It is in keeping with the desire to flatter them. At the same time, the moralization of the gods cannot be taken too seriously without hampering their ability to uphold the laws of the city against criminals, traitors, and other enemies of the state.
8. McPherran, *The Religion of Socrates*, pp. 132–133, tells us that new gods must be "vetted" by the state.
9. Robert Parker, *Athenian Religion: A History* (New York: Oxford University Press, 1996), pp. 215–16; Louise Bruit Zaidman and Pauline Schmitt Pantel, *Religion in the Ancient Greek City*, transl. by Paul Cartledge (New York: Cambridge University Press, 1992), p. 11.
10. We assume unthinkingly that freedom of religion is a good thing. But is it? I have argued elsewhere that it is not. See "Is Freedom of Religion a Mistake?" *Free Inquiry*, Vol. 32, No. 3 (April/May 2012), pp. 19, 44, & 45.

11. Homer, *Iliad*, Bk. 2.420ff.
12. According to Hesiod, this tradition has its source in a trick played by Prometheus on Zeus to benefit humanity: *Theogony* and *Works and Days*, trans. By M. L. West (New York: Oxford University Press, 1988), p. 19. On other accounts, the smoke sufficed to nourish the gods. See Zaidman and Pantel, *Religion in the Ancient Greek City*, p. 49.
13. Herodotus, *History*, 9.33, 9. 36–37.
14. Emily Kearns, *Ancient Greek Religion: A Source Book* (Oxford: Wiley-Blackwell, 2010), p. 183.
15. Ibid, p. 165.
16. Sarah B. Pomeroy, et al., *Ancient Greece: A Political, Social, and Cultural History* (New York: Oxford University Press, 2012), p. 280.
17. Kearns, *Ancient Greek Religion*, p. 163.
18. Taylor, *Varia Socratica*, p. 16.
19. Zaidman and Pantel, *Religion in the Ancient Greek City*, p. 11.
20. Ibid, p. 12.
21. MacDowell, *The Law in Classical Athens*, p. 200.
22. Robert Parker, "Law and Religion," in Michael Gagrin and David Cohen (eds.), *The Cambridge Companion to Ancient Greek Law* (New York: Cambridge University Press, 2005), p. 67. In *Athenian Religion: A History*, pp. 209, Parker suggests that the decree of Diopeithes might have been merely the invention of the comic stage. Nevertheless, Parker believes that the trial of Socrates was a case of the persecution of ideas; and MacDowell, *The Law in Classical Athens*, p. 200.
23. McPherran, *The Religion of Socrates*, p. 88, claims that atheism is the "black thread" that links the prosecutions of Diagoras, Protagoras, Anaxagoras, and Socrates.
24. Parker, *Athenian Religion: A History*, p. 208.
25. I. F. Stone, *The Trial of Socrates*, (Toronto: Little Brown & Co., 1988) p. 232. I am convinced by the outstanding case made by I. F. Stone refuting all these allegations (pp. 231–47). However, I do not share Stone's view that the trial of Socrates was somehow a unique case of the persecution of ideas.
26. Ibid, p. 233.
27. Taylor, *Socrates*, p. 60.
28. As claimed by Pomeroy, et al., *Ancient Greece*, pp. 289, 361.
29. Stone, *The Trial of Socrates*, pp. 231–247.
30. Michael J. O'Brien, "Protagoras," in Rosamond Kent Sprague (ed.), *The Older Sophists* (Columbia, South Carolina: University of South Carolina Press, 1972), p. 3. Also, Taylor, *Socrates*, p. 62.
31. *Meno*, 91d.

32. Gregory Vlastos, *Socrates: Ironist and Moral Philosopher* (New York: Cornell University Press, 1991), pp. 295 ff.
33. As Parker rightly points out, when the Bacchanalia was suppressed in Rome, it was not a matter of defending "theological orthodoxy," *Athenian Religion: A History*, p. 217.
34. E. R. Dodds, *The Greeks and the Irrational* (Berkeley, California: University of California Press, 1951), p. 201, note 63.
35. M. I. Finley, "Socrates and Athens," in *Aspects of Antiquity* (New York: Penguin Books, 1977), pp. 65–6.
36. Parker, *Athenian Religion: A History*, p. 217.
37. Walter Burkert, *Greek Religion*, transl. by John Raffan (Cambridge, Mass.: Harvard University Press, 1985), p. 156.
38. Pomeroy, *Ancient Greece*, p. 344.
39. Thucydides, *History of the Peloponnesian War*, VI.27.
40. Emily Kearns, *Ancient Greek Religion*, p. 143.
41. Robert Parker, *Athenian Religion: A History*, p. 206.
42. Thucydides, *History of the Peloponnesian War*, VIII.45–56, VIII.65–68.
43. Erwin Rohde, *The Cult of Souls and Belief in Immortality among the Greeks* (New York: Harcourt, Brace, & Co., Inc., 1925), p. 219.
44. Ibid, pp. 221–22.
45. Jane Harrison, *Prolegomena to the Study of Greek Religion* (London: Merlin Press, 1962), pp. 539 ff.
46. Rohde, *The Cult of Souls and Belief in Immortality among the Greeks*, p. 223.
47. J. R. Watmough, *Orphism* (New York: Cambridge University Press, 1934), pp. 62–3.
48. Rohde, *The Cult of Souls and Belief in Immortality among the Greeks*, p. 222.
49. Taylor, *Socrates*, p. 96, note.
50. *Euthyphro*, 3b.
51. Harrison, *Prolegomena to the Study of Greek Religion*, p. 2.
52. See Stone, *The Trial of Socrates*, p. 147: the dialogue is described as a "metaphysical—and semantic—wild goose chase" that has "almost nothing to do with the trial of Socrates"; R. E. Allen, *Plato's 'Euthyphro' and the Early Theory of Forms* (New York: Humanities Press, 1970), pp. 89, 112; Terence Irwin, *Plato's Moral Theory: The Early and Middle Dialogues* (New York: Oxford University Press, 1977), p. 22: "the dialogue fails to show how it [piety] can be distinguished from justice as a whole." Richard Kraut, *Socrates and the State* (New York: Princeton University Press, 1984), p. 245 and p. 252: "I conclude that the *Euthyphro* contains no answer, explicit or implicit,... Socrates clearly says in the *Euthyphro* that he does not know what piety is, and no passage in this or any other dialogue forces us to take his avowals at less than face value."

53. Brickhouse and Smith, *Plato's Socrates*, pp. 64 ff.; Mark L. McPherran, *The Religion of Socrates*, pp. 54ff. See Bibliography for more details.
54. This is the view of many philosophers, including my colleague Bela Szabados, to whom I am indebted for his generous comments on this section.
55. I do not wish to conflate Homer with the traditional practice of Greek religion in general. Homer is a brilliant intellect in his own right, and should not be held responsible for all the shortcomings of the religious practices of the Greeks. However, it is difficult to avoid this mistake because Plato often conflates them.
56. *Euthyphro*, 4c–d. I. F. Stone takes issue with this way of seeing the situation in which Euthyphro finds himself. He argues that Euthyphro's position is superior to that of Socrates because he takes his moral obligation seriously. *The Trial of Socrates*, pp. 147, 149.
57. *Euthyphro*, 6a. McPherran, *The Religion of Socrates*, p. 35, regards Euthyphro as a "Homeric sectarian," but also recognizes that he has some things in common with Socrates—namely that they are both "diviners," meaning privileged recipients of divine information (p. 33).
58. Homer, *Iliad*, Bk. 21.464.
59. Interestingly, this made the mortals fascinating, tragic, and heroic; they had so much to lose, so much on the line, so much at risk, because death was always looming. In contrast, the gods could not be either tragic or heroic because they are strangers to death.
60. R. F. Walton, "Hybris," in *Theological Dictionary of the New Testament* (Grand Rapids, 1972), seems to confuse *hubris* with sin; Ninian Smart, *The Religious Experience of Mankind* (New York: Charles Scribner's Sons, 1969), p. 252, describes Zeus as punishing the sinner. This view of *hubris* has been popularized by Thomas Cahill, *Sailing the Wine-Dark Sea: Why the Greeks Matter* (New York: Random House, 2003), p. 122. This view has been rightly challenged by Kaufman in *Tragedy and Philosophy*. See also N. R. E. Fisher, *Hybris: A study in the values of honor and shame in ancient Greece* (Warminster, England: Aris & Phillips, 1992). See Bibliography for more details.
61. See Walter F. Otto, *The Homeric Gods: The Spiritual Significance of Greek Religion,* transl. from the German by Moses Hadas (London: Thames and Hudson, 1954), pp. 66, 241. See also Jasper Griffin, *Homer on Life and Death* (Toronto: Clarendon Press, 1980), p. 155; and Jasper Griffin, *Homer* (Toronto: Oxford University Press, 1980). Even though the latter provides an excellent introduction to Homer, it makes the unperceptive observation that the Trojans started the war (presumably because Paris seduced Helen) and therefore deserved to lose. This leads to the strange conclusion that the story is moralistic (p. 27).

62. For example, F. M. Burnyeat regards Euthyphro as a fanatical supporter of the old religion, "The Impiety of Socrates" in Brickhouse and Smith, *The Trial and Execution of Socrates: Sources and Controversies*, p. 140.
63. Stone, *The Trial of Socrates*, p. 147.
64. *Euthyphro*, 6c.
65. Ibid, 7d–8a. In Greek literature, the gods do in fact disagree about what human beings ought to do. For example, in Euripides' *Electra*, Orestes is commanded by the Delphic oracle to go to Argos and avenge the murder of his father (Agamemnon) by his mother (Clytemnestra). But no sooner does he do what he is obligated to do, then he is dubbed "a shedder of kindred blood" and pursued by the Furies.
66. *Euthyphro*, 10a.
67. Ibid, 12e.
68. Ibid, 14b.
69. Xenophon, *Memorabilia*, II.1.28.
70. Thucydides, *History of the Peloponnesian War*, V.116.
71. Ibid, VII.77.
72. Aeschylus II, *Prometheus Bound*, transl. by David Grene (New York: Washington Square Press, 1967).
73. Aeschylus, *Prometheus Bound*, 255.
74. Plato, *Protagoras*, 321c.
75. Ibid, 322c–323a. This new version of the story fits the theme of the dialogue where Protagoras argues that the gift of justice is given to all, not just to a select few—while Socrates challenges Protagoras with his usual claims about the special knowledge of justice that makes only a select few fit to rule.
76. Hesiod, *Works and Days,* p. 43.
77. Ibid, pp.43–44.
78. *Euthyphro*, 15b.
79. Ibid, 13c.
80. *Republic*, 335b–c.
81. *Euthyphro*, 13e.
82. Ibid, 14c.
83. Thomas C. Brickhouse and Nicholas D. Smith, *Plato's Socrates*, p. 66.
84. Ibid, p. 64, Brickhouse and Smith acknowledge that Socrates saw his own vocation, as a "mission he performs for the god"; they surmise that his mission was to spread wisdom (p. 67). The problem is that the authors take the Socratic profession of ignorance seriously (p. 124). So how can he spread wisdom when he has none? They solve the puzzle in the conventional way, by maintaining that at least Socrates knew his ignorance, which made him modest and cautious, while others, believing that they were wise, forged blithely ahead (pp. 124 ff.).

85. McPherran, *The Religion of Socrates*, is the only scholar to my knowledge who is aware of the pitfalls involved in this conception of piety. He makes a heroic effort to disentangle Socrates from the radicalism involved. See Bibliography for more details.
86. *Apology*, 22a, 30a.
87. Ibid, 26c.
88. Ibid, 26d.
89. *Symposium*, 215b.
90. *Apology*, 26c–27a; *Euthyphro*, 6a–b.
91. *Apology*, 18a.
92. *Phaedo*, 96a.
93. Ibid, 97b–98c.
94. Taylor, *Socrates*, pp. 64–65.
95. The connection between philosophical views and political proclivities is made by Alban D. Winspear and Tom Silverberg, *Who Was Socrates?* (New Jersey: The Cordon Company, 1939), pp. 42–44. See Bibliography for details.
96. Brickhouse and Smith, *Plato's Socrates* are a recent example.
97. Taylor, *Varia Socratica*, ch. 1, "The Impiety of Socrates," pp. 14–16.
98. *Phaedo*, 80e–81a; *Gorgias*, 523a ff.; *Symposium*, 220c–d; *Phaedrus*, 242b, 245c; *Meno*, 81b, ff.; *Republic*, 614b. Even though the *Euthyphro* contains no Orphic myths, the moralization of the gods is an important element of Orphism.
99. Taylor, *Socrates*, p. 5.
100. Stephen L. Harris and Gloria Platzner, *Classical Mythology: Images and Insights* (New York: McGraw-Hill, 2012), pp. 270–72.
101. I am simplifying and weaving together information from the following sources: W. K. C. Guthrie, *Orpheus and Greek Religion* (London: Methuen & Co. Ltd.1935); Erwin Rhode, *Psyche: The Cult of Souls and Belief in Immortality Among the Greeks*, (New York: Harcourt, Brace & Co. Inc., 1925); J. R. Watmough, *Orphism*, op.cit.; Clifford Herschel Moore, *Ancient Beliefs in the Immortality of the Soul* (New York: Longmans, Green and Co., 1931); A. D. Winspear, *The Genesis of Plato's Thought*, op.cit., ch. 4.
102. Rohde, *Psyche: The Cult of Souls and Belief in Immortality Among the Greeks*, p. 339.
103. Moore, *Ancient Beliefs in the Immortality of the Soul*, p. 8; Watmough, *Orphism*, pp. 53–4.
104. Moore, *Ancient Beliefs in the Immortality of the Soul*, p. 9.
105. Ibid, pp. 9–10.
106. Rohde, *Psyche: The Cult of Souls and Belief in Immortality Among the Greeks*, 342–3.

NOTES 69

107. Taylor, *Socrates*, pp. 50–51: Taylor tells us that Orphic beliefs were kept alive by the Pythagoreans at Thebes and Phlius with whom Socrates consorted. See also Alban Dewes Winspear, *The Genesis of Plato's Thought*, pp. 47–49. Winspear also maintains that Orphism had a conception of justice as transcendent and eternal that was allied with Zeus—a concept of justice that is central to Socratic thought.
108. Plato, *Alcibiades I*, 129c, in *The Dialogues of Plato* (vol. I), transl. by B. Jowett (London: Oxford University Press, 1931) in 4 vols.; *Republic*, 610c.
109. Plato, *Phaedo*, 65a–d; 80a–c, 83e.
110. Ibid, 83d. In the *Gorgias* (493a) Socrates says that he heard a wise man say that our body is a tomb.
111. *Phaedo*, 81a.
112. Ibid, 82c ff.
113. This idea is central to the distinctively Platonic view of justice developed in the *Republic*. See the criticism of this concept by David Sachs discussed in Section 3.7.
114. *Phaedo*, 81d ff.
115. *Gorgias*, 523a ff.
116. *Odyssey*, Bk. 11.
117. Taylor, *Varia Socratica*, pp. 21–23.
118. Ibid, p. 16.
119. Ibid, p. 20.
120. Ibid, pp. 27–8.
121. Ibid, p. 21.
122. Ibid, p. 27.
123. Ibid, p. 25; Watmough, *Orphism*, p. 27. That is not my reading of the play. It is true that Hippolytus is rather smug, arrogant, and obnoxious. He is a master of misogynistic diatribes. Yet, there is nothing objectionable about his desire to live a celibate life. He does not hurt or oppress anyone. He has no wife to insult with his misogynistic opinions. He does not belong to a pernicious institution whose highest officials spread these venomous anti-female attitudes throughout the world with the intention of recruiting a priestly cast. Hippolytus' ascetic proclivities are quite harmless in comparison to the monkish perversity familiar to us from Augustine to the present (see my criticism of Aquinas' asceticism in *Aquinas and Modernity*, chapter 4). Nevertheless, Aphrodite is offended by his boastful purity and sets out to destroy him. The fate of Hippolytus is dreadful—it is certainly not a fate that he deserved. To my mind, the play is a classic tragedy—a case of innocent suffering.
124. Guthrie, *Orpheus and Greek Religion*, p. 33.
125. Watmough, *Orphism*, p. 31.
126. Ibid.

127. I make this argument in *Terror and Civilization* (New York: St. Martin's Press, 2004) and *Aquinas and Modernity: The Lost Promise of Natural Law* (Lanham, Maryland: Rowman & Littlefield, 2008).
128. Robert Parker, *Athenian Religion: A History*, p. 211: "we hear nothing of repression of skeptics."
129. J. B. Bury, *A History of Freedom of Thought* (New York: Henry Holt and Company, 1913), pp. 35, 50–51.
130. Plato, *Gorgias*, 527b: Socrates concludes that the truth of these tales should lead us to be "more on our guard against doing than suffering wrong." The lesson is familiar, since it anticipates turning the other cheek: let them strike you with a "humiliating blow,... for you will suffer no harm thereby if you really are a good man and honorable" (527c–d).
131. See my discussion of John Bunyan, in my *Terror and Civilization*, pp. 22ff.
132. *Republic,* 604b–c.

CHAPTER 3

The Defense

Plato and Xenophon represent two different strategies for the defense. The two strategies involve two different kinds of denial. As noted earlier, both Xenophon and Plato understand that Socrates was guilty by association. Xenophon denies that Socrates was a close associate of Alcibiades, Critias, or Charmides. In contrast, Plato does not deny that Socrates was a close associate and mentor of these shady characters. Plato's strategy for the defense is nevertheless a form of denial—denial that the ideas of Socrates had anything to do with the conduct of Alcibiades, Critias, or Charmides; denial that Socrates had any wisdom to impart; and denial that virtue can be taught.

In this chapter, I will start by focusing on those aspects of Plato and Xenophon's defense that are relevant to the historical context in which the charges were made. I will then proceed to examine the legend created by Plato, which has been echoed by philosophers through the ages. Socrates would never have had the grip on the philosophical imagination of the West without the dialogues of Plato, who built an edifice around the character of Socrates that is truly formidable. The success of Plato's account is due in no small part to the captivating tropes used by Plato to buttress his defense. In this chapter, I hope to show that these tropes are flawed and cannot sustain the plausibility of the legend, despite the verdict of the ages.

1 Xenophon's Denial

Xenophon realizes that Socrates is guilty by association and does his best to undermine this association by denying that Socrates was a close associate of Alcibiades, Critias, or Charmides. In his *Memorabilia*, Xenophon presents Alcibiades as a crafty and unruly character. He describes a conversation between the young Alcibiades and his guardian, Pericles, in which the young Alcibiades mirrors some of the attitudes of the Old Oligarch.[1] In the conversation reported by Xenophon, Alcibiades brings Pericles to acknowledge that there is a difference between a government's ability to use persuasion to enact laws and the despot's use of force. They agree that the laws enacted by the despot without persuasion are not valid. Alcibiades then applies the same reasoning to a majority passing laws that are not acceptable to the minority. From that, he derives his *modus operandi*:

> It follows then that whatever the assembled majority, through the use of its power over the owners of property, enacts without persuasion is not law, but force?[2]

Pericles laughs off the cleverness, which regards any laws enacted by the *demos* to be identical with force, and therefore illegitimate. Like the Old Oligarch, Alcibiades did not recognize the legitimacy of the laws enacted by the *demos*. As far as he was concerned, the laws of the majority are not binding on him, or people of his class.

Xenophon claims that Alcibiades was a lawless individual at an early age, so Socrates cannot be held responsible for his conduct. He admits that Critias was a violent and murderous fellow, who inflicted great harm on Athens.[3] However, he insisted that his political extremism had nothing to do with Socrates, and that he only came to Socrates to learn how to get the better of others in argument, then left him when he thought he had learned his techniques.[4] The same for the others: they only sought Socrates in the hope of learning how to attain power. When they had learned a few things from him, they went on their way in pursuit of power. As long as they were close to Socrates, he was able to keep them under control. But once they parted company with him, they returned to their evil ways, and there was nothing that Socrates could do about it.[5]

Xenophon claims that when he went to Thessaly, Critias fell in with some bad company that corrupted him and loosened the grip of Socrates on his character.⁶ However, other ancient sources contradict Xenophon. Philostratus tells us that Critias corrupted the Thessalians, and not the other way around. Indeed, he

> rendered their oligarchies the more grievous by conversing with those in power there and by attacking all democracy. He slandered the Athenians, claiming that they, of all mankind, erred the most. Consequently, upon reflection, Critias would have corrupted the Thessalians rather than the converse.⁷

Xenophon's strategy is to distance Socrates from Alcibiades, Critias, and Charmides, in the hope of absolving him from what he saw as the crux of the charges—incitement of or complicity in their crimes. Xenophon's defense is based on the claim that the evils suffered by Athens were not inspired by Socrates. They were bad characters from the start; Socrates tried to rein them in, but without success.

Xenophon's defense must be rejected on two grounds. First, his blanket denial that Alcibiades, Critias, and Charmides were not close to Socrates is not credible. It is contradicted by Plato, who does not deny the long and close association of Socrates with these shady characters. Xenophon's denial that Socrates exercised any influence over them is also contradicted by Plato's description of the spellbinding effect that Socrates had on his students, as described by Alcibiades in Plato's *Symposium*. Second, Xenophon's account inadvertently cast a dark shadow on Socratic teaching. If these men wished to acquire power and position in the democracy, why seek out Socrates? There were better teachers who specialized in public speaking. Xenophon indicates that they thought Socrates could teach them a few tricks that would help them destroy their political opponents. Clearly, they were people who were so hungry for power that they had no intention of playing by the rules. They must have seen in Socrates a kindred spirit—someone who would teach them how to subvert the system, not how to excel in it. In short, Xenophon's defense is neither credible nor flattering.

Xenophon continues his strategy of denial in his effort to defend Socrates against the charge of impiety. In his *Memorabilia*, Xenophon presents Socrates as a very pious man in the conventional sense of the term—a man who was wholeheartedly devoted to the gods of the city and the rituals required to pay them homage.⁸ In short, Xenophon flat out denies the charge of impiety on its own terms. Scholars have dismissed

Xenophon's defense for being neither interesting nor believable. As J. Burnet points out, if the picture of Socrates that Xenophon presents is true, then the charge of impiety would have no basis whatsoever in reality.[9] Gregory Vlastos agrees. He argues that if Xenophon's claim is true, no Athenian jury, "for whom the cult-centered conception of piety is *de rigeur*," could have convicted Socrates, because he could have easily been able to cite the kind of evidence that such a jury would have found compelling.[10] But if we take Plato seriously, as Vlastos does, then the conception of piety that Xenophon attributes to Socrates is the very conception of piety that Socrates rejects in the *Euthyphro*.[11] This is why Xenophon's defense is not convincing.

2 Edict of the Thirty Tyrants

According to Xenophon, Critias hated Socrates for criticizing his relationship with Euthydemus, and for trying to check his evil inclinations. So, when he came to power, he passed a law making it "illegal to teach the art of speech."[12] In other words, Critias passed a law forbidding the teaching of rhetoric. Xenophon claims that this law was intended to prevent Socrates from teaching, and in so doing, undermine his influence over the young men of Athens.[13]

Despite having discredited Xenophon's account of the trial, despite dismissing him (as so many scholars have done) for indulging in whitewashing, concealment, and the falsification of the circumstantial evidence, Gregory Vlastos nevertheless takes Xenophon's claim on trust that this piece of legislation was indeed directed at Socrates. This is questionable because Socrates did not teach the art of speech; it was taught by the likes of Protagoras. It was useful for those who wished to succeed within the democracy, not those who wished to overthrow it. Socrates was not interested in making winning speeches in the assembly. So, the edict could not have been directed at stalwart anti-democrats such as Socrates. The legislation was clearly intended to suppress the democratic enemies of the Thirty.

3 The Case of Leon of Salamis

Plato made an effort to distance Socrates, *not* from Critias and Charmides, but from their reign of terror. He claimed that Socrates refused to cooperate with the Thirty and displayed courage and integrity in the course of this dark chapter in the history of Athens.[14] The case of Leon of Salamis was meant to be a significant illustration. In the Plato's *Apology*, Socrates defends himself by saying

> When the Oligarchy was established, the Thirty summoned me to the Hall, along with four others, and ordered us to bring Leon from Salamis, that he might be executed. They gave many such orders to many people, in order to implicate as many as possible in their guilt. Then I showed again, not in words but in action, that, if it were not rather vulgar to say so, death is something I couldn't care less about, but that my whole concern is not to do anything unjust or impious. That government, powerful as it was, did not frighten me into any wrongdoing. When we left the Hall, the other four went to Salamis and brought in Leon, but I went home. *I might have been put to death for this, had not the government fallen shortly afterwards.*[15]

Both Taylor and Stone interpret this incident as proof of Socrates' moral integrity, his "courageous defiance" (Taylor's words), or "civil disobedience" (Stone's words). They are totally credulous about how Socrates expected to pay for his disobedience with his life.[16] Stone takes this act of disobedience as an indication that Socrates was politically neutral where the conflict between the oligarchic and democratic parties in Athens was concerned because he thought of all politics as a defilement of the soul.[17]

The idea that Socrates would have been put to death "had the government not fallen shortly afterwards" has been denied by Ellen and Neal Wood. As they rightly point out, the Thirty had time enough to kill Theramenes, who was opposed to the arrest of Leon of Salamis, and "time enough to expel citizens...and time enough to establish an even more extreme oligarchy,... *after the arrest and execution of Leon.*"[18]

The fact is that no one else could have gotten away with refusing to do the bidding of the Thirty. This is why the audience could not have been too impressed with Socrates' description of events. The suggestion that Critias and Charmides would put their beloved Socrates to death must have been as implausible for an Athenian audience as it is for those of us who know the powerful spell that Socrates cast on his associates.[19]

A better version might have been as follows:

> My fellow Athenians, I need not tell you that failing to co-operate with the Thirty meant certain death. I am sure you have friends and family who perished for refusing to co-operate. I might also have been put to death for my refusal to co-operate, were it not for the fact that Critias and

Charmides were very close friends of mine. They shared my view that care of the soul is the one thing needful. They were in possession of the royal art. As physicians of the soul, they were bent on purifying Athens. Once in power, I was stunned at the violent intensity of the regime and refused to participate in its crimes.

That would have been a more believable statement—but it would have required Socrates to wonder if he misled them. However, as portrayed by Plato and Xenophon, he had no second thoughts and no regrets. Socrates prides himself on the fact that he did not do their bidding but went home. That is precisely the problem. Going home was not good enough for the Athenians who lost fathers, husbands, and brothers at the hands of these thugs. Socrates was in a position to call off his dogs. He was in a position to rebuke them. He was in a position to correct them and bring them to their senses. Going home was not good enough because he could have stopped them. Far from exonerating him, this incident reveals his close association with the criminal regime, and the serious moral failing implied by this error of omission, which displayed callous indifference to the sufferring of his fellow citizens.

4   The Case of the Generals at Arginusae

In 406 BCE, Athens narrowly escaped a defeat at the battle of Arginusae. However, the victory had cost 25 vessels and 4000 men. Unhappily, it was believed that many of these men were alive when they were abandoned in the water by the generals, who should have rescued them. Apologists for Socrates assume that the sailors were dead, which leads to the conclusion that the outrage over not rescuing bodies at sea in a storm was overblown.[20] If the sailors were dead, then the outrage toward the generals is a function of the importance that the Greeks placed on the honor of burial due to fellow citizens.[21] However, the outrage of the lower classes may not simply have been a function of the Greek pre-occupation with the proper way to treat dead bodies. The source of the fury is that the sailors were alive and "victorious" in the battle; Xenophon referred to them as men not bodies. He tells us that these victorious men were left to drown in their ships without oars or any way of escaping.[22] In this light, the anger and indignation was not a matter of superstition about how to treat the bodies of the dead, but an understandable anger by those whose fathers and brothers were left to die after their victory. The generals claimed that stormy seas made the rescue impossible. The Assembly suspected that the generals just did not bother to pick them up, and left them in the water to die instead.[23] Some historians believe that the storm was just an excuse, and that the conduct of the generals was a treasonous effort to assist the oligarchic cause by weakening the fleet and its sailors, which was the source of the power of the democracy.[24] The prosecution decided to put the generals on trial by the whole citizen Assembly. They wanted the fate of all eight generals to be decided *en bloc*. The committee, whose business was to preside over the trial, protested that the proposal was a direct infringement of the constitution, and that the generals should be tried before a separate law court and not the whole Assembly.[25] Socrates was a member of the committee and protested along with the rest of them—it was the only occasion in which he was politically engaged in the democracy. The committee was overwhelmed by the public outrage at the generals and agreed to ignore the unconstitutionality of the procedure. Socrates remained unmoved, but was defeated. The generals were tried as a body and found guilty. Eight generals were deposed, and the six that had not escaped from Athens were executed.[26]

Socrates used this case at his trial as an example of his devotion to law and justice and the courage to take an unpopular stand and upbraid the Athenian Assembly for its disgraceful behavior.[27] However, it is important to note that the only time that Socrates participated in the democracy, he bravely stood up for the aristocratic few (i.e., the generals) against the poor sailors who manned the naval ships and were left to die.[28] Viewed from the democratic vantage point, this incident might not have been proof of Socrates' high-mindedness, but a "loyal piece of factional work."[29]

5 UNWILLINGNESS TO ESCAPE

Plato portrays the trial of Socrates as a case of grave injustice. Yet, Socrates refuses to escape from jail, even when the opportunity presents itself. In the *Crito*, Plato presents Socrates as accepting his punishment out of loyalty to Athens and her laws.[30] His refusal to escape is intended to display Socrates' respect for law—even when it condemns him unjustly. The *Crito* is usually understood as an account of political obligation. This account is not credible, either as a theory of political obligation or as a defense of Socrates.

In the *Crito,* Socrates conducts a conversation with the personification of the Laws of Athens. They tell Socrates that he owes them obedience for having nurtured him, and he agrees. He owes obedience to the laws of Athens because he has benefitted from her largess. However, it does not follow from the fact that he has benefitted from being a citizen of Athens that his obligation to the laws is unconditional. The argument assumes that the justice of the regime is irrelevant to the question of moral obligation. The same argument could be used to justify obedience to the laws of the Thirty. It implies that those who complied with the laws of the Thirty had a moral obligation to do so as citizens of Athens and beneficiaries of her largess.

Plato's *Crito* is often regarded as the basis of the social contract theory of government. By accepting the benefits bestowed by the state, individuals tacitly consent to obey the laws. However, any reasonable account of the social contract between the citizen and the state must be two-sided. Like any other contract, the social contract becomes null and void when one party breaks the agreement. In dealing with the question of political obligation, Sophocles presents a more plausible view in his *Antigone* where the obligation is dependent on the justice of the regime. If Athens has broken the contract by unjustly putting Socrates to death, then he has no obligation to obey the death sentence. By presenting Socrates as a man whose devotion to his city is unconditional, Plato hoped to distance him from the treasonous oligarchic coup that with whom he was associated. It may have been a clever defense, but it was a bad theory.

It is certainly true that there would have been no Socrates without the freedom that Athens accorded sophists, philosophers, and scientists. Without the freedom of Athens, the cultivation of Socrates' philosophical talents would not have been possible. Unfortunately, this is not a view that was shared by Socrates. As a philo-Laconian or lover of Sparta, he claimed that it was Sparta and Crete (not Athens) that were the "most ancient and fertile homes of philosophy among the Greeks."[31] This sounds like a surprising view, but as we shall see in Section 4, Socrates regarded the Spartan passion for philosophy as a well-kept secret. His claim is that philosophers are better off in Sparta where they are highly esteemed, and where they rule, not openly, but behind the scenes. In Athens they are judged and condemned by the mob, which can neither understand nor appreciate them. As we shall see, for Socrates, being a philosopher is akin to being divinely inspired—a state of affairs that does not require social nurturing. So, it is not clear that he owes Athens anything of any significance.

Crito was in a position to bribe the guard and provide Socrates with the privileges that were accessible to Athenian oligarchs. On the whole, it was easy for oligarchs to escape prosecution. Once they realized that they were in political trouble, they could live in exile with their friends in oligarchic states—a situation facilitated by the institution of *xenia* or guest-friendship.[32] The institution allowed individual oligarchs from one city to bind themselves in loyalty and friendship to oligarchs in other cities. When one of them got in political trouble, the other promised to offer him refuge and invite him to live on his estate in the style to which he was accustomed. If an oligarch was exiled by his city, he was assured of a hospitable place to live in the same grand style. Even in situations of war between two rival cities, two guest friends who encountered each other in a battle were duty bound to refrain from killing one another, even though they continued to slaughter other men from the rival city. The institution of *xenia* can be compared to a political insurance policy for the upper classes. Thucydides and Xenophon were themselves Athenian exiles who lived among their oligarchic friends in other Greek city-states.

So, why did Socrates refuse Crito's offer to escape? Surely it was not because the theory of political obligation was so compelling. There is a more obvious reason. Had he escaped, his honor and reputation would have been besmirched forever, since he was given numerous opportunities to depart legally, before and during the trial. With so many oligarchic friends in enemy cities, he could have gone voluntarily into exile before the trial—and there would have been no trial. During the trial, he could have proposed banishment as an alternative to the death penalty suggested by the prosecution; but he did not. The suggestion that his penalty should be free meals at the Prytaneum for the rest of his life must have been offensive to the Assembly, since the Prytaneum was where the heroes who gave their lives to overthrow the Peisistratid tyranny in the sixth century were honored by the democracy.[33] Clearly, this *hubris* did not help his case with the jury.

Contrary to the political theory espoused in the Crito, the trial provided no evidence of Socrates' respect for law. Instead of defending himself, Socrates disparaged the court, heaped scorn on his fellow citizens, made a charade of the proceedings, and forced the jury to convict him. His conduct at the trial was more defiance than defense. Nevertheless he was convicted only by a small majority of 60 votes, which means that as many as 220 out of about 500 jurors voted to acquit him—under the circumstances, that's hardly a vicious mob.[34] Not surprisingly, many of those who wished to acquit him became convinced during the proceedings that he was incorrigible, unrepentant, and more determined than ever to continue radicalizing the youth. This explains why more people voted for the death penalty than voted that he was guilty in the first place—360 jurors voted for the death penalty, while 140 *were still willing to let him go*. So, having passed up all the legal opportunities to live happily and comfortably in the company of his adoring oligarchic friends in other cities, having had every opportunity to escape legally, it would have been disgraceful for Socrates to escape at the eleventh hour by breaking out of jail.

6   Plato's Legend

Plato's legend presents Socrates as a divinely inspired man. It was commonplace for him to go into a trance in the middle of a walk, or a dinner, or a conversation, and listen to a heavenly voice.[35] The voice was like a guardian angel; it warned him when he was about to make the wrong decision.[36] So, when it came to impiety or the corruption of the young, the charges were patently absurd. Socrates was a model of virtue, who did everything in his power to improve the souls of the youth he came into contact with.[37] He was sent by a god, to wake Athenians from their moral slumber, so they would care for their souls.[38]

By some strange quirk of fate, this great sage, supreme in goodness, managed to acquire a dreadful reputation among the citizens of his beloved city. This paragon of virtue was slandered—supposedly by the envy and malice of his fellow citizens.[39] He was so reviled by them that one day, when they could tolerate his presence in their midst no longer, they charged him with impiety and with corrupting the young. They concocted these trumped up charges, in the hope that he would flee, or go into voluntary exile. But he decided to stand trial. He was not only innocent of the charges, he was also infinitely superior to the ignorant mob that shamelessly convicted and put him to death. The question is why? The answer provided by Plato is that society finds goodness as intolerable as truth.[40] But how could that be? Surely, the good man does not harm his fellow citizens. Surely, they have nothing to fear from the good man. That is the crux of Plato's legend. The trouble is that the

Athenians had plenty to fear from Socrates. So, they could not have convicted him for his goodness.

Plato's defense of Socrates is closely tied to the scenario imagined in the *Republic*, of the just and righteous man who suffers from the consequences of a bad reputation all his life, but is nevertheless happier than the bad man who reaps the benefits of a good reputation. The *Republic* is meant to show that the just man is happier than the unjust man, come what may. Supposedly, justice alone suffices for happiness, because of its beneficial effect on the soul—without any reference to the social and political advantages that a reputation for justice might bring.

Philippa Foot has rightly objected that Plato errs in taking on such unrealistic portraits. She argued that even though it may be possible for an unjust man to reap the benefits of a sterling reputation for some time, it is impossible to sustain this deception over a lifetime. The character of the unjust man will eventually be found out because it is impossible to fool all the people all the time.[41] In my view, Plato insists on these implausible circumstances because the perfectly just man with a dreadful reputation who is treated with contempt by everyone—mirrors the plight of Socrates, as understood by Plato. As the *Apology* makes clear, Socrates is the good man who has suffered from a *lifetime* of so much ill repute that he finds himself face to face with the hemlock. However, the idea of a perfectly good man who suffers from a bad reputation all his life is as unlikely as the wicked man who enjoys an unassailable reputation as long as he lives. Just as the bad character of the unjust man is bound to be uncovered, so the good character of the good man is bound to shine through.

It is conceivable that a good man may be slandered by malicious gossip. He may even be portrayed in a negative light in a popular farce —the way that the young Socrates was portrayed in Aristophanes' *Clouds*—a foolish scientist floating on a cloud, mocking Zeus, and corrupting impressionable youth. Is it possible for such a lie to succeed for a lifetime? Surely, over his long life, those who came into contact with Socrates would realize what a good man he was. Surely, they would realize that his sole mission in life was to improve the souls of others—as everyone from Plato to Gregory Vlastos, W. K. C. Guthrie, A. E. Taylor, and others have maintained. Surely, those who came into contact with him would debunk these malicious lies. Nor could his perpetual questioning of figures of authority have garnered him the animosity of the populace in a democratic society that was not inclined to revere authority. Nor was his line of questioning particularly spiteful, if Plato's dialogues are any indication. At the very least, the good conduct of his students and close associates would have been living proof that the malicious gossip had no basis in reality. And there's the rub. Far from undermining the effects of the malicious gossip against him, the conduct of his students confirmed it.

Plato's legend leaves us with unfathomable riddles because it is divorced from historical reality. We know from Xenophon's *Memorabilia* and the pamphlet of Polycrates that Socrates was prosecuted for being the teacher of Alcibiades, Critias, and Charmides.[42] How could the sage who taught virtue be the teacher and close associate of the treasonous and self-serving Alcibiades, or the ruthless and bloodthirsty Critias, the leader of the infamous Thirty Tyrants? How can a man of such impeccable integrity be surrounded by such scoundrels?[43] How can a man who was wholeheartedly devoted to the mission of improving the soul, fail so spectacularly when it came to his most intimate friends and associates? How can a man of such superlative virtue acquire such a bad reputation that even a lifetime of goodness could not dispel? The legend of Plato does not begin to answer these puzzling questions. Nevertheless, the legend has prevailed—thanks largely to Plato's literary ingenuity.

7   Tropes in Plato's Defense of Socrates

Plato concocted some very beguiling tropes in support of his legendary defense of Socrates. We have already discussed the gadfly and the horse (Section 1.7). Others include: (1) the medical analogy, (2) the parable of the ship, and (3) the care of the soul. All are equally flawed, as we shall see.

(1) *The Medical Analogy.* It is well known that Socrates was fond of the medical analogy when it came to politics. For him, the political art required specialized knowledge akin to medicine. Like the latter, the political art had as its goal the health and wellbeing of the patients, and did not cater to their desires or pleasures.[44] In the *Gorgias*, Socrates describes his trial as that of a doctor prosecuted by a cook before a jury of children. Then he tells us to imagine what the cook would say:

> children of the jury, this fellow has done all of you abundant harm,... by surgery and cautery, and he bewilders you by starving and chocking, giving you bitter draughts and compelling you to hunger and thirst, whereas I used to feast you with plenty of sweet meets of every kind.[45]

The point he is making is that democratic leaders are akin to cooks and candy-makers who flatter the people instead of improving them. In contrast, the statesman, like the doctor, has to do unpleasant things for the health of the patient—unpleasant things that the patient does not like or enjoy—bitter pills, even "amputations" that are deemed necessary to save the body politic.[46]

Even in his late work, Plato never abandoned the medical analogy for understanding politics. In the *Statesman*, Plato endorsed the necessity of a purge by a true statesman for the good of the city.[47] In his quest to define the true statesman, Plato struggled to distinguish him from the tyrant. There were seven constitutions identified in the dialogue: monarchy vs. tyranny, aristocracy vs. oligarchy, and constitutional democracy vs. simple democracy. In each case, the critical distinction between the noble and ignoble forms of government is rule according to law over willing subjects, versus rule without law over an unwilling population. However, where the seventh form of government or rule by the true statesman is concerned, then all the relevant distinctions in the understanding of constitutions become obsolete.[48] The highest form of government is in a class by itself and "must always be exalted, like a god among mortals, above all other constitutions."[49] When it comes to the truly gifted ruler, the one who possessed the true art of ruling, then

> it makes no difference whether their subjects be willing or unwilling; they may rule with or without a code of laws.... It is the same with doctors. We do not assess the medical qualifications of a doctor by the degree of willingness on our part to submit to his knife...or other painful treatment. Doctors are still doctors whether they work according to fixed prescriptions or without them...So long as they control our health on a scientific basis, they may *purge* as reduce us or they may build us up, but they still remain doctors. The one essential condition is that they act for the good of our bodies to make them better instead of worse...[50]

Like doctors, true statesmen

> may *purge* the city for its better health by putting some of the citizens to death or banishing others. They may lessen the citizen body by sending off colonies like bees swarming off from a hive.[51]

Comparing the true statesman to a doctor who amputates a leg to save the patient misses the mark. The medical analogy fails because a real doctor gets the consent of the patient before amputating. In an effort to force the analogy to fit his view of the "true statesman," Plato claims that the doctor who amputates *against the will of the patient* is a true doctor nevertheless.[52] Plato is wrong. The doctor who amputates a leg against the wishes of the patient is indistinguishable from an assailant. The medical analogy makes medicine indistinguishable from assault.

In the *Statesman*, Plato tries to distinguish between the true statesman and the tyrant to no avail.[53] He admits that the difference is hard to discern, and that is why he warns against Sophists, because they look amazingly like the real thing, but they are tricksters. The whole discussion is reminiscent of Jesus warning us against false prophets, who prophesy in his name and do miracles in his name, and sound a lot like him. Neither Jesus nor Plato can give us any way of distinguishing the real from the counterfeit, the best from the worst. The arrogant lawlessness of the "true statesman" explains why it must have been hard for the Socratic circle to regard Critias as a tyrant.

It may be objected that all this talk of tyranny and murderous purges flies in the face of the Socratic dictum that it is never just to harm anyone,[54] and that "it is worse to do than to suffer wrong."[55] However, the Socratic conception of harm provides a loophole. For Socrates, harming others is making them worse. This gives the self-proclaimed wise man, the physician of the soul, the one who knows, a great deal of leeway in dealing with others. Critias no doubt thought he was making his city better.

If Plato's *Gorgias* is any indication, Socrates spoke of killing, banishing, and confiscating the property of people as a "*good thing*" and a "*just action*" when the consequences were deemed advantageous by those who know.[56] Unlike Machiavelli, Socrates does not consider these violent extrajudicial actions as "necessary evils," but as *just* actions. Close associates of Socrates no doubt imbibed his *hubris*—an arrogant self-assurance that leads to criminality on a large scale. He seduced his students into thinking that they were physicians of the body politic. They alone knew what was best for the city; they alone could rule the unruly multitude; they alone were fit for power; they were true statesmen who could do no wrong; they were gods among men. Meanwhile, those who ruled in accordance with law and with the consent of the people were charlatans. Far from defending Socrates, the medical analogy supports the case for the prosecution.

(2) The *parable of the ship* is one of the cornerstones of Plato's grandiloquent defense of Socrates—as well as its Achilles heel. Imagine a ship with a wise and skillful captain saddled with a bunch of drunken sailors.

The captain relies on the stars for navigation, but the drunken sailors assume that he is a useless star gazer and throw him overboard.[57] The result is disastrous for the ship. It does not take much imagination to recognize that the captain is Socrates, the ship is Athens, and the drunken sailors are the "Athenian mob" that convicted Socrates. In the context of this parable, Socrates mourns that the superior few suffer dreadfully at the hands of the inferior many: "what the best among men experience in relation to their city is so difficult that there is no single other experience like it."[58] On that occasion, Socrates' interlocutors seem a little more skeptical than usual; they object to the Socratic claim that philosophers are a blessing to their cities, on the grounds that it runs afoul of the general consensus that philosophers were not only useless to the city, but also "altogether vicious." This is clearly a reference to the reputation of Socrates and his crowd. Socrates acknowledges the difficulty of showing why he is right and everyone else is wrong. So, he sidesteps the matter by resorting to the parable.

The parable of the ship is intended to mirror Plato's perception of the plight of Socrates at the hands of the Athenian *demos*. The key element in the parable is not only that the sailors are drunk, but also that the merits of the true navigator are invisible to them, since they do not know that being a "star gazer" is integral to navigation. In the same way, Socrates has special knowledge that is integral to the art of ruling; but the Athenian *demos* is as oblivious to the importance of this knowledge as the drunken sailors were to star gazing. All appearances to the contrary, Socrates is the superior one; he is the true benefactor of the city; and his fellow citizens are the drunken sailors. Plato's tale implies that the Athenians should have surrendered uncomprehendingly and with gratitude to the captain's superior wisdom. The parable fails to provide any rebuttal of the widely held view that philosophers are "vicious." It fails to give us any reason why Socrates is right and everyone else is wrong. It simply asks us to take it on his authority that his case is analogous to that of the innocent stargazing navigator—but why should we?

The parable misses the mark. Plato makes navigation so mysterious and incomprehensible that a competent captain can manage the ship only with the absolute, total, and *uncomprehending* subordination of his sailors. Surely, even the most ignorant sailors should be able to distinguish between a captain who is competent and one who is not. They should be able to distinguish between a ship that is afloat and one that is sinking. They should be able to differentiate between a captain who can bring the ship to its destination, and one who cannot. It makes no sense for sailors to throw a captain overboard when he is keeping the ship afloat and headed to its destination. This is why Plato had to make the sailors not only ignorant but also drunk.

The implication of the parable is that the rule of the wise is both *unassailable* and *unrecognizable*. It follows that the sailors should surrender *uncomprehendingly* to the rule of the captain. Having been the captain of a sailboat myself, I can testify that having an ignorant crew with no knowledge of sailing whatsoever makes the task of being captain difficult, unpleasant, and dangerous. In other words, the parable fails because the total ignorance of the sailors in comparison to the captain is neither reasonable nor desirable for the captain, the sailors, or the ship. Just as the medical analogy is based on a fallacious understanding of the practice of medicine, so the parable of the ship is based on a misconception of what it takes to be a captain of a ship large enough to require sailors.

It may be objected that the image of the uncomprehending surrender to the all-knowing captain runs afoul of Plato's conception of Socrates as the divinely inspired man who lifts others out of the cave and into the sunlight of knowledge. Of course, it is only the very few that are lifted out of the cave. So, it is natural to surmise that these would be his closest associates. It must have been obvious to the Athenians who convicted Socrates that the Athenian ship of state was not afloat when the Socratic tyrants were at the helm. This was clear for all to see because neither the Athenians nor the historians who recorded these events were drunken sailors. They could see clearly that the ship of state was floundering. So, they had every reason to throw the Socratic navigators overboard. The relevant question at the trial was: did Socrates intend to cultivate more of these political monsters? His unrepentant demeanor made it clear that the answer was in the affirmative.

(3) *The care of the soul.* Just as the art of medicine improves the body, so true statesmanship improves the soul. This leads Socrates to tell Callicles that he is "one of very few Athenians, not to say the only one, engaged in the true political art, and that of the men of today I alone practice statesmanship."[59] He explains that the criterion for being a true statesman is the ability to make the citizens as good as possible. He tells Callicles (his interlocutor) that to be fit for a political career, he must answer the following question in the affirmative:

> Is there any man who previously was evil, unjust, undisciplined, and senseless, and through Callicles has become an upright and worthy man, be he

stranger or citizen, slave or free?... Tell me,... Callicles what man will you claim to have improved by your *company*?[60]

If that were the criterion of public office, then Socrates could not possibly qualify. Even if the standard were made considerably lower, Socrates would still not qualify. Lowering the standard, the question would be: Is there anyone who, as a result of the company of Socrates, became evil, unjust, undisciplined, and senseless? The answer is—yes, there have been such men.

According to Plato, Socrates made his mission to implore all who came into contact with him to care for their soul as the one thing needful, as the most important thing. So, how could he be responsible for what Critias, Charmides, or Alcibiades did? A. E. Taylor said it was his "misfortune" to have been associated with these characters.[61] In other words, the political case against Socrates was merely circumstantial. It was guilt by association, as Plato and Xenophon maintained.

A better explanation is that there is something deeply flawed in the Socratic conception of justice or righteousness. The latter has its roots in the Orphic project of withdrawal from the attachments to the world and control over the desires of the body. Plato developed this conception of justice in the *Republic*. It is well known that Plato's conception of justice differs rather dramatically from the ordinary conception of justice. In the ordinary or common sense view, justice is about our relations with others. Treating others fairly and decently means paying debts, keeping promises, not lying, cheating, deceiving, or taking advantage of others. In other words, the ordinary conception of justice involves abstaining from certain types of acts—treachery, violence, thievery, betrayal, deception, and the like. In contrast, justice in the peculiarly Platonic sense is a condition of the soul; it is about the relation between different parts of the soul; it is about self-mastery understood as the rule of reason over the appetites. The assumption is that this conception of justice as self-mastery is a pre-requisite for justice in the ordinary sense of refraining from sacrilege, temple-robbing, adultery, embezzlement, kidnapping, and the like.[62] However, as David Sachs has pointed out, nowhere does Plato make an *argument* to that effect.[63] In his brilliant essay, Sachs illustrates that it is possible to be just in the Platonic sense without being just in the ordinary sense of treating others well; by the same token, it is possible to treat others well without being just in the Platonic sense of the term. Sachs gives two important reasons why neither one of these two concepts of justice necessarily implies the other. First, "intelligence, courage, and self-control are,... compatible with a variety of vulgar injustices and evildoing... the most that can be said on behalf of Plato's argument is that crimes and evils could not be done by a Platonically just man in a foolish, unintelligent, cowardly, or uncontrolled way."[64] Second, there is no reason for thinking that those who are just or righteous in the ordinary sense must also have Platonically well-ordered souls. For example, it is possible to be kind and fair to others while being self-indulgent when it comes to food, drink, or sex.

Even though Sachs does not say so, his essay is extremely relevant to the case against Socrates. Plato maintained that Socrates could not have corrupted his three infamous students because he was a man of exceptional self-mastery—a man with a well-ordered soul, a man who is virtuous in the distinctively Platonic sense of the term. However, if the argument fails on a purely theoretical level as Sachs has illustrated, then it also fails at the practical level—as a defense of Socrates. Simply because Socrates had exceptional self-mastery, simply because his soul was characterized by the rule of reason over the appetites, simply because he was just in the peculiarly Platonic sense of the term, it does not follow that he was just in the ordinary sense of the term. In other words, even if Socrates had complete mastery over himself, it does not follow that he treated others fairly. The same goes for his students. The Athenians who convicted him did not think that he or his students treated them fairly. There is no indication that Socrates treated Alcibiades fairly,[65] let alone Xanthippe or the children. By sweeping away the ordinary conception of justice and replacing it with an Orphic understanding of morality, Socrates encourages those who believe that they have a share in divine wisdom to think of themselves as exceptions to the standard rules of morality. There is every indication that Alcibiades, Critias, and Charmides thought that the ordinary rules of morality did not apply to them.[66]

8   Socrates and Jesus

Plato opened the door to Christianity. But the success of the latter also made Socrates more appealing. Indeed, the veneration with which Socrates has been regarded in the history of Western thought makes him second only to Jesus in virtue, integrity, and righteousness.[67] Voltaire called Socrates the Jesus Christ of Greece, and thought of Jesus as the Socrates of Palestine. Gregory Vlastos thought that even though Socrates fell short of Christ as a moral teacher, he was truly great because his ideas anticipated Christianity—the personal god, the immortality of the soul, and the punishments of the after-life. In other words, he was a Christian *avant la letter*.[68]

Since Christianity has triumphed and paganism has been defeated (it would be more accurate to say that paganism was mercilessly and violently suppressed by the Church), the reputation of Socrates has profited immensely by being on the right side of history. The fate of Jesus of Nazareth mirrors the fate of Socrates, as described by Plato. Plato's claim that Socrates was persecuted for his wisdom and goodness was a precursor to the Jesus narrative at the heart of Christianity. The triumph of Socrates, much like the triumph of Jesus, is due in no small measure to the ability of zealous disciples to silence the critics and expunge their reproaches from the historical record. The case against Jesus of Nazareth was made in a "lost" work, *True Word*, by Celsus, which we know only through the refutations of Oregon of Alexandria. Likewise, Polycrates made the case against Socrates explicitly in a "lost" pamphlet, *Accusation of Socrates* (393 BCE), which we know only through the denunciations of Socrates' disciples—especially Plato and Xenophon.[69] Purging, burning, destroying, and censoring the writings of the opposition to shield the hero from all criticism invite legitimate suspicion. If a persuasive case can be made in defense of Socrates and Jesus, then it would not be necessary to silence the critics for all eternity. However, it was necessary in both cases to expunge all criticism from the record in order to show that in both cases they were persecuted for their *goodness*.

The persecution of goodness is not to be confused with the miscarriage of justice, where an innocent man is convicted of a crime he did not commit and is unjustly put to death. Socrates and Jesus were supposedly put to death for their goodness, because human beings are so perverse that they hate having such good men in their midst. The idea is as bewildering as it is familiar. The notion that a man would be persecuted for his goodness is readily accepted in a Christian culture in which human depravity is paramount. The idea is the founding myth of Christianity. This founding myth explains the grip that the Platonic portrait of Socrates continues to have on the imagination of the West.

The idea that the world cannot tolerate goodness allows the fate of Socrates to dovetail with the fate of Jesus. The people preferred a convicted felon such as Barabbas because they could not endure the perfect goodness of Jesus. Accordingly, Jesus warned his disciples against just such a fate, saying that they will be maltreated just as he was maltreated, because like him, they are not of this world (John 15:18–20). Not surprisingly, the early Christians claimed that they were persecuted by the Romans for their goodness. It did not occur to them that those who looked with longing and eagerness for the destruction of the world by their God, and were in some cases willing to help God get on with it by building great fires to hasten the apocalyptic event, would be regarded with legitimate suspicion. Christians were insensible to the threat that they posed to their community. Like Socrates and Jesus, they were convinced that the world hated them because they were witness to truth, goodness, and justice, not because they were fire hazards, or because they refused to swear allegiance to the empire and were therefore potential traitors. For Christians, the persecution of goodness was the norm in a fallen world. It did not occur to them that they were in any way culpable.

Even though the persecution of goodness cannot withstand rational scrutiny, it has nevertheless penetrated so deeply into the fabric of Western thought that it is difficult to fathom how radical it is, or to grasp its bleak implications. The latter include the development of a culture preoccupied with human depravity and the pervasiveness of ignorance and sin. To remedy this defect, priests, who have special access to divine wisdom, are entitled to rule others without persuasion or understanding. These ideas were the basis of the dark authoritarianism anticipated by the work of Plato. The totalitarian tyranny of the Catholic Church that engulfed Europe in the middle ages was but a Christianized Platonism—Plato's dystopia realized in the world.

9   Verdict of the Ages

When it comes to Socrates, the verdict of the ages has been almost entirely a footnote to Plato. Every age paints the persecution of Socrates in its own image as the persecution of an emerging truth struggling to supplant the decadence of an old order.[70] Socrates was not only co-opted by Stoics, and beloved by Christians, he also played a prodigious role in the history of rationalism, liberalism, and the Enlightenment. Condorcet expressed the sentiments of the Enlightenment philosophers when he wrote that the death of Socrates was "the first crime announcing the war between philosophy and superstition, which still continues today."[71]

In his iconic *On Liberty*, J. S. Mill used the example of Socrates to defend the absolute and inviolable freedom of thought and speech.[72] Mill's argument was at its best when the dissenting opinion was true and the received opinion was false. He took it for granted that the wisdom of Socrates represented the truth, whereas the received opinions of his fellow Athenians were falsehoods. In silencing him, he argued, the Athenians robbed themselves of the opportunity of exchanging error for truth. Mill assumed that the trial was about ideas. He assumed that Socrates was put to death simply because he challenged the received opinions of his time. Thanks to Mill, Socrates became a champion of the liberty of thought and speech,[73] and the trial became a supreme example of the extraordinary individual, who stands on principle against the tyranny and vengeance of the mob. For Mill, Socrates is a champion of liberty in an age of democracy, and the threat of the tyranny of the majority. Mill was right in pointing to the need to defend liberty in an age of democracy. However, Socrates was no champion of liberty.

If the legend of Socrates as the champion of intellectual liberty is to be plausible, Socrates has to be separated from Plato. It follows that the division of Plato's dialogues into early, middle, and late is intended to show that the real Socrates appears only in the early dialogues where the *elenchus* or dialectical refutation is dominant. In this way, those who consider Plato a harbinger of totalitarianism can still cling to Socrates was a champion of freedom of thought and speech. For example, Karl Popper regarded Socrates as a poster-child for the open society, and denounced Plato for turning the Socratic love of truth, reason, and liberty on their head, in the most spectacular case of intellectual sabotage in history.[74] The Oxford liberals, as represented by A. E. Taylor and Ernest Barker, also thought that Socrates was a champion of liberty, even if he was not a champion of democracy.[75]

Most scholars agree that crimes of thought were virtually unknown in the ancient world. Gregory Vlastos tells us that those who held unorthodox views were not prosecuted. He points to the example of Aristodemus who openly ridiculed those who made sacrifices to the gods.[76] Vlastos surmises that the difference between Socrates and Aristodemus is that the latter did not make any effort to teach his impious views. Vlastos thinks that Socrates was prosecuted because he was a *teacher* of unorthodox views. Socrates was prosecuted for the "aggressiveness of his public mission," which Vlastos understands as teaching virtue.[77] This mission, with its focus on the soul, instead of on sacrifices, was unorthodox.[78]

Vlastos provides as evidence that Socrates was prosecuted for his teaching the fact that fifty years after the event, Aeschines declared in his *Contra Timarchum*: "Men of Athens, you executed Socrates the Sophist because he was shown to have been the educator of Critias, one of the Thirty who subverted the democracy."[79] This is indeed a pregnant quotation, but it does not succeed in showing that Socrates was prosecuted merely for teaching an unorthodox conception of virtue. In defense of Socrates, Vlastos says that he was not as great a moral teacher as Jesus, and adds that he might not have been particularly successful. It would have been more accurate to say that the failure of Socrates to teach virtue was staggering.

Vlastos is no doubt correct to claim that Socrates was prosecuted for his teaching. However, it was not for teaching an unorthodox morality. The immorality of his students was what the Athenians held against him. They had to endure the treachery, brutality, and utter moral depravity of his students. That is what irked them. Socrates did not simply fail to improve his students, he corrupted them—he harmed them in the genuinely Socratic sense of the term, by making them much worse than they would have been otherwise.

What divides scholars is whether the persecution of Socrates was a unique case. E. R. Dodds thinks that the trial of Socrates was not unique, but was part of a witch-hunt directed at philosophers, sophists, scientists, and freethinkers, that took place in the "Great Age of Greek Enlightenment," which he compares to the McCarthy era in the United States.[80] I. F. Stone provides a powerful refutation of Dodds' claim.[81] He denies that there was a general crackdown on intellectuals. Stone believes that the trial of Socrates was an unusual case in which historical and political circumstances led Athens to betray her own ideals.[82] Despite his comprehensive knowledge of the historical events, Stone believes that Socrates was innocent and the charges were bogus.

The fact that there were no witch-hunts of intellectuals does not mean that the trial of Socrates was a singular or unparalleled case in which Athens betrayed her ideals, as Stone maintains. We know that Antiphon, the famous Sophist, was tried for his life as the inspiration behind the oligarchic coup of 411 BCE.[83] In so far as Socrates was regarded as the inspiration behind the oligarchic coup of 404 BCE, then the trial of

Socrates is neither part of a broad persecution of ideas that gripped Athens in an age of freedom, as Dodds maintains; nor was it totally unprecedented, as Stone believes.

My objection to Stone is that he romanticizes democracy. He associates it with freedom, open public debate, devotion to reason, persuasion, and the rule of law. He thinks that one of the gods of Athens that Socrates offended is Demos, but provides little evidence for such a god. Somehow, the deification of the demos does not strike terror in Stone's heart. In my view, the conflict between Socrates and Athens is a conflict between two claims, each claiming superior authority—the demos on one hand and, the self-proclaimed, divinely inspired man on the other—both claims are equally terrifying.

It may be argued that the best way to defend Socrates is to confront his anti-democratic reputation head on. After all, there was much to criticize about democratic Athens, and some of the criticisms of Socrates had validity. This would have been Plato's strongest line of defense at the trial. Socrates was indeed a critic of democracy. What of it? How else can a wise man improve his society?[84] After all, being a critic is not the same as being a traitor or a conspirator. Plato could not use this argument in the *Apology* because the disciples of Socrates were traitors, conspirators, and great villains.[85]

It is natural for modern scholars to think of the trial of Socrates in terms of the persecution of ideas because their models of persecution are intellectual: the Inquisition, the Stalinist purges in Russia, and the McCarthy era in the United States. All these were efforts to root out ideas. I do not believe that the trial of Socrates can be understood in these terms.[86] If the trial were simply about ideas, then all the historical events would be irrelevant and would provide no insight into the case for the prosecution. Then, the only way to explain the conviction of Socrates would be in terms of gratuitous evil, the resentment of the inferior many, and the unfathomable hatred of wisdom and goodness—in short, the legend of Plato. In truth, Socrates was feared because of his capacity to nurture oligarchic radicals bent on treachery, sedition, and political violence. There was legitimate fear of what Socrates inspired and could still inspire.

Contrary to what Stone, Dodds, Vlastos, and others maintain, the trial was not an inquisition intended to clamp down on unorthodox ideas as such.[87] Socrates was implicated in the *deeds* of his students, close friends, and associates. As Xenophon tells us in the *Memorabilia*, he was accused because of his association with Critias, Charmides, and Alcibiades.[88] It was not a crime of thought, but of *incitement* to crimes and misdemeanors.[89]

Even the most uncompromising defender of freedom of speech, John Stuart Mill, recognized that there are forms of speech that overlap with action, and that such speech cannot belong to the domain of absolute freedom, even in the most liberal society:

> No one pretends that actions should be as free as opinions. On the contrary, even opinions lose their immunity when the circumstances in which they are expressed are such as to constitute their expression a positive instigation to some mischievous act.[90]

Incitement to harm others, or put them at risk, is a legitimate object of legal censure, even in the most liberal society imaginable. In prosecuting Socrates, Athens was not criminalizing his opinions, but making sure that he would cease and desist from inciting young oligarchs to violence against the state. Unfortunately, he made it clear at the trial that he had no intention of changing his ways.

The opponents of Socrates saw him as the consummate intellectual puppeteer who pulled the strings behind the scene. Leaders of the newly re-established democracy feared his ability to incite another bloody coup. Athens had already suffered two oligarchic coups in the same decade. Contrary to the claims of his adoring fans, Socrates was not a threat because of his unrivaled virtue.[91] He was a threat because he cultivated young men who had an appetite for autocratic rule, who preferred Spartan authoritarianism to Athenian freedom, and who had such a visceral abhorrence of Athenian democracy that they were willing to subvert it by violent means.

Legend has it that the Athenians repented the condemnation of Socrates, and that Meletus was killed for the role he played in the affair. However, there is no evidence that the Athenians repented.[92] The relevant fact is that Socrates was unrepentant. According to the accounts of the trial by both Plato and Xenophon, Socrates showed no remorse or regret. In the face of such a colossal fiasco, he did he apologize for what might have been the unintended consequences of his teaching. He categorically denied that he corrupted anyone—intentionally or unintentionally.[93] He refused to take any responsibility, on the ground that he had no knowledge to impart.[94] Plato offers us nothing that could explain how the students of Socrates came to be so dreadfully corrupted.

Did Socrates inspire the lawlessness of Alcibiades and the crimes of Critias and Charmides? Was Socrates responsible for politically radicalizing these young men? Did he make them unwilling to live on equal terms with others? Did he make them unwilling to live by the rules to which others were subject? Did he make them feel that they were beyond equality? Did he make them averse to accepting even a moderate democracy in which the rich and well-born rule by the consent of the many? Absolutely.

Does that mean he supported the regime of the Thirty? According to some scholars[95] he probably shared the sentiments expressed in Plato's *Seventh Letter*, where he says that he was enthusiastic about the revolution that endowed the Thirty with supreme power because he thought they would "lead the city from an unjust life." However, he soon realized that "these men made the former government look in comparison like an age of gold."[96] In other words, he was in favor of the regime when it started, then shrank with horror at its crimes and refused to participate.

I reject this seemingly plausible scenario, because if it were true, then recognizing his complicity, the remorseful Socrates would have left the city, and there would have been no trial. His enthusiasm for the medical analogy leads me to believe that he regarded the crimes of the regime as a necessary amputation to save the body politic.

If Socrates was horrified by the crimes of the regime, yet did not leave the city either during the reign of the Thirty or after the restoration of the democracy, but decided to stand trial, then he would have had to admit that he corrupted his students unwittingly. If so, then he would have shown some remorse for what transpired, and taken some responsibility. But he categorically denies corrupting them wittingly or unwittingly, had no remorse, and took no responsibility.[97] Instead, he displayed a callous disregard for the sentiments of his fellow citizens who lost their relatives in the bloodbath initiated by his students. All this leads me to suspect that his only regret was that the coup did not succeed in permanently ridding Athens of her democracy.

Why did the great sage not turn his critical eye on his own ideas—ideas that were so potent, yet so lacking in measure and moderation, that imparting them to the likes of his students—rich, spoiled, and disgruntled oligarchs—was bound to court disaster. Why was he not more introspective? Why did he insist on carrying on exactly as before? How could the man who was famous for saying that "the unexamined life is not worth living"[98] fail to examine his own life and teachings? Is this not the height of irony? The ingenious narrative concocted by

Plato and bequeathed to posterity does not begin to answer any of these questions.

10   Socrates and Heidegger

There is a similarity between the unease of democratic Athens with Socrates and the apprehension with which Germany regarded Heidegger after the defeat of the Nazis. When asked by the de-Nazification Commission whether Heidegger should be allowed to teach at the university, one of Heidegger's best friends and colleagues, Karl Jaspers, said that he did not think that the German students were strong enough to withstand the intellectually seductive style that Heidegger employed.[99] Like the Germans, the Athenians were concerned about Socrates' intellectually seductive influence. Both Germany and Athens were determined to force their respective philosophers to stop teaching and retire to the obscurity of the contemplative life. Heidegger complied; but Socrates refused, and in so doing, forced the Athenians to condemn him. Thanks to Plato, he became a martyr, endowed with an aura of honor and glory. But Heidegger was not so lucky; his name is shrouded in opprobrium and ill repute, even though Hitler was not a student of Heidegger, nor was he a close friend or associate.

In our time, the predicament of Socrates is not unlike the predicament of a radical Islamic Imam whose disciples have committed acts of terror on a grand scale. Would any of us be inclined to find the Imam innocent? Would we be as charitable as the Athenian demos? Surely, we would demand that he be removed from our midst. His defenders might say that the Imam was unjustly accused, and that he was not responsible for the conduct of his students because he was preaching a religion of peace and goodness. That was Plato's defense of Socrates. Is it any more credible in the case of Socrates as in the case of the Islamic Imam? Is a teaching not known by its fruits?

Plato has created a formidable legend around the figure of Socrates by extricating his ideas from the crimes of Critias and Charmides. He has convinced posterity that Socrates was prosecuted for challenging received opinion. Then he spent a lifetime proving that the ideas of Socrates were superior to those of his contemporaries.

In the forthcoming chapters, I will challenge Plato's defense on its own terms. Far from exonerating Socrates, I believe that Plato's dialogues legitimize the case for the prosecution.

Notes

1. Xenophon, *Memorabilia* (Cambridge, MA: Loeb Classical Library, Harvard University Press, 1923), I. ii.42–46.
2. Ibid.
3. *Memorabilia*, I. ii.12.
4. Ibid, I. ii. 15.
5. *Memorabilia*, I. ii. 24–25.
6. Ibid, I. ii. 24.
7. Philostratus in Rosamond Kent Sprague, *The Older Sophists* (Columbia: University of Carolina Press 1972), p. 243.
8. Xenophon, *Memorabilia*, I. ii.64.
9. J. Burnet, "Socrates," *Hastings Encyclopedia of Religion and Ethics* (New York: Charles Scribner's Sons, 1928), Vol. xi. Burnet rightly maintains that if Socrates was indeed the man described by Xenophon, he could never have been prosecuted for impiety, or anything else for that matter. Vlastos makes the same point in *Socrates: Ironist and Moral Philosopher* (New York: Cornell University Press, 1991), pp. 290–91.
10. Vlastos, *Socrates: Ironist and Moral Philosopher*, pp. 291–93.
11. Ibid, p. 290.
12. *Memorabilia*, IV. iv.3.
13. Ibid, I. ii.64.
14. *Seventh Letter*, 324 d–325 a.
15. *Apology*, 32 c–d. My Italics.
16. Taylor, *Socrates* (Westport, Connecticut: Hyperion Press, Inc., 1979), pp. 101–102; I. F. Stone, *The Trial of Socrates* (Toronto: Little, Brown & Co., 1988), p. 113.
17. Stone, *The Trial of Socrates*, p. 111–114, argues that Socrates "stood apart from the political life of the city," because he thought politics in general was sinful. I think this reading is mistaken. If he really was an apolitical ascetic, why were his students so overwhelmingly political and oligarchic?
18. Ellen Meiksins Wood and Neal Wood, "Socrates and Democracy: A Reply to Gregory Vlastos," *Political Theory*, Vol. 14, No. 1 (February, 1986), p. 74, my italics. See Bibliography for more details.
19. See the discussion of Plato's *Symposium* in Section 4.2.
20. Thomas C. Brickhouse and Nicholas D. Smith, *Plato's Socrates* (New York: Oxford University Press, 1994), assume that the sailors were dead, pp. 162–63.
21. This was connected to the belief that the souls of the unburied can find no rest, and therefore haunt the land where they are unwillingly detained. This may be dreadful for the living; if they happen to live on the land where the dead are detained against their will, which would not have been the case for

the Athenians. See Erwin Rohde, *Psyche: The Cult of Souls and Belief in Immortality among the Greeks* (New York: Harcourt, Brace & Co., Inc., 1925), pp. 162–63.
22. Xenophon, *Hellenica*, I.7.9–10. The case is dealt with exhaustively in Douglas M. MacDowell, *The Law in Classical Athens* (New York: Cornell University Press, 1978), pp. 187–89.
23. Alban D. Winspear and Tom Silverberg, *Who Was Socrates?* (New Jersey: The Cordon Company, 1939), pp. 65–66.
24. Alban Dewes Winspear, *The Genesis of Plato's Thought* (New York: Dryden Press, 1940), p. 165: Winspear is here relying on the account of G. Grote, *History of Greece*, ed. by Mitchell and Caspari (London, 1908), p. 750.
25. Winspear and Silverberg, *Who Was Socrates?* p. 67.
26. Stone, *The Trial of Socrates*, pp. 111–112; Taylor, *Socrates*, p. 98. Taylor takes this incident to be proof of Socrates' "sterling integrity and fearless devotion to the cause of law."
27. *Apology*, 32 a–b. Stone, *The Trial of Socrates*, p. 113: points out that the Assembly later agreed that he was right, so he was eventually given credit for his stance by the *demos*.
28. Bernard Williams claims that the treatment of fighters at the hands of their generals and commanders was a sensitive issue that was dramatized by Sophocles' *Philoctetes*. In that play, Odysseus represents the callous inhumanity of the generals. See Section 6.3 for my discussion of the play.
29. Winspear and Silverberg, *Who Was Socrates?* p. 67.
30. Gregory Vlastos, "The Historical Socrates and Athenian Democracy," in *Political Theory*, Vol. 11, No. 4 (Nov. 1983), pp. 495–516, thinks that the dialogue proves that Socrates was not an oligarch, but was totally committed to the democratic constitution of Athens and did not blame the laws for the injustice done to him, but the people who administered the laws. This thesis was thoroughly debunked by Ellen and Neal Wood, "Socrates and Democracy: A Reply to Gregory Vlastos." *Political Theory*, Vol. 14, No. 1 (February, 1986), pp. 55–82. See also J. Peter Euben, *The Tragedy of Political Theory: The Road Not Taken* (Princeton, New Jersey: Princeton University Press, 1990), who claims that Socrates was totally devoted to Athenian democracy and was eager to improve it. The same argument appears in Thomas C. Brickhouse and Nicholas D. Smith, *Plato's Socrates*, p. 163. See Bibliography for more details.
31. *Protagoras*, 342 a–d.
32. For an excellent discussion of this institution, see Gabriel Herman, *Ritualized Friendship and the Greek City* (New York: Cambridge University Press, 1987).
33. Stone, *The Trial of Socrates*, pp. 188–9.
34. Taylor, *Socrates*, p. 118.

35. *Symposium*, 220c–d; *Phaedrus*, 242b–c.
36. *Apology*, 31d.
37. Ibid, 31b.
38. Ibid, 31a.
39. Ibid, 23e–24b.
40. Ibid, 24b.
41. Philippa Foot, "Moral Beliefs," in Foot (ed.), *Theories of Ethics* (London: Oxford University Press, 1967), p. 100.
42. *Memorabilia*, I. ii.12–16.
43. In *Plato's Socrates*, Brickhouse and Smith suggest that Socrates sought out the worst of the worst in order to improve them (p. 171). See my response to this argument in the Bibliography.
44. *Gorgias*, 521a ff.
45. Ibid, 521e–522a.
46. Ibid, 521e.
47. *Statesman*, 293b–c. I am using the translation by J. B. Skemp in *The Collected Dialogues of Plato* (eds.) Edith Hamilton and Huntington Cairns (New York: Princeton University Press, 1961).
48. Ibid, 293b.
49. Ibid, 303b.
50. Ibid, 293b–c. My italics.
51. Ibid, 293d. My italics.
52. Ibid, 296b.
53. Ibid, 301c.
54. *Republic*, 335e.
55. *Gorgias*, 473a.
56. Ibid, 470a–b. It may be argued that Critias is the perfect Machiavellian figure who could benefit his city because he did not have to choose between his city and his soul; in contrast, Socrates appears to care about his soul and his salvation. But this is not the case because Machiavelli was candid enough to consider extra-judicial killing as a necessary evil, not a "just action," regardless of the advantages anticipated. In the American election of 2016, Ben Carson, a surgeon and a real doctor, who ran for the Republican Presidential nomination, invoked the need for political amputations. Needless to say, he was one of the scariest people running for office in a year where there was no shortage of scary people contending.
57. *Republic*, 488a.
58. Ibid.
59. *Gorgias*, 521d.
60. Ibid, 515a–b. My italics.
61. Taylor, *Socrates*, pp. 100, 115.
62. *Republic*, 442e–443b.

63. David Sachs, "A Fallacy in Plato's *Republic*," *The Philosophical Review*, Vol. 72, No. 2 (April 1963), pp. 141–158.
64. Ibid, pp.154–155.
65. According to Alcibiades' account in *Symposium*, to be discussed in the next chapter.
66. I am grateful to Professor Mark Rigstad of Oakland University for alerting me to this important work.
67. It may be argued that Jesus apes Heracles, not Socrates. Heracles was the son of god (Zeus), who helped humanity by slaying monsters. However, the similarities are superficial because Jesus was not focused on this world. Instead of slaying monsters, Jesus brings back the chthonic gods of eternal torment. Nevertheless, the similarities gave the new religion a familiarity that took the edge off its strangeness.
68. Gregory Vlastos, "The Paradox of Socrates," in Vlastos (ed.), *The Philosophy of Socrates: A Collection of Critical Essays* (Notre Dame, Indiana: University of Notre Dame Press, 1971, 1980).
69. Alban D. Winspear and Tom Silverberg, *Who Was Socrates?* p. 85. They rightly point out that the case against Socrates, like the case against Jesus, has not come down to us in unified form; also Taylor, *Socrates*, p. 112; and Emily Wilson, *The Death of Socrates: Hero, Villain, Chatterbox, Saint* (London: Profile Books, 2007), p. 4.
70. This is the theme of Emily Wilson, *The Death of Socrates*.
71. Quoted in Peter Gay, *The Enlightenment: The Rise of Modern Paganism* (New York: W. W. Norton & Co., 1966), p. 82.
72. John Stuart Mill, *On Liberty*, 1859 (New York: Liberal Arts Press, 1956), ch. 2.
73. Arlene W. Saxonhouse, *Free Speech and Democracy in Ancient Athens* (New York: Cambridge University Press, 2006), regards Socrates as a democrat because he loved to speak his mind freely.
74. Karl R. Popper, *The Open Society and Its Enemies*, Vol. 1, *The Spell of Plato* (Princeton, N.J.: Princeton University Press, 1966), pp. 128–137; R. H. S. Crossman, *Plato Today* (New York: Routledge, 1937, 1959). Crossman regards Plato as a totalitarian and links him with Hitler's Germany, while regarding Socrates as a martyr for freedom of speech; Thomas C. Brickhouse and Nicholas D. Smith, *Plato's Socrates*, p. 157.
75. W. K. C. Guthrie, *Socrates* (New York: Cambridge University Press, 1971), p. 95. Guthrie tells us that the Oxford liberals are close to the truth about Socrates. See also E. A. Havelock, *The Liberal Temper in Greek Politics* (New Haven: Yale University Press, 1957).
76. Vlastos, *Socrates: Ironist and Moral Philosopher*, p. 295.
77. Ibid, p. 297.

78. Vlastos, "The Paradox of Socrates," in Gregory Vlastos (ed.), *The Philosophy of Socrates: A Collection of Critical Essays* (Notre Dame, Indiana: University of Notre Dame Press, 1971, 1980).
79. Vlastos, *Socrates: Ironist and Moral Philosopher*, p. 296.
80. Dodds, *The Greeks and the Irrational*, p. 189.
81. Stone, *The Trial of Socrates*, pp. 231–47.
82. Ibid.
83. Antiphon, *The Speeches*, edited by Michael Gagarin (Cambridge University Press, 1997), pp. 247 ff.
84. This is the argument made by J. Peter Euben in *The Tragedy of Political Theory*. See Bibliography for more details.
85. In Aristotelian terms they would be examples of the *megaloponeroi* as opposed to petty criminals. See discussion of *hubris* in Section 5.7.
86. Even Stone, *The Trial of Socrates*, ch.1, regards the trial as the persecution of ideas.
87. Ibid, pp. 231–247: Unlike Dodds, Stone claims that the trial of Socrates was an exception in an otherwise tolerant society.
88. *Memorabilia*, I. ii.12–16.
89. Thucydides, *History of the Peloponnesian War*, VI. 27. Thucydides tells us that the mutilation of the Hermae was regarded very seriously as evidence of "a revolutionary conspiracy to overthrow the democracy."
90. J. S. Mill, *On Liberty* (New York: Library of the Liberal Arts, 1859, 1956), ch. III, p. 67.
91. James S. Hans, *Socrates and the Irrational*, pp. 53, 63, 65, 73.
92. Taylor, *Socrates*, p. 128.
93. *Apology*, 26a.
94. Ibid, 33b.
95. Ellen and Neil Wood, "Socrates and Democracy: A Reply to Gregory Vlastos," *Political Theory*, Vol. 14, No. 1 (February, 1986).
96. *Seventh Letter*, 324c–d.
97. *Apology*, 25d–26a.
98. Ibid, 38a.
99. Karl Jaspers, "Letter to the Freiburg University Denazification Commission," December 1945, in Richard Wolin (ed.), *The Heidegger Controversy: A Critical Reader* (New York: Columbia University Press, 1991).

CHAPTER 4

How Plato Legitimizes the Case for the Prosecution

Plato's portrait of Socrates has cast such a spell on the imagination of the West that even those who see in Plato's political philosophy a sinister totalitarianism nevertheless regard Socrates as the liberator of the mind.[1] This view presupposes a radical divide between Socrates and the mature Plato. This division is in turn sustained by the conventional distinction among scholars between the early, middle, and late dialogues. The assumption is that the early dialogues present an accurate portrait of Socrates, while the middle dialogues represent Plato's own ideas albeit under the spell of Socrates; but in the late dialogues, Plato departs from the ideas of Socrates. So much so that Socrates would have been put to death in the regime recommended by Plato in the *Laws*. Contrary to those who share Karl Popper's view that Plato represents the greatest case of sabotage in history, I will show that the ideas attributed to Socrates in the early dialogues are inseparable from the dark authoritarianism of Plato's later work.

I am not suggesting that Plato had no original thoughts of his own. As W. D. Ross has rightly argued, it would be very strange if a philosopher like Plato were a mere reporter and not someone using the dialogue form as a literary devise.[2] I follow most scholars in thinking that Plato's early dialogues and the work of Xenophon may embellish the life of Socrates, but they cannot be totally inventive since many of the people who were expected to read these dialogues knew Socrates and were present at his trial and even his death. Plato and Xenophon also tell us something about the philosophical questions that occupied the historical Socrates: the unity of the virtues, the relationship of knowledge and virtue, the impossibility of teaching virtue, the importance of caring for the soul, the nature of the gods, the need for political expertise, and the analogy of statecraft with other crafts. All these themes re-appear in the early, middle, and late dialogues of Plato. This does not mean that Plato was simply the mouthpiece for Socrates. His original contribution was in his brilliant capacity to work out the political, moral, metaphysical, and epistemological implications of Socratic assumptions. He developed Socratic intuitions, but he did not depart from the basic assumptions—not even in the *Laws*.

In this chapter, I will argue that far from exonerating Socrates, the Platonic dialogues lend credibility to the case for the prosecution. Plato's insistence on the innocence of Socrates does not follow from the evidence provided by his own dialogues. Reading Plato's dialogues—especially the *Symposium*, the *Protagoras*, and the *Laws*—allows us to see the legitimacy of the case for the prosecution. At the heart of the matter is the Socratic paradox—namely, that virtue is knowledge but cannot be taught.[3] This paradox is the key to Plato's defense of Socrates. If virtue cannot be taught, then Socrates cannot be blamed for failing to teach his students virtue. The paradox is clearly outlined in the *Protagoras*, but the mystery of it is resolved only in the *Laws*. The close link between these two dialogues undermines the idea that Plato departed from Socrates in his later work. Indeed, Plato's repressive regime in the *Laws* is a logical consequence of the alliance of Socratic religion with politics—an alliance required by the Socratic mission of "care of the soul." It follows that Socratic ideas are dangerous and subversive, not only for democratic Athens, but for any regime that aspires to peace, order, and a modicum of liberty.

1   THE SOCRATIC PARADOX

No one has explained the "Socratic paradox" better than Gregory Vlastos. As he has rightly maintained, there are two aspects of Socrates that come into conflict with each other. On the one hand, we have a man with "an evangel to proclaim, a great truth to teach: our soul is the only thing in us worthy of saving, and there is only one way to save it: to acquire knowledge."[4] Clearly, he has a message that is nothing short of the "elixir of life." Yet, he claims repeatedly that he has no knowledge to impart. Therein lies the paradox: on the one hand, Socrates tells us that knowledge is necessary for salvation, and on the other hand, he tells us that he has no knowledge to impart. To make things even more paradoxical, he adds that even if he had the requisite knowledge, it is not the sort of knowledge that can be imparted or taught in any case. What makes him wiser than others, in his own estimation, is that he is under no illusion that he has the requisite knowledge. Unlike others, he is aware of what he lacks. As Vlastos explains, the paradox deepens because Socrates goes calmly to his death confident that "no evil thing can happen to a good man."[5] Since that good man is himself, Vlastos is moved to ask: "Can this be the same man who believes that no one can be good without knowledge, and that he has no knowledge?"[6]

Is Socratic ignorance just bogus and false modesty? Vlastos does not think so. This leads to even greater paradoxes. In Vlastos' view, Socrates not only says things that "contradict the role of the preacher and teacher of the care of the soul," he also "acts in ways that do not seem to fit this role."[7] His characteristic activity is the "elenchus" or the refutation. You say A and he shows you that A implies B and B implies C, and then he asks you, did not you say D before, and does not D contradict C? Then, far from clarifying the matter, he "leaves you with your shipwrecked argument." As we have seen, that is what he did to Euthyphro. He left him no better off than he found him. Vlastos thinks that Socratic tactics are at the very least "unfriendly."[8] In short, his "customary conduct" as a "pitiless critic" and "heartless intellectual" contradicts the role of the evangelist that he attributes to himself in the *Apology*. As Vlastos rightly observes, the paradox is even apparent from his conduct during the defense.

So, how can he claim to improve anyone? Vlastos proposes to solve the paradox as follows:

> Socrates the preacher turns out to be a man who wants others to find out his gospel so far as possible by themselves. Socrates the teacher now appears as a man who has not just certain conclusions to impart to others, but a method of investigation.[9]

Vlastos' claim is not convincing—not even to Vlastos. There is nothing in the method that would lead to any conclusions, let alone specific ones about the care of the soul. Vlastos is aware of the failure of the method to accomplish the mission of the evangel. He accuses Socrates of a "failure of love" and compares him unfavorably with Jesus for lacking the latter's love for humanity; far from shedding any tears for Athens, Socrates scolds, exhorts, and condemns her.[10] He is equally heartless when it comes to his interlocutors. For Vlastos, the problem is that the Socratic method is not good at attending to the empirical facts. Anyone who attends to the facts would know that knowledge is neither necessary nor sufficient for virtue.

Laches had courage even though he could not define it. And, as far as Socrates' courage in the face of death is concerned, Vlastos rightly attributes that to some sort of religious faith, not knowledge.[11]

Despite all these devastating criticisms, Vlastos nevertheless tries to explain why Socrates was truly great. He argues that Socrates advances humanity by making moral inquiry open to everyone. The expert can only offer guidance, but the decision belongs to each one who must be free to "make his own choice between right and wrong, not only in action, but in judgment."[12] The chance that one can be wrong is a "calculated risk" that Vlastos thinks is the price one must "pay for being free."[13] According to Vlastos, Socrates made people realize, for the first time, that moral inquiry is the business of everyone. Until then, people considered morality to be a function of class; people of the lower strata of society, which included not only slaves, but free-born manual workers, were not expected to know how to behave properly.[14] In that sense, Socrates is a "great reformer of morality" because he redefines the virtues in such a way as to make them "human qualities" and not "class attributes." In so doing, he paves the way for the liberating message of Jesus.[15]

The claim that Socrates wanted people to think for themselves in order to be free is spurious. It implies that Socrates is not only a democrat, as Vlastos maintains, but a liberal who celebrated individuality and freedom of thought, not just for the few, but for everyone. However, if Socrates was really eager to advance the reasoning powers of ordinary people, if he really wanted everyone to deliberate, and thought they really could, including the lower classes, he would have been a champion of the democracy. Far from being a champion of the democracy, he loathed it as an absurdity that was contrary to the natural order of things. He rejected the claim of Protagoras that politics was the business of everyone because Zeus distributed knowledge of justice and a sense of decency to all.[16] For Socrates, only those with special expertise in the political art were fit to rule. Turning Socrates into a democrat and a liberal (as Vlastos does) is senseless.[17]

Vlastos makes the Socratic Paradox even more paradoxical than he found it. It is not just the case that Socrates failed to improve the likes of Euthyphro, the troubling thing was that his closest associates were moral monstrosities—bloodthirsty killers, self-serving traitors, and fanatical oligarchs who were totally contemptuous of ordinary people—the very people that Vlastos thinks Socrates served by urging them to improve their souls. The real paradox is that a man of great moral virtue, whose mission was the improvement of the soul, failed so miserably to improve the morals of his closest friends and associates.

2 Resolving the Paradox I: Divine Inspiration

Socrates thought that virtue is un-teachable only because he flattered himself into believing that it was a special kind of wisdom—a divine gift from the gods to exceptional individuals such as himself. In the *Meno*, Socrates says: "virtue will be acquired neither by nature nor by teaching. Whoever has it gets it by *divine dispensation*."[18] Such a man, Socrates adds, "would be a solid reality among shadows."[19] The trances that Socrates was famous for serve to highlight his special relationship to the divine.[20] The claim that he had no knowledge to impart is nothing but false humility that cannot be taken seriously. Socrates is the paradigm of Aristotle's "ironic man" who affects a "mock-modesty" that "looks like self-advertisement."[21] Aristotle rightly rejects this man almost as much as he rejects the braggart because they both lack the veracity and candid honesty of the authentically virtuous person. The only grain of truth in the Socratic dictum that virtue is knowledge that cannot be taught is that the knowledge in question is not discursive—it is knowledge by acquaintance—his special acquaintance with the divine, and the acquaintance of his companions with Socrates. His companions were no doubt convinced that only through their acquaintance with Socrates could they get a glimpse of his peculiar wisdom. Socrates tells Phaedrus that he is divinely inspired, and Phaedrus agrees.[22] It is no wonder that Alcibiades accuses Socrates of "insolence" and "infernal arrogance."[23]

The relationship between Socrates and Alcibiades, as described by Plato, reveals not only the intimacy between them, but also the influence of Socrates on so many other young men. The portrait that emerges is not of someone who had nothing to teach, or who was eager to make his students think for themselves. In the *Symposium*, when Alcibiades enters the dinner party in a drunken state, Socrates immediately makes room for him on the couch and calls on Agathon for protection, because Alcibiades cannot keep his hands to himself! Socrates jokingly complains about how dreadful it is to be in love with Alcibiades, since the latter is madly jealous. Clearly, Socrates is teasing Alcibiades, but his intimacy with him is undeniable. After some cavorting back and forth, Alcibiades gives a long tribute to Socrates describing both the sexual and the intellectual effect that Socrates had on him and on many other good-looking young men—Plato informs us several times that Socrates had a special appreciation of the boyish beauties of his day and spent much of his time enjoying their company.[24]

Sexually speaking, Alcibiades compares Socrates with Marsyas, the ugly but sensual satyr who challenged Apollo in playing the flute. Like Marsyas, Socrates had a mesmerizing effect on the youth who came into contact with him. But unlike the satyr, Socrates did not need a musical instrument to enchant and seduce, all he needed was a few words and "we're staggered and bewitched... I'd swear on oath what an extraordinary effect his words have had on me—and still do."[25] The young and handsome Meno, in Plato's dialogue by that name, makes the same complaint. Meno accuses Socrates of "exercising magic and witchcraft upon me and positively laying me under your spell until I am a mass of helplessness." He advises Socrates not to go abroad lest he be arrested as a wizard.[26] Alcibiades compares Socrates to the Sirens, so powerful is his attraction. Alcibiades is speaking as a grown man about his close relationship with Socrates when he was young, yet it is clear that he is still in love with Socrates. He tells Agathon and the rest of the attendees at the drinking party that being in love with Socrates was like being

> bitten by something much more poisonous than a snake; in fact, mine is the most painful kind of bite there is. I've been bitten in the heart, or the mind, or whatever you like to call it, by Socrates' philosophy, which clings like an adder to any young and gifted mind it can get hold of, and does exactly what it likes with it.[27]

Alcibiades adds that those who are at the *Symposium* know what he is talking about since they have also experienced Socrates' "philosophical frenzy" and tasted that "sacred rage."[28] It seems that the source of much of this frustration is not simply intellectual, but also sexual. Despite being smitten by Socrates and finding every opportunity to spend the night with him, Alcibiades admits, much to his humiliation, that his sexual advances came to naught, even when he slept all night under the cloak of this "godlike and extraordinary man."[29] Socrates just laughed and jeered at his youthful beauty. Alcibiades is spellbound and hopelessly in love with Socrates, despite his recognition of the latter's impudence and conceit.[30] His humiliation notwithstanding, Alcibiades declares his admiration for the self-control and strength of mind that Socrates displayed in resisting his advances. The whole experience left Alcibiades "at his wits end" and in "utter subjection" to Socrates than ever.³¹ On some translations, Alcibiades' love for Socrates made a "slave" out of him.³² Now that Agathon, the handsomest youth at the party, has taken up with Socrates, Alcibiades warns him lest he suffer the same heartbreak, humiliation, and abject servility.

What is troubling about this eulogy to Socrates is that neither Plato nor the contemporary admirers of Socrates realize how incriminating it is. W. K. C. Guthrie makes the bizarre inference that what Meno and Alcibiades experienced at the hands of Socrates was the result of being introduced to the "force of rational argument."³³ Since when does the force of rational argument have such a stupefying effect?

What did Plato have in mind? How can this eulogy, and the rest of the dialogue, provide one more defense of Socrates, one more testimonial to his greatness, his virtue, and his innocence? Perhaps Plato thought that by highlighting Socratic self-mastery in the face of such disarming beauty, he was refuting the charge that Socrates was guilty of corrupting the young. Simply because Socrates had exceptional self-mastery, simply because his soul was characterized by the rule of reason over the appetites, simply because he was just in the peculiarly Platonic sense of the term, it does not follow that he was just—in the ordinary sense of the term (Section 3.7). Even though Socrates had complete mastery over himself, it does not follow that he treated others fairly. He was not fair to Alcibiades. We fail to recognize this because of our aversion to pederasty. If the relations involved were heterosexual, which is to say that if a woman had treated Alcibiades as Socrates had treated him, it would be obvious to us that she was leading him on, and that she was a selfish and self-absorbed tease.

The message of the *Symposium* is that Socrates had transcended the desires of the body. As the wise and mysterious Diotima explained to Socrates, love is a longing for the good and the beautiful. Since the gods already have wisdom, truth, goodness, and beauty, it makes no sense for them to long for what they already have.³⁴ This is why love occupies a place intermediate between gods and men ³⁵ It is a mediator between wisdom (which belongs to the gods) and ignorance (which belongs to ordinary humanity). It follows that love is integral to the Socratic understanding of philosophy as longing for divine wisdom.³⁶ As Diotima explains, the ascent to wisdom, truth, and beauty is a gradual initiation that begins with the devoted love of a single beautiful body, followed by "devotion to boyish beauties" in general—we know that Meno, Agathon, Phaedo, Charmides, and Alcibiades had more than their fair share of boyish beauty. In the long run, this devotion to boyish beauty is transcended as the philosopher ascends from the body to the spirit. Having been initiated in the "mysteries of Love," the philosopher soars to the "loftiest thought" and reaps the "golden harvest of philosophy." Mounting "the heavenly ladder," he draws closer to the "final revelation" and is overwhelmed by the "wondrous vision" which is beauty itself in all its "everlasting loveliness" and "eternal oneness" that neither flowers nor fades.[37] Having reached this lofty juncture, the philosopher becomes a "friend of god."[38] In this super-human condition, he will no longer be seduced by "comely boys or lads just ripening to manhood," but will care nothing for the beauty that "used to take his breath away."[39] The dialogue does not lead to Guthrie's conclusion that Socrates "is not given to pederasty."[40] On the contrary, it is a necessary step in the ascent to wisdom, and a window into the erotic intensity of his relationship with his students.

In the *Charmides,* the latter is described as a great beauty that Socrates is eager to meet. When he is introduced to him by Critias, Socrates admits to losing his composure, and when he gets a glimpse inside his garments, Socrates is "aflame" and could hardly control himself. As Socrates reveals, "I felt that I had been overcome by a wild-beast appetite."[41] Ironically, the dialogue is about temperance. We are to surmise that this is the wild beast that Socrates managed to tame in his later years, when he was finally able to resist the advances of Alcibiades. He has not always been able to resist the advances of Alcibiades. In the *Gorgias,* Socrates tells us that the two great loves of his life were Alcibiades and philosophy.[42] The relationship between Socrates and Alcibiades dates from the time when Alcibiades was a mere boy and Socrates a man in his thirties.[43] So, the idea that he had no influence on Alcibiades cannot be seriously entertained.

In a dialogue by Aeschines describing the relationship between Socrates and Alcibiades, Socrates compares his love for Alcibiades to Bacchic possession.[44] In the *Gorgias,* Socrates declares that he is in love with Alcibiades as much as with philosophy.[45] The *Protagoras* also begins by extolling the beauty of Alcibiades even though his beard has started growing and he is on the verge of manhood. Socrates is surprised by the fact that he is more interested in listening to the wisdom of Protagoras, who was visiting Athens, than chasing after Alcibiades—suggesting that his preferences have matured.[46]

Alcibiades I provides yet another portrait of the intimate relationship between Socrates and Alcibiades.[47] Socrates is presented as the lover who promises Alcibiades that he will be true and will continue to love him when his physical beauty fades and when all the other lovers have abandoned him, because he knows that as his beauty is fading, his soul, which is his true self, is gaining in wisdom and knowledge. Jowett comments that the relationship between Socrates and Alcibiades as presented there contradicts the one in the *Symposium*. However, this is not necessarily the case. Alcibiades makes it clear in the *Symposium* that Socrates was once his lover. His sense of abandonment in the *Symposium* coincides with the adoption by Socrates of a sexual asceticism that is compatible with his Orphic religion.

Socrates must have gradually transcended his preoccupation with beautiful boys in favor of a higher and more spiritual kind of beauty—hence his callous treatment of Alcibiades. One assumes that Socrates reached that stage by the time of his death—although the scene of his execution as presented by Plato in the *Phaedo* raises some suspicions: Socrates summarily dismisses his wife Xanthippe and his child, so that he can converse with his disciples and fondle the lovely locks of Phaedo.

As Diotima explains, in the *Symposium*, ordinary mortals are ensnared by the beauty of the body, and never ascend to the lofty heights of the philosopher. Being mortals, love drives them to seek what they lack—immortality—through procreation.[48] Diotima thinks that procreation is the prosaic version of the quest for the eternal, which reaches its height in the philosophical quest for divine wisdom.[49] The analogy is suspect because it makes philosophy and teaching philosophy analogous to procreation—as if by teaching one is reproducing oneself. This sort of teaching can create only individuals who are chronically incapable of independent thought—a predicament that Alcibiades describes so vividly as a state of abject servility.

Socrates failed so spectacularly to improve his students because he convinced them that he had a special access to divine wisdom, which he could not impart to them. It led Alcibiades and the rest of them to think he was a man unlike any other, on whose every word and gesture they must dote. Far from enlightening or improving the souls of his students, lovers, and close associates, far from introducing them to the force of rational argument, far from teaching them to think for themselves, Socrates leaves them rationally dumfounded, intellectually servile, and psychologically unhinged. In this way, he seduces them into surrendering their independence and becoming his puppets—just what the Athenian accusers of Socrates suspected. In other words, even if it is the case that virtue is knowledge that cannot be taught (because it depends on divine inspiration), it does not follow that Socrates was in no position to educate, guide, influence, or inspire these men. In short, Plato's account of the relationship between Socrates and his students legitimizes the case for the prosecution.

3 Resolving the Paradox II: Statesmanship

There is something odd about saying that virtue is knowledge that cannot be taught—but there is nothing paradoxical about it, once the meaning of the terms are understood. Plato's *Protagoras* provides the clearest account not only of the Socratic paradox, but also of the arguments of its detractors. When Socrates proclaims that virtue cannot be taught,[50] Protagoras, the great sophist, provides a devastating refutation. He rightly declares that the Socratic claim is at odds with what we all know from experience.[51] Our parents teach us virtue at an early age. Indeed, parents never tire of telling their children what is right and what is wrong, what is honorable and what is disgraceful, what is holy and what is impious.[52] It would be extremely irresponsible for parents to neglect their children when it comes to this most important aspect of their education, the want of which would lead them to be ruined or "punished by death or exile."[53] The very fact that society punishes people who lack virtue—a sense of justice and respect for others—is itself proof that virtue can be taught, if not by parents, then by punishment at the hands of the state. If the reform of wrongdoers were impossible, then punishment would be mere vengeance. Protagoras thinks that punishment must reform the offender. It follows that "virtue can be instilled by education," either gently through parental guidance, or not so gently through the punishment of the state.[54]

Protagoras is not suggesting that everyone is morally equal—only that everyone must have some share in virtue if the state is to survive.[55] He compares the teaching of virtue to the teaching of flute-playing. Imagine a society that can only survive if everyone was a flute-player.[56] Everyone would learn to play the flute and teach everyone else. Naturally, the wealthiest would hire the best teachers. However, the children of the wealthy may not necessarily become the best flute players because they may not have as much natural ability as their parents. Nevertheless, everyone in that society, including the worst flute-player, would still be very good compared to the untrained savage who is untutored by society. It follows that the worst men in society are better than savages.[57]

Protagoras claims to be a teacher of virtue. What he means by virtue is "helping a man acquire a good and noble character."[58] This includes justice, moderation, and respect for others. It also means sagacity, wisdom, prudence, and the ability to handle his affairs as well as the affairs of state. Interestingly, what Protagoras and Socrates mean by virtue is the same. For both, the apex of virtue is the "art of politics."[59] The difference is that Socrates claims that this art cannot be taught, while Protagoras is busy teaching it everyday. However, not everyone who studies with Protagoras will be a statesman of the same caliber as Pericles; just as every flute player will not become a virtuoso.

Faced with this knockdown argument, Socrates resorts to his characteristic irony. He pretends to gaze at Protagoras "spell-bound" and speechless.[60] When he finally collects himself, he tries to trick Protagoras into self-contradiction with his usual antics. However, Protagoras is not easily defeated, and Socrates emerges as jealous, destructive, and immature. He thought he could defeat Protagoras by asking him about the unity of the virtues—by all accounts, one of Socrates' favorite topics.[61] Are the virtues the same as parts of a gold coin are the same, or are they different as parts of a face are different? Protagoras opts for the face analogy. This leads to all sorts of conclusions that Protagoras rejects, such as the holy is not just and the just is not holy. Socrates thinks that the just and the holy are the same (a questionable idea), but Protagoras is neither willing to say that justice is identical with piety nor that they are totally different; the same goes for wisdom and courage. Protagoras thinks that the relation between different virtues is complex. Socrates bullies him into a straightjacket forcing him to declare that knowledge and virtue are totally different. So, how can Protagoras claim to teach virtue when he also regards it as something totally different from knowledge?

Contrary to Socrates' triumphalism, Protagoras's position is not so easily vanquished, but can be salvaged by saying that virtue does not *require* knowledge. Children can be taught to be moderate, kind, and considerate, even though they cannot define any of these concepts.[62] Meanwhile, Socrates defends a crude hedonism that leads to the conclusion that no one does evil willingly, but only out of ignorance. If wickedness is a function of ignorance, it follows that virtue must be a function of knowledge. Socrates concludes the dialogue with his famous paradox that virtue is knowledge, but cannot be taught.

In their efforts to defend Socrates against his accusers, Plato and Xenophon claim that Socrates was interested in morality, not politics. However, the idea that Socrates was concerned with morals, and not with politics, does not stand up to scrutiny. He did not separate virtue from the art of politics. In the *Protagoras,* Plato makes it clear that for Socrates, virtue is identical with the "political art."[63] In the *Symposium*, the divine wisdom attained by the philosopher at the summit of the "heavenly ladder" is about "the ordering of society."[64] The identity of virtue and statesmanship is also made clear in Plato's *Meno*. There, virtue is defined as "managing the city's affairs capably."[65] In the *Euthydemus*, Socrates asks, what does the "royal art," the "art of kings," or the "art of politics" accomplish? The answer is that it is the art "by which we shall make other men good" as well as happy.[66] Understood in this light, the peculiar Socratic mission of "caring for the soul" must be understood as a political mission by those in possession of divine knowledge.

Unlike Protagoras, Socrates is not interested in ordinary flute-players; he is interested only in virtuosos. It is certainly the case that people can be taught to play the flute, but no one can be *taught* to be a virtuoso. The same is true for statesmanship. No one can be taught to be a statesman—not everyone will be capable of it no matter how much teaching they get. To show that virtue (understood as statesmanship) cannot be taught, Socrates uses the example of Pericles, who could not impart his skill to his two sons.[67] So understood, there is nothing paradoxical about saying that virtue (understood as statesmanship) cannot be taught.

In the *Republic* as well as the *Laws*, Plato was working out the full political implications of the Socratic understanding of statecraft understood as "care of the soul." The political art *par excellence* is making sure that people are both good and happy. It follows that the political art does not aim at freedom, wealth, or security, but virtue. The point of statecraft is to make people good; for only by being good, can they be happy in this world as well as the next.

In conclusion, the Socratic paradox is not paradoxical once virtue is understood as a special knowledge belonging to the divinely inspired (or those who think they are), and the "care of the soul" is understood as the political mission of these divinely inspired statesmen. This Socratic attitude to statecraft, which was fully worked out by Plato, is open to a twofold interpretation—one innocuous, the other deadly. I will begin with the innocuous before proceeding to the deadly. It is the latter that needs to be confronted and acknowledged, for it is the one that can explain how a man like Socrates could mislead the likes of Alcibiades, Critias, and Charmides.

4 The Sunny Side of Plato's Politics

Although scholars do not normally put it in such simplistic terms, the innocuous political implications of Socratic ideas, as worked out by Plato, are as follows. In Plato's mature works, he continued to believe that

Socrates was right in thinking that the highest virtue is wisdom, which is necessary for those who would manage the affairs of state—and that is a special kind of knowledge, which is accessible only to the few. However, Plato was not only pre-occupied with virtuosos or statesmen, he was also concerned with the virtues of ordinary human beings. He thought that moderation is at the heart of ordinary virtue and is closely allied with justice. It is not the exclusive reserve of the wise, but is widely dispersed through education; it can and has been taught. Indeed, moderation must be a priority if the state has any chance of being harmonious and just. The importance of education as the key to the dissemination of virtue is as true for Plato's *Republic* as it is for his *Laws*, where the minister of education is the most important government official.[68] Citizens must be just if the state is to be ruled by persuasion rather than force. In the *Republic*, Plato provides a heroic argument to the effect that justice leads to happiness for societies as well as individuals. However, he is not confident that ordinary people will necessarily be motivated by the power of reason. So, the *Republic* ends with the myth of Er, which is intended to motivate those who are not likely to be convinced by the argument. In short, Plato's mature position is a refinement of the Socratic view.

Despite the emphasis on the dissemination of moderation throughout the state, in both the *Republic* and the *Laws*, Plato insists that those in power give the state its character. No state can be just if the rulers are not *supremely* just, because power is like the ring of Gyges, which has the ability to make people invisible. This immunity from detection allowed Gyges to enter the palace, kill the king, seduce the queen, and usurp the kingdom.[69] In the myth of Gyges, the ring represents the temptation that political power provides—the temptation to do injustice with impunity. The myth makes us wonder if any of us can get through the trial with our characters intact. From the Platonic point of view, the abuse of political power is the supreme political problem. Plato's solution is to separate power from wealth and to ally it with the highest virtue (i.e, wisdom). In this sunny world, those in power will be wise enough to know that justice is the key to happiness. They will therefore not be tempted to abuse the immunity from detection that power affords. To that end, he makes his argument that the just man is the happy man. Some cynical commentators believe that the argument is just propaganda intended for popular consumption. In my view, the very opposite is the case, the argument is intended for the wise few, the rest are presented with the puerile incentive for justice that belief in the torments of the afterlife affords. Plato's argument that justice leads to happiness is overstated and needs to be qualified, but that is another matter. The point is that some version or other of this sunny interpretation of Plato has been at the heart of his enduring popularity in the history of the West. Unfortunately, there is a serious flaw at the heart of the sunny side of Plato's politics that drives it to the dark side.

5 THE DARK SIDE OF PLATO'S POLITICS

Socrates was Plato's prototype of the divinely inspired man, the one who lifts others out of the cave so they can see the truth. In view of the collective comfort of the cave, Plato surmised that the process of education is akin to the arduous task of climbing a steep slope out the cave. Unfortunately, human beings are inclined to relish their captivity; the prisoners are not motivated to leave the soothing twilight of the cave. A prisoner, who escapes the darkness and emerges into the spectacular light of the sun, must be *dragged* out. Clearly, the process is so onerous that only very few can be hauled out. The real puzzle is how the first prisoner managed to escape in the first place. In other words, who is the un-dragged dragger? Plato marvels at the virtuosity of the first prisoner who escaped from the cave and witnessed the beauty of the truth beyond. He surmises that this un-dragged dragger must have been divinely inspired. For Plato, that extraordinary individual was Socrates. The wisdom of Socrates was a divine gift that set him above ordinary humanity—it was the kind of wisdom that Plato believed made a man peculiarly fit to govern his fellow human beings. This special knowledge of the "kingly art" or the "art of politics" made him a "physician of the soul." This is the Socratic mission that is described as "care of the soul."

The political implications of these assumptions were fully worked out by Plato in the *Laws*. The latter has a gloomy realism that is lacking in the fantasy world of the *Republic*.[70] This realism has its source in the fact that the regime described in the *Laws* is closely modeled on Sparta. Socrates (and his crowd) admired Sparta, despite the latter's hostility to sophists and philosophers. In the *Protagoras*, Plato tells us that Socrates did not accept the commonly held view of Sparta as hostile to philosophers. On the contrary, he thought that

> the most fertile homes of philosophy among the Greeks are Crete and Sparta, where are to be found more Sophists than anywhere on earth. But

they conceal their wisdom like the Sophists Protagoras spoke of, and pretend to be fools, so that their superiority over the rest of Greece may not be known to lie in wisdom, but seems to consist in fighting and courage.[71]

In other words, Socrates challenges the commonly held view that what made Sparta and Crete so powerful is iron discipline and military training. Instead, Socrates claims that philosophy, not military training, accounts for Sparta and Crete's stunning success. Apparently, Sparta and Crete valued philosophy above all else and were in the habit of meeting secretly with philosophers to learn from them how to improve their society. So great is the Spartan love of philosophy that the wisdom of Greece, including that of Solon (the Athenian law-giver), had its source in the philosophers of Sparta. Socrates associates philosophy with the "Laconic brevity" or pithy sayings inscribed in Apollo's temple at Delphi—"Know thyself" and "Nothing too much."[72] It follows that his own brevity (in contrast with the long-winded speeches of Protagoras and other Sophists) makes him a true philosopher in the Laconian tradition. In contrast, Sophists such as Protagoras are imposters; Spartans know the real thing when they see it.

In the beginning of the dialogue, Socrates went to see Protagoras with one of his young friends, who (much to the dismay of Socrates) was very excited about the prospect of studying with Protagoras. Socrates hoped to talk him out of it by going with him to see Protagoras and asking him some pointed questions that would undermine Protagoras' reputation. When they got to the house, Socrates asked Protagoras if he would prefer to speak with them in private, or openly in front of the rest of the company.[73] It was then that Protagoras revealed his distaste for Sophists who adopted a "disguise," operating "under cover" in the hope of escaping the malice of the authorities.[74] Protagoras thought that these covert Sophists failed to accomplish their purpose because they "did not pass unobserved by the men who held the reins of power in their cities."[75] For Protagoras, being secretive, pretending not to be philosophers "turns the attempt into sheer folly, and cannot fail to arouse even greater hostility."[76] One cannot help thinking that Protagoras was describing Socrates—a Sophist who denied he was a Sophist; an educator who denied he had anything to teach; and a political agitator posing as a devout man preaching the "care of the soul," who was nevertheless found out by the authorities. Protagoras regarded anyone who behaved like this as an "unprincipled rogue."[77] Protagoras was for openness, not esotericism. So, he had no desire to speak to Socrates in secret.

In contrast, Socrates admired the secretive philosophers who have made Sparta great and whose wisdom is supposedly the foundation of Greek culture. Socrates claimed that when they are tired of consulting with their philosophers in secret, the Spartans "expel all resident aliens" and "converse with the Sophists unbeknown to any foreigners."[78] In this way, the rest of Greece has no idea that Sparta has any philosophers. They are so secretive that they even pretend to be incapable of eloquent speech, even though their eloquence is occasionally revealed in spite of themselves. In this way, Sparta has fooled everyone into thinking that being a Spartan means having a taste for physical not intellectual exercise. Nothing could be further from the truth. So, what is the point of all this secrecy? Why does Sparta go to such ridiculous lengths to keep her wise men clandestine?

All these bizarre claims about Sparta's secret love of her philosophers, men who pretend to have neither wisdom nor eloquence, underscores a few important points. Socrates admired Sparta; he could not imagine that Sparta could be great without consorting with philosophers like him. He could not imagine a well-ordered state that was not ruled (covertly if not overtly) by a true philosopher. But why were Spartans secretive about their need to consult philosophers? The obvious answer is that their passion for philosophers was not indiscriminate. They did not want just any Sophist to enter their city. Nor did they care to have Sophists speaking openly to all, but only to those who held the reins of power. The meeting between the Spartan, the Cretan, and the Athenian Stranger in Plato's *Laws* was precisely such a meeting. Sparta and Crete were allies with very similar societies. The Spartan and the Cretan in the *Laws* talk as if they are the most dull-witted men on the planet. If we believe what Socrates says in the *Protagoras*, they must be faking it. Even though they seem like cloistered simpletons, they are keenly interested in the wisdom of the Athenian. They suspect that he might help them improve their societies. This is an important link between the *Protagoras* and the *Laws*.

It follows that the Athenian Stranger in the *Laws* is not just any philosopher—he is Socrates, or someone very much like him. He is the true philosopher that according to Plato's *Protagoras* is secretly consulted by the Spartans—a fact that accounts for the excellence of their polity. Like Socrates, the Athenian Stranger admires Sparta—but he also thinks she has a fatal flaw. That flaw has its source in the fact that all the discipline in that society has an external source; it lacks self-control or moderation. In both the *Republic* and the *Laws*, Plato insists that moderation is a virtue that must be widely dispersed in society and that it does not necessarily require wisdom. In the *Laws*, the emphasis on moderation is even more explicit than in the *Republic*.[79] Moderation is so important that the Athenian Stranger suggests drinking parties as a way to develop temperance.[80] Does that mean that Plato modified the Socratic insistence on the unity of the virtues? Yes—but not altogether, as we shall see.

The whole point of the *Laws* is to illustrate what would be involved if a divinely inspired man like Socrates was to team up with two powerful lawgivers from Sparta and Crete, who share his conception of the art of politics or the kingly art as a special craft. As physicians of the soul, these men believe that politics has a single goal—the cultivation of virtue, or the "care of the soul." In the *Laws*, the Athenian Stranger and his interlocutors agree that the goal of politics is not freedom, wealth, order, or empire. Virtue is its "single object."[81] Even in this dialogue, Plato is still addressing Socratic questions: Can virtue be taught? Is virtue possible without wisdom?[82] His answer, in the *Laws* as in the *Republic*, is that there is a superior type of virtue that belongs to the physicians of the soul, and cannot be taught, and an inferior type of virtue that belongs to those who need their services. In other words, there is the virtue of those who rule, and the virtue of those who are ruled. The superior virtue is divinely inspired and therefore *cannot be taught*, while the inferior virtue can indeed be taught.[83] The trouble is that the inferior virtue is not "incorruptible" and, as a result, is not altogether reliable. Therefore, great care must be taken to preserve it. And that care—the care of the soul—is what the art of politics is all about. Even in the *Laws*, Plato never tires of the craft analogy.[84] For Plato, as for Socrates, politics continued to be a craft that involves specialized knowledge and required a divine wisdom that cannot be taught.

At first, the regime described in the *Laws* appears to be a compromise between Athens and Sparta. It is a "mixed regime" in the sense of having monarchical as well as democratic elements.[85] Wardens of the law who sit on the ruling council are elected based on their merits, as long as they are between fifty and seventy years of age[86]; commanders are nominated by law-wardens, other government officials are chosen by lot—which is the distinctively democratic approach in Greek politics.[87] This best attainable regime is certainly not an oligarchy, which means that wealth is not the foundation of political power. In contrast, Plato displays a decided hostility toward wealth. The wealthy do not control the reins of power. Extremes of wealth and poverty are meticulously avoided as destructive to social order and harmony.[88] Property is equally distributed among the citizens—no one can increase that initial allotment more than fourfold and no one can sell the allotment and descend into penury. Usury is totally outlawed.[89] In this way, the richest cannot have more than four times what the poorest have. The best realizable regime described in the *Laws* is more democratic than oligarchic because it is characterized by a startling degree of equality in wealth and power among the citizens.[90] Of course, it is important not to exaggerate this equality, since the ideal state is not free from slavery. The latter is taken for granted—without which the citizens would not have the leisure to govern and defend themselves—there are no professional politicians, no professional lawyers, no professional judges, and no professional soldiers; all these duties must be shouldered by the citizens. Plato also insists that the citizens treat the slaves as well as they treat each other—a far cry from the way Sparta treated its slave population—the Helots.[91] In short, Plato's political position is antithetical to oligarchy and the claims of wealth; he sees wealth mainly as corruptive. He assumes that anyone who gets too rich must be either involved in shady dealings, or is niggardly. Plato is not sympathetic to the Old Oligarch—he does not confuse wealth and excellence. He might not be as inclined to pander to the oligarchs that Socrates cultivated.

As I have argued earlier (Section 1.5), the mature Plato is politically more moderate than Socrates where democracy and oligarchy are concerned. However, when it comes to religion, Plato's philosophical mission can be described as an effort to wed Socratic religion with politics. Plato's *Laws* is a logical working out of the political implications of the Socratic assumptions about the gods, piety, and care of the soul. As the dialogue proceeds, darkness sets in. The concern with moderation and self-control at the beginning of the dialogue morphs into state control of the internal landscape of the psyche. External conformity of conduct with the law is rejected as insufficient; instead, the goal of the law is to ensure conformity of thoughts, feelings, beliefs, and attitudes. State control of education becomes an all-consuming affair. The minister of education is by far the most important government official.[92] The goal of education is to ensure that children will have no "pains or pleasures in contradiction to the laws."[93] As presented, education is indoctrination. The youth are not allowed to explore ideas that challenge the values of their society. Fear of intellectual contamination is paramount. Immigrants are rejected, for fear that they will bring strange customs, habits, and ideas that might undermine the existing order.[94] Even when war or disease ravages the population, immigrants are still shunned. Commerce (which was the basis of Athenian wealth) is spurned as a potential source of contagion; the economy is based on agriculture (as it was in Sparta).[95] Sophists are not allowed to enter the city lest they pollute the state with their ideas.[96] Young people (under forty) are not allowed to travel, lest they become enamored with different regimes and lifestyles.[97] Those over forty who are allowed to travel must, upon their return, tell "the youth that the political institutions of other cities are inferior to their own."[98] Those who are corrupted by their travels and think that other cities are better, must be disciplined, re-programmed, or put to death if they make any attempt to meddle in education or the laws.[99]

In general, dissidents are admonished, isolated, and "converted" through persuasion by the wisest members of the "Nocturnal Council," which meets every day between dawn and sunrise.[100] If dissidents fail to be persuaded, they must be put to death. The state that emerges has an endless appetite for monitoring, manipulating, and policing the citizens with a relentless apparatus of state surveillance and control. Plato compares the state with the skull where the young wardens are the eyes, intelligent and nimble, they survey the state from the top.[101] As they watch, the young wardens report their perceptions of everything that goes on in the state to the organs of the memory, represented by the elder wardens. The old wardens are to the state what reason is to the head.[102] All citizens are rewarded for being informants.[103] The abuse of such a system by "grudge informers" is not seriously considered—a problem that was rampant in the dark ages when Europe was subjected to the brutality of the Catholic Inquisition, and again under the Nazi regime in Germany.[104]

Modeled on Sparta, Plato's best realizable regime is characterized by discipline, religiosity, military training of women and men, common meals, want of commerce, absence of luxury, and hostility to scientists and sophists.[105] The freedom associated with Athens, the freedom that modern people associate with democracy, is altogether absent. The separation of public and private domains that is the cornerstone of liberty is missing. Plato's regime has a stranglehold on the private lives of citizens—no freedom of thought or speech, no freedom of inquiry, no private dining, no same-sex unions, and no bachelors—at least not without a stiff fine.[106] Plato recognized that the regulation of private life is the hardest thing for people to accept and therefore the hardest thing to accomplish.[107] Living constantly in the public eye, as the Spartans did, is the key that makes it possible to control citizens by the power of social reprobation.

In the *Laws*, impiety is re-defined as intellectual dissent. Belief in religious dogmas is required by law. The laws against impiety do not simply apply to conduct, but also to thoughts, opinions, and attitudes. These laws are as harsh as they are extensive.[108] It is the duty of the secret philosophers, the most senior members of the "Nocturnal Council," to "minister" to the souls of the impious in the hope of converting or reforming them.[109] Even when no injuries or harms are committed, even when the impious are men of good character, the death penalty is nevertheless required for unbelievers.[110] The reason given by Plato for such harshness is the same reason given by Aquinas in defense of the Catholic Inquisition—the very existence of people with these dissident ideas will contaminate, pollute, or corrupt, the community.[111] People with dissident ideas cannot even express them privately, since everyone is a potential informer.[112] Magistrates who fail to prosecute offenders against the laws of impiety will themselves be charged with impiety.[113]

Following Socrates, Plato allied religion with morality. He declared that bad people are people who do not believe in the gods, or do not have the correct ideas about them.[114] Since the wrong religious ideas lead people astray, it follows that the correct religious beliefs are necessary for moral virtue. Plato therefore proceeded to make the religious ideas of Socrates compulsory—citizens were required by law to believe that the gods exist, that the gods are good and just, that they take an interest in human affairs, that they punish the wicked and reward the righteous, and that they cannot be swayed by bribes or sacrifices.[115] Plato was convinced that these religious dogmas are necessary for the well-being of the state.[116] The mandatory propagation of incredulous religious beliefs requires violent institutions. The grotesque invention of crimes of thought was necessary to sustain the alliance between the religion of Socrates and the state. In other words, Plato was the intellectual father of the Inquisition, long before it became a reality under the barbarous tyranny of the Catholic Church.[117]

Contrary to popular belief, Socrates would not be prosecuted for impiety in the society of the *Laws* because his religious ideas have become the orthodoxy—enforced with a vengeance. It is not Socrates who will meet death at the hands of the state, but his intellectual opponents.[118] Sophists will not be tolerated. Scientists will be censured, since they are the cause of what Plato calls a "plague of impiety."[119] Even poets and dramatists will be compelled to use their art to support the Socratic dogmas—that the gods are good, that the just man is the happy man, and that injustice does not pay.[120] Stories, chants, and music will be the most important allies in the inculcation of these doctrines among the youth.[121] For art must be guided by utility, not pleasure.[122] The Homeric gods are banished. The tragic poets are silenced. All artists are forced to turn their art into propaganda for the new regime of truth.

Despite the fear of science and philosophy as the sources of dangerous innovations that threaten the religious dogmas, Plato has no intention of shutting philosophy out of the well-ordered state altogether. A select handful of old men among the law wardens who have distinguished themselves in wisdom and virtue by word and deed, and who are altogether "incorruptible" are required to travel with the express purpose of seeking out what Plato calls the "divinely inspired." As Plato explains:

> Amongst the mass of men there always exist—albeit in small numbers—men that are *divinely inspired*, intercourse with such men is the greatest value, and they spring up in badly-governed states just as much as in those that are well governed. In search of these men it is always right for one who dwells in a well-ordered state to go forth on a voyage of enquiry by land and sea, if so be that he himself is incorruptible, so as to confirm thereby such of his native laws as are rightly enacted, and to amend any that are deficient. For without this inspection and enquiry a State will not permanently remain perfect, nor again if the inspection be badly conducted.[123]

By conversing with the Athenian Stranger, this is indeed what the Spartan and the Cretan are doing. In the regime described in Plato's *Laws,* the wisest and most virtuous, who set out in search of the "divinely inspired," are also those who control the strings of power in the form of the "Nocturnal Council."[124] They are the only ones allowed to "meddle" with the divinely established laws and change or improve them in light of their intercourse with the "divinely inspired." Indeed, the success of the regime described in the *Laws* is due to the alliance of power and philosophy—the kind of philosophy that understands what is necessary for the "care of the soul." But why are all these repressive policies necessary for the care of the soul?

In view of the fact that the virtue of ordinary people is of an inferior and corruptible variety, and in view of the fact that the circumstances under which virtue can be corrupted or destroyed are innumerable, great care must be taken to guard against the corruption of the soul. The difficulty involved in guarding the fragile virtue of ordinary folks necessitates this plethora of repressive policies. Plato does not notice the ominous, totalitarian qualities of his "divine Synod" because its political wisdom conforms to the ideas of Socrates. The *Laws* is the working out of the political implications of the Socratic premises in the most realistic detail. This is why the dichotomy—between the Socrates of the early dialogues and the totalitarian Plato of the late dialogues—cannot be sustained. The *Laws* is merely the drawing out of the logical and necessary implications of the alliance between the religion of Socrates and political power.

The sunny understanding of Plato described in the previous section requires the alliance of *virtue* and political power. That is a dream whose appeal no one can deny. But the dark reading of Plato's philosophy requires the alliance of the wisdom of the divinely inspired with political power. The Platonic fascination with the alliance of Socratic philosophy and political power explains Plato's adventures in Syracuse. If the *Seventh Letter* has any authenticity, Plato could not resist "converting" Dionysus II, the tyrant of Syracuse, to philosophy. His friend Dion, who was close to the tyrant, led Plato to believe that such a conversion was possible because Dionysus was "all on fire with philosophy."[125] Dion was eventually killed, and Plato's hopes were dashed. Despite his disappointment, Plato continued to dream of the coincidence of philosophy and political power as the only hope for humanity.[126]

In the *Laws*, he imagines a conversation between the "divinely inspired" Athenian and the receptive clandestine philosophers from Sparta and Crete after a "deluge," when most of the people are wiped out and those who remain are innocent and not yet familiar with the free and corrupt ways of city life. The "deluge" is a golden opportunity to actualize the wedding of Socratic religion with politics. In the absence of a natural catastrophe of such gargantuan proportions, a bold despot is the best hope, because only such a daring man can accomplish the "purge" necessary if all the obstacles to the realization of the well-ordered state are to be removed by exile and assassination.[127]

From his early to his latest dialogues, Plato was convinced that the alliance of Socratic religion with politics was the key to the well-ordered state whose priority is the care of the soul. If the Socratic mission was indeed a political mission, then Socrates must have regarded Critias and Charmides as the bold and daring despots who could effect the radical changes that a city such as Athens required to transform her into a well-ordered polity where virtue is supreme. The war, the plague, the decimation of the fleet at Syracuse, the disastrous defeat at the hands of Sparta, and the colossal loss of life, were the closest thing to a "deluge." Such circumstances provide the perfect opportunity for accomplishing the radical reforms required. It can only be a blessing when bold and daring despots, who are friends of the true philosopher, are at hand to execute the necessary exiles and assassinations that would sweep away the obstacles to the realization of a new civic order.

If the *Seventh Letter* is authentic, then Plato did not learn much from the experience of the terror under the Thirty. He tells us that he came to the conclusion that no matter how dreadful he finds his city, the wise man should not lead a revolution.[128] However, if he has the opportunity to influence a despot, he should not relinquish the opportunity, because

> if anyone were ever to attempt to realize my ideals in regard to laws and government, now was the time for the trial. If I were to convince *but one man*, that in itself would ensure complete success.[129]

It seems that the political brutality of his relatives did not dampen Plato's enthusiasm for the coincidence of philosophy and political power. Nor can we blame his youth for his ardor. Plato was neither the first nor the last to suffer from the gargantuan conceit of philosophers who are convinced that that they can do wonders in politics if only they could have a free hand or have access to someone whose hand is as free as it is fearless. Time and again, philosophers have been disillusioned by their darling despots.

In conclusion, what we learn from the darkness of Plato's *Laws* is that understanding the supreme function of the state as the inculcation of virtue, by the divinely inspired who have access to an absolute, inviolable, and transcendent truth, is a guarantee of human misery on a grand scale; for it is a recipe for the sanctification of the most foul and self-righteous types of criminality.

Far from being a betrayal of Socrates, the dystopia in the *Laws* is the logical consequence of what the Socratic "care of the soul," as understood in the early dialogues, requires. Socrates was not a moral evangel urging individuals to care for their own souls. His mission was as political as it was religious. All his denial notwithstanding, he was indeed a teacher. The Socratic paradox—that virtue is knowledge that cannot be taught—turns out not to be paradoxical in the least. The virtues of ordinary humanity can indeed be taught. The paradox applies only to the divinely inspired, whose mission is to bestow on ordinary humanity the political conditions required for the "care of the soul."

As a teacher, the effect that Socrates had on his students was as mesmerizing as it was stupefying. So, the argument made by Plato in the *Apology* that he did not approve of the conduct of the Thirty, yet was powerless to influence them, cannot be taken seriously. Instead of exonerating Socrates, the dialogues of Plato—early as well as late—support the case for the prosecution, because Socratic ideas invite violence and treachery on a grand scale.

Notes

1. Karl R. Popper, *The Open Society and Its Enemies* Vol. I, *The Spell of Plato* (Princeton, N.J.: Princeton University Press, 1966); R. H. S. Crossman, *Plato Today* (New York: Routledge, 1937, 1959). The same tactic is used by Biblical scholars who attribute all the nasty aspects of Christianity to St. Paul so that they can create their own fiction, which they call the "historical Jesus."
2. W. D. Ross, "The President's Address: The Problem of Socrates," *Proceedings of the Classical Association,* Vol. 30 (1933), pp.7–24. Ross suggests that Socrates was in search of definitions, and that Plato developed this search into his the full-fledged theory of forms. He does not think that Plato invented the immortality of the soul single-handedly, and that Socrates must have shared these Pythagorean ideas about the soul as Taylor and Burnet argue so convincingly; John Burnet, "The Socratic Doctrine of the Soul," *Proceedings of the British Academy,* Vol. VII, January 1916; A. E. Taylor, *Socrates* (New York: Doubleday, 1953), pp. 50–51.
3. *Apology,* 33 b; *Meno,* 99b.
4. Gregory Vlastos, "The Paradox of Socrates," in Gregory Vlastos (ed.), *The Philosophy of Socrates: A Collection of Critical Essays,* (Notre Dame, Indiana: University of Notre Dame Press, 1971, 1980), p. 7.
5. *Apology,* 41 d.
6. Vlastos, "The Paradox of Socrates," p. 7.
7. Ibid.
8. Ibid.
9. Ibid, p. 12.
10. Ibid, p. 16.
11. Ibid. p. 16.
12. Ibid, p. 20.
13. Ibid, p. 21.
14. Ibid, p. 19. The egalitarianism of Socrates is over-stated. Even if it were true (I will show that it is not), Euripides challenged the notion that morality is a function of class in *Electra.*

15. Ibid, pp. 16, 18.
16. *Protagoras,* 322 c–323 a.
17. Gregory Vlastos, "The Historical Socrates and Athenian Democracy," *Political Theory,* Vol. 11, No. 4 (Nov., 1983), pp. 495–516: see Bibliography for more details.
18. *Meno,* 99e–100a, my italics, translated by W. K. C. Guthrie.
19. Ibid.
20. *Symposium,* 215b.
21. Aristotle, *Nicomachean Ethics,* 1128 (Bk. IV, ch. 7). Aristotle is non-committal about Socrates, but he recognizes the appeal that the ironic man has because, unlike the braggart, he does not distort the truth for personal gain. Taylor does not think that Socrates fits the Aristotelian description of the ironic man because he is convinced that his profession of ignorance was genuine: Taylor, *Socrates,* p. 47, note 1.
22. *Phaedrus,* 238c.
23. *Symposium,* 219c.
24. *Protagoras,* 309a; *Symposium,* 175d; *Charmides,* 154a.
25. *Symposium,* 215d–e, 216d.
26. *Meno,* 80a–b.
27. *Symposium,* 218a.
28. Ibid, 218b.
29. Ibid, 219c.
30. Ibid.
31. *Symposium,* 219 e. Alcibiades' eulogy to Socrates goes far beyond the latter's sexual self-restraint and catalogs all the other virtues of Socrates—his ability to stand all night in a trance, his ability to withstand bitter cold and walk barefoot on the ice, his courage in battle, and the fact that he saved Alcibiades' life during the campaign, but insisted that Alcibiades get the decoration from the authorities. Before putting this long eulogy in the mouth of Alcibiades, Plato makes sure to remind us that drunks always tell the truth.
32. Guthrie thought that Socrates exerted this effect unconsciously. But Vlastos thought it was a conscious effort to make himself attractive despite his appearance in a society that worshipped physical beauty. Although Vlastos does not mention Nietzsche, the latter has a similar view. Being ugly in a society that placed a premium on physical beauty, Socrates consciously and purposefully shifted the emphasis from physical prowess, beauty, and display, to inner purity of heart—a shift that Nietzsche associated with the decline of Western civilization. See W.K. C. Guthrie, *Socrates* (New York: Cambridge University Press, 1971), p. 79; Gregory Vlastos (ed.), *The Philosophy of Socrates: A Collection of Critical Essays,* p. 17.

33. Guthrie, *Socrates*, p. 82.
34. *Symposium*, 204a.
35. Ibid, 203a.
36. Ibid, 204a.
37. Ibid, 210c–211c.
38. Ibid, 212a.
39. Ibid, 211d.
40. Guthrie, *Socrates*, p. 75.
41. *Charmides*, 155d–e.
42. *Gorgias*, 481d.
43. Taylor, *Socrates*, pp. 48–49.
44. Aeschines, *Alcibiades*, discussed in Taylor, *Socrates*, p. 49, notes 1 and 3. Taylor insists on the "absolute moral purity of Socrates" and tells us that all this sexual banter is just play and not to be taken literally.
45. *Gorgias*, 481d.
46. *Protagoras*, 309a.
47. *Alcibiades I*, 132a, in Vol. I of *The Dialogues of* Plato (4 vols.), translated by B. Jowett (London: Oxford University Press, 1931).
48. *Symposium*, 208b.
49. Ibid, 209a–e.
50. *Protagoras*, 319b, 320b.
51. Ibid, 324b–c.
52. Ibid, 325b ff.
53. Ibid, 325c.
54. Ibid, 324a–c.
55. Ibid, 324e and 327d.
56. Ibid, 327a.
57. Ibid, 327d, 322c–d.
58. Ibid, 328a–b.
59. Ibid, 319a–e.
60. Ibid, 328d.
61. Ibid, 329e.
62. As Gregory Vlastos rightly points out, Laches is courageous even though he cannot define courage. But Vlastos is solidly in the Socratic camp, and had no intention of coming to the aid of Protagoras.
63. *Protagoras*, 319a–e.
64. *Symposium*, 209b.
65. *Meno*, 71e.
66. *Euthydemus*, 292c–e, 291c. In that dialogue, Socrates gets a taste of his own medicine. The eristic style of his interlocutors forces him to agree to things that he does not really care to affirm. As a result, he ends with absurd conclusions. The whole exercise is comparable to the way he treated Protagoras.

67. *Protagoras,* 319d.
68. *Laws,* 765d. For Plato, a society that spends more money on prisons than on education is the height of folly.
69. *Republic,* 359d. The myth might have some historical basis; Herodotus tells us that Gyges became the king of Lydia by killing the king and seducing his queen, *Histories,* I.8ff.
70. *Republic,* 472c–d; see also, *Laws,* 739c–d, where the Athenian Stranger rejects the common ownership of land and wives as an unworkable model.
71. *Protagoras,* 342a–b.
72. Ibid, 343b.
73. Ibid, 316c.
74. Ibid, 316d.
75. Ibid, 317a.
76. Ibid, 317a.
77. Ibid, 317b. One wonders if Plato is not putting in the mouth of Protagoras a common Athenian opinion of Socrates.
78. Ibid, 342d.
79. *Laws,* 710a–b.
80. Ibid, Bks. I–II.
81. Ibid, 963a.
82. Ibid, 963d–964a.
83. Ibid, 710b.
84. Ibid, 962a.
85. Ibid, 756c–e.
86. The ruling Council is made up of 360 wardens of the law, with 90 from each of the four propertied classes.
87. *Laws,* 759b–c. However, those chosen by lot are "tested" to make sure they are fit to serve.
88. Ibid, 744d ff.
89. Ibid, 743d.
90. Ibid, 756b.
91. Ibid, 777a.
92. Ibid, 765d.
93. Ibid, 659d.
94. Ibid, 950a–b.
95. Ibid, 949e.
96. Ibid, 937e ff.
97. Ibid, 950d–951a.
98. Ibid, 950d–951a.
99. Ibid, 952c.
100. Ibid, 969b–c.
101. Ibid, 964e–965a.

102. Ibid, 965a.
103. Ibid, 730d–e.
104. The problem of grudge informers was one that the German courts had to deal with after the collapse of the Nazi regime in Germany. In contrast, the Catholic Church has never been required to make amends for relying on grudge informers to supply it with victims for its Inquisition. See Lon L. Fuller, *The Morality of Law* (New Haven: Yale University Press, 1964).
105. *Laws,* 634d–e.
106. Ibid, 720a–b, 774a.
107. Ibid, 780a.
108. Ibid, 907d–910d.
109. Ibid, 909a.
110. Ibid, 908c–909a.
111. On Thomas Aquinas's defense of the Inquisition, see my *Aquinas and Modernity: The Lost Promise of Natural* Law (Lanham, Maryland: Rowman & Littlefield, 2008), chs. III.7, III.8, and V.1.
112. *Laws,* 730d–e, and 907d ff.
113. Ibid, 907e.
114. Ibid, 885b.
115. Ibid, 907d –910d.
116. Ibid, 885b–c, and 888b; *Republic,* 364 b ff.
117. E. R. Dodds, *The Greeks and the Irrational* (Berkeley, California: University of California Press, 1951), p. 224: Dodds claims that there is an important difference between the Catholic Inquisition and the trials for impiety recommended in Plato's *Laws.* Whereas the Inquisition was intended to save people's souls in the beyond, Plato's goal was the good of the civic order. In other words, Plato's version of the Inquisition had some concrete purpose that the Catholic Inquisition lacked.
118. *Laws,* 662c.
119. Ibid, 890a, also, 886d.
120. Ibid, 661c–d.
121. Ibid, 664a and 665c.
122. Ibid, 667b–c.
123. Ibid, 951b–c. My italics.
124. Ibid, 951d–e.
125. *Seventh Letter,* 340b–c.
126. *Laws,* 710 c; *Seventh Letter,* 326b, 328a. See also M. I. Finley, "Plato and Practical Politics," in M. I. Finley, *Aspects of Antiquity: Discoveries and Controversies* (New York: Penguin Books, 1977), pp. 74–87.
127. *Laws,* 735b ff., 835c.
128. Ibid, 331d.
129. Ibid, 328b–c. My italics.

CHAPTER 5

Plato's Critique of Homer Repudiated

The claim that history is written by the victors has never been truer than in the victory of Christianity over pagan religion. Socrates began the assault on the gods, which Christianity continued without any scruple or regard for truth, let alone charity.[1] If we are to appreciate the significance of the religious triumph of Socrates and Plato in Western civilization, we must come to grips with what has been defeated. As the target of Socratic and Platonic ire, Homer is the key to understanding what was lost in the triumphal march of Socratic thought. Only by recognizing the sophistication, humanity, and refinement of Homer can we grasp the calamity involved in the defeat of his perspective. Only in comparison with Homer can we grasp the dark and disturbing nature of the religious innovations of Socrates—only then can we see Socrates without rose-colored glasses. I have no intention of providing an exhaustive account of Homeric religion or doing justice to the vast scholarly literature on Homer; my goal is merely to show that Plato's criticisms of Homer are unfounded, and his claims to intellectual superiority are highly dubious. Throughout this discussion, it is important to keep in mind that criticism of Homer was no crime. No matter how influential, the books of Homer were not the bible of the Greeks; they were not sacred texts protected by an ecclesiastic authority that fetters the mind. Rejection of Homeric ideas could not (in and of itself) be the basis for criminal charges. Nevertheless, Plato's disparagement of Homeric ideas, in comparison to Socratic ones, has been his most powerful defense, especially from the point of view of posterity. Plato has convinced posterity that Socrates was silenced for having unorthodox ideas—ideas that were superior to those of his contemporaries—especially Homer and the tragic poets that Homer inspired.

In this chapter, I will argue that Plato's critique of Homer is partial, unjust, and unjustified. I will examine six distinct criticisms leveled by Plato. First, Plato objects that Homer's myths have no regard for the truth (5.1). Second, Plato rejects Homer's heroes for thinking that death as the worst fate; but death does not hold such terror for those who know that the cosmos is so ordered that no evil can befall a good man—if not in this life, then in the next (5.2). Third, Plato is critical of Homer's gods on the ground that they are the source of both good and evil. Instead, he insists that the gods should be presented as the source of good only; meanwhile, the source of evil must be sought elsewhere (5.3). Fourth, Plato complains that Homer's gods are not assiduous in punishing the wicked and rewarding the righteous; so, their love of justice is questionable (5.4). Fifth, Plato thinks that Homer's gods are morally degenerate and therefore provide poor models for human conduct (5.5). Sixth, Plato denounces Homer's tendency to blame the gods for the wrongdoing of human beings as a contemptible form of self-deception or "lie in the soul" that allows individuals to escape responsibility (5.6). These are the reasons that Socrates thinks Homer must be censored.[2] Is he right? Or, is the veneration of Socrates simply a manifestation of the self-satisfaction of triumphant ideas? I will conclude with some reflections on the supposed shift in Western civilization from the manly virtues of Homer to the feminine virtues of Socrates.

1   Religion Without Lies

Plato has the temerity to denounce Homer's myths as lies. At first blush, it seems hypocritical for Plato to object to Homer for being a mythmaker. Plato is a consummate mythmaker himself—the myth of metals, the myth of the cave, the myth of Gyges, and the myth of Er, are a few examples. However, Plato distinguishes between two kinds of myths—true and false myths. He regards Homer's myths as false, while his own myths are true—supposedly because they contain a deep reality beyond the superficial details of the story.[3] In other words, the literal details are not important; what makes a myth true or false is the message it contains. Bluntly stated, Homer's myths do not fit the Orphic vision of life and death to which Socrates and Plato were committed. Plato has the boldness to suggest that myths about what happens after death, something that no one can possibly know anything about, contain more truth and validity than Homer's stories whose naturalistic gods are modeled on human beings, and rooted in human experience of the only world we know.

In denouncing the lies of Homer, Plato says "truth must be highly esteemed," because "untruth is of no use to the gods, though *useful to men as a kind of medicine.*"[4] In other words, we prefer truth, but when lies are more useful, then we should forget about truth and embrace the lies, since they are the medicine human beings need. Then he adds that when it comes to medicine, "we must allow physicians to use it, but not private citizens."[5] We know that "physicians" is a code word for Socratic politicians who understand themselves as physicians of the soul.

It follows that the criterion of how myths are to be evaluated is by their utility. Utility for what, you ask? The Socratic answer is utility in cultivating the virtues that will contribute to political harmony in the state. Truth is of value only to gods, but human beings need "necessary lies" or "noble fictions."[6] Plato certainly thought that Orphic tales about the immortality of the soul and its fate after death are useful for promoting virtue in the soul and harmony in the state.[7] However, by the time of Plato's birth, Orphism had deteriorated into trafficking in pardons and indulgences.[8] Plato was aware of this. In the second book of the *Republic*, Adeimantus complained that:

> begging priests and prophets frequent the doors of the rich and persuade them that they possess a god-given power to remedy by sacrifices and incantations...any crime that the rich man or any of his ancestors may have committed...They offer in proof a mass of writings by Musaeus and Orpheus,...in accordance with these they perform their ritual...both for the living and the dead, there are absolutions and purifications for sin...- which free from punishments yonder, where a dreadful fate awaits the uninitiated.[9]

Orphic tales invite this sort of decadence, but Plato continued to peddle them anyway.

Plato defends these tales as true myths—myths that contain a deep underlying truth that can be detected by looking into one's soul. In truth, they depend on religious dogmas with no foundation in human experience—dogmas that can only be sustained by the threat of death for unbelievers.[10]

In contrast, the myths of Homer are grounded in the world. The gods of Homer are modeled on human beings. They are a totally understandable human fantasy—blessed in abundance with all the good things that human beings desire—beauty, prowess, and exuberant health. The gods lived eternally in the bloom of youth, without the dread of old age, or the fear of death. These beautiful gods were simultaneously a product of fantasy and realism. They were not threatened by atheism because faith in them was neither necessary nor relevant. At the same time, it was easy to believe in them because they were natural rather than supernatural. The naturalistic quality of the gods meant that denying their existence or claiming *not to believe* in them is foolish. Believing or not believing in Poseidon, Aphrodite, Athena, Demeter, Hades, Sleep, or Death makes no difference. You can deny the existence of Poseidon, but you are bound to experience the wildness of the sea. You can deny the existence of Aphrodite, but you are bound to experience the power of erotic love, or your own inner Aphrodite. You can deny the existence of Demeter, but you are bound to experience the bounty of the Earth at harvest time. You can deny the existence of Hades, but you cannot avoid the sting of death. So, the reality of the gods cannot be denied without absurdity.

Especially in the *Iliad*, Homer avoided the magical or miraculous. The gods travel around the world with breathtaking speed; sometimes they use flying horses that cover in one leap the distance a man can see from a watchtower.[11] Nevertheless, their effects on the world were not miraculous. Almost everything the gods did by way of intervening in human affairs could be explained in naturalistic terms, or as the result of chance. Ares filled some men with a fighting spirit; Aphrodite filled others with sexual desire; Sleep engulfed the tired fighters; the darkness of death descended on the fallen warriors; Athena inspired her favorites with tireless courage; Zeus turned a brave man into a coward and made him run for his life; Apollo made every arrow hit its mark; Hera covered the battlefield with a mist to cause confusion. These elements of human experience do not require the denial of observed reality. Believing in the gods is not a matter of faith in the unknown or unknowable. How can anyone not believe in the reality of sky, wind, storms, death, desire, sleep, and the other forces of nature that the gods personify?[12] How can anyone deny the reality of rage, anger, vengefulness, lust, courage, and a myriad other human passions that they also represent?

This is not to suggest that the role the gods played in human life was in any way either insignificant or devoid of mystery. Their effect on human life was as significant and as mysterious as the role played by the haphazard, and contingent.[13] Like the latter, the gods may help or hinder human enterprises, for individuals as well as communities.

Those who believe in Zeus think that when they are lucky, Zeus is helping them, and when they are unlucky, that he has abandoned them. Those who do not believe in Zeus will find that luck is sometimes with them, and sometimes not. So, believing or not believing in Zeus makes no difference; either way, the role that luck plays in human life is both prodigious and unfathomable. Zeus is an artistic representation of the inescapable reality of chance in human life.[14] Those who believe in Zeus hope that lavish gifts and offerings may inspire his benevolence, but this is not necessarily the case. The Trojans made the most extravagant gifts and sacrifices to Zeus, but their city was annihilated anyway. It follows that whether Zeus is with them or against them has little to do with their merits.

It may be argued that the difference between attributing whatever happens to luck, and attributing it to Zeus is akin to the difference between believing that the world is arbitrary and haphazard, and thinking that whatever happens is always the result of a conspiracy. The popularity of conspiracy theories may well be due to the need to escape from the anxiety inspired by the arbitrary, indiscriminate, and haphazard contingency of existence. Homer's mortals always assume that whatever happens is the deliberate work of the gods—but Homer knows better.

In the *Iliad*, the action takes place on two levels: heaven and the Earth, the divine and the human. As readers, we are privy to what happens on earth as well as in heaven. We are therefore cognizant of the connection between human and divine events. In contrast, Homer's earthlings see only their own reality and are not privy to the divine drama. As a result, they misinterpret events. They attribute their changing fortunes to the capriciousness of the gods; they believe that the gods are the cause of everything that happens—but we know that the gods are not collaborating to control events; they tend to work at cross-purposes; so what happens is not exactly what any of them intended. It follows that the gods are integral to a world that is haphazard and contingent.

In contrast to Homer, Socrates claims to have knowledge of the inscrutable nature of reality; he claims to have penetrated the deepest recesses of existence. He claims to *know* that the heart of being is reason and goodness, not arbitrariness and caprice. He claims to have access to a moral order that is perfect, eternal, universal, and supersedes all others.

He claims to know that the human soul has a special kinship with the divine principle that is at the heart of reality. He claims to know that the soul is deathless.[15] The religion of Socrates requires faith in abstract and invisible phenomena that have no basis in human experience—a faith without a shred of evidence, a faith that flies in the face of lived experience. In contrast, the religion of Homer does not run afoul of observed reality—namely, that the good and the just does not always hold sway, human beings are not immortal, and arbitrariness, not reason and goodness, are the foundations of reality. All these truths can be confirmed by human experience. It stands to reason that the myths of Homer cannot be denied without absurdity. In contrast, the myths of Socrates cannot be affirmed in the absence of the threat of death.[16] So, which are the true myths?

2 Religion Without Asceticism

Plato objected to Homer's attitude to death. In the *Republic*, Socrates refers to the passage in the *Odyssey* where the ghost of Achilles tells Odysseus that he would rather be a landless peasant toiling in the fields than a king in the land of the dead.[17] Equally objectionable was the description of the world beyond the grave as "fearful, dank, hated even by gods."[18] These descriptions of death are incompatible with the Socratic view that death is not anathema but the goal; and that philosophy is the "practice of dying."[19] Plato also objects to all the lamentations of Achilles after his friend Patroclus was killed by Hector.[20] He thinks that a hero should not be presented as so attached to his friend that he laments his death so pitifully. Heroes must be detached from everything that weds human beings to the world of the here and now; they should know that death is not a dreadful thing for a good man. On the contrary, the good man is better off in the beyond, because the world is ordered in such a way that no harm can befall him.[21] As some scholars have argued, Socrates believes that we are all better off dead.[22] It follows that great men should not shrink from death because it is not the evil that Homer imagines it to be.

For Homer, death was loathsome, not because it was filled with terrors, but simply for lacking the sunny exuberance and vitality of life. In that light, the Socratic enthusiasm for death and the Socratic understanding of the highest life as the practice of dying, are as incomprehensible as they are irrational. Socrates replaces the sunny gods that celebrate life in this world with an abstract asceticism that undermines the natural human attachments to the world. Instead, he is wedded to a conception of life that regards the body with loathing as the tomb of the soul, from which it is necessary to escape.[23]

The gods of Homer acknowledged the primacy of copulation. When Zeus took Hera in his arms, the "divine earth sent up spring flowers beneath them, dewy clover and crocuses and a soft crowded bed of hyacinths, to lift them off the ground. In this they lay, covered by a beautiful golden cloud, from which a rain of glistening dewdrops fell."[24] Zeus and Hera represent the exuberant beauty of life in this world. Nor did the gods reserve the enjoyment of the world to themselves. They loved to see mortals singing, dancing, and dining in their honor. When Homer talks about "sacrifices" to the gods, he means that the mortals were feasting, drinking, relaxing, and enjoying themselves.[25] Unlike the monotheistic god who followed, the gods of Homer were not interested in celibacy, fasting, foreskins, and other self-mortifications.

The Olympic gods did not create the world, but they loved it. They would not dream of destroying it, even if they could. They did not regard life in the world as a test or a punishment to be endured, but a delight to be enjoyed. This love of the world stands in marked contrast to the Orphic antipathy to life. It is also at odds with the Christian hope for the ever-anticipated, always impending, destruction of the world by its creator.

3 Religion Without Dualism

Plato objects to the gods of Homer because they are the source of both good and evil in the world. He objects to Homer's story about Zeus holding two jars, one filled with good, and the other with evil fates.[26] He insists that the gods should be the source of "good only" and totally "guiltless of evil."[27] For "evil things we must find some other cause, not the god."[28] In this search for a source of evil, human beings generally settle on their political enemies. Homer does not fall prey to this inclination. He does not see the world in dualistic terms. He does not regard the war between the Greeks and the Trojans as a cosmic struggle between good and evil. He does not depict the battle as a conflict between right and wrong, heroes and villains—all the combatants are heroes in the Greek sense of warrior-chieftains.[29] There are no villains in the epic. There is heroism and disgraceful conduct on both sides. What is striking to the modern reader is that the non-Greek enemies (the Trojans) are neither primitive nor savage; they are not demons deserving destruction. On the contrary, the epic is named after Ilium, the glamorous and wealthy Trojan city, and is as much about the defeat of the Trojans as the triumph of the Greeks.

Nothing illustrates the absence of dualism more than Homer's portrait of Hector, the leader of the Trojan army. He is the son of the king and queen of Troy—Priam and Hecabe (often Romanized as Hecuba). He is responsible for defending his city and his family. He is cognizant of the terrible danger presented by the massive Greek army gathered outside the city walls. He is determined to fight the "war-loving Greeks" in defense of the women and the little children of Troy, even unto death.[30] He does not curse the Greeks as evil demons who have sailed across the "dark wine sea" to raid the riches of Troy. He blames the despicable conduct of his brother, Paris, for provoking them by seducing Helen, the wife of Menelaus, when he was a guest at Menelaus' home. He calls his brother a sex-crazed seducer with bedroom eyes, a good for nothing without redeeming qualities, and he compares him most unfavorably with Menelaus whose luscious wife he stole.[31] As leader of the Trojan forces, Hector shoulders the grim consequences of his brother's imprudent escapades.

Mostly, the epic reads like the screen play for an action film that is full of gore, with men being decapitated, having their eyes gouged out, their limbs severed form their bodies, grasping their innards as they fall screaming face down into the dust and blood of the battlefield, where they are trampled by horses and chariots and engulfed by the darkness of death. The dying men are nameless and faceless, and the war seems like a sport—soccer or football. However, when Achilles kills Hector, the war takes on a dark reality.

In a heartbreaking scene of conjugal love, Hector bids farewell to his wife, Andromache, and his child, who is oblivious to the dangers at hand. The farewell of Hector and Andromache is one of the few times that the human cost of the war is on display. Hector and Andromache are painfully aware of the fact that they might never see each other again. They know that if Hector cannot keep the Greeks at bay, it will mean death for him and slavery for her. The worst does indeed come to pass.

Throughout the epic, Homer uses stock phrases to describe Hector in heroic terms as "Hector of the flashing helmet," "god-like," "glorious," and "handsome." In physical prowess and beauty, Hector is compared to Achilles—the legendary Greek hero and son of a goddess and a mortal man. After Hector kills Patroclus (who was wearing Achilles' armor),

Hector puts on the armor. Homer tells us that it fit his body perfectly, which means that his physique was every bit as fabulous as that of the matchless Achilles. When Achilles kills Hector, Zeus grieves for him.[32] In the heat of the battle, Zeus was tempted to intervene to save Hector, and he would have done so were it not for the disapproval of the other gods and the strife in heaven that would ensue.[33]

Apollo, the most iconic Greek god, is also distressed by Hector's fate. He cannot understand why Achilles is such a darling of the gods. He thinks Achilles has no pity and no respect for others. Apollo scolds his fellow gods for supporting Achilles so unconditionally and calls them "monsters of cruelty."[34] Hera responds in self-defense saying that Achilles is the son of a goddess whereas Hector is but a mere mortal. Nevertheless, Zeus stands up for Hector and compares him favorably to Achilles. Like Apollo, Zeus finds Achilles' abuse of Hector's body intolerable. So, he intervenes and forces Achilles to accept a ransom from Priam (Hector's father), for Hector's body. The gods loved Hector so much that they took measures to restore his body to its pristine beauty despite the abuse inflicted on it by Achilles.[35] Even the proud Achilles tells Zeus in a prayer that he would have rather been killed by Hector, a man as good and as worthy as himself, than die fighting against the impersonal force of Scamander, the River-god.[36]

It is not only the gods and Achilles who recognize the magnificence of Hector, but also all of Hector's enemies—the Greek warriors—pay tribute to his magnificence. When Hector dies at the hands of Achilles, the other Greeks gathered around his body and "gazed in wonder" at his stature and stunning good looks.[37] So, even in death, Hector is admired by his enemies. It is not just the Greeks who admired the Trojans; the reverse was also the case. When Priam arrived at the tent of Achilles to deliver a ransom for his son's body to warm Achilles' cold heart, he could not help but notice how large and fine Achilles was. Even the cold-hearted Achilles dwelt with admiration on the nobility of Priam.[38] All this admiration for the enemy is puzzling, especially to a Christian civilization accustomed to regard war as a crusade against evil. Homer's treatment of the enemy highlights the gulf between his worldview and our own, which is a legacy of Socratic religion.

For Homer, the war was akin to a sport where it is necessary to have two equally good opponents to make the sport worthwhile. Only with a good opponent is a triumph an achievement. This attitude involves respect for fellow warriors not only for their skill and valor, but also for the courage with which they face death. This is a view of war that is foreign to us. The best example of this attitude in recent history is the attitude of the Zulus. When the British invaded Zululand in South Africa, they had contempt for the Zulu warriors. Their goal was to demolish the Zulu culture as hopelessly primitive and inferior to the technological advances and superior Christian values of the West. In the famous battle of Rorke's Drift on January 22, 1879, 140 British soldiers with cannon fire defeated 3,000 Zulu warriors. The battle was immortalized in the film *Zulu* (1964, starring Michael Cain). In the film, the Zulus, who played themselves, were exquisite human specimens, agile, swift, and spritely with long legs and lean silhouettes; they leapt over the British fortifications with ease and grace, fired their arrows at their formidable enemy, and met their death with cannon fire without flinching. The carnage was hideous. Nevertheless, the Zulu warriors kept coming. They came in waves. The British could hear them coming because they would always sing before they attacked the British fort. The British soldiers found the singing extremely disconcerting; it made them anxious and angry; they thought that the Zulus were taunting them. A white African in the British camp, who understood the Zulu language, explained to them that the song was a salute to the valor and sacrifice of the British soldiers as fellow warriors. There was something of Homer in the Zulu attitude that the British found simply incomprehensible. A serenade in their honor by the Zulu warriors made no sense to the British for whom war was not an opportunity to display physical prowess or courage in the face of death, but the a *mission civilisatrice*—spreading the values of civilization to the savage and primitive nations of the world.

The arrogant condescension of the British for the Zulu warriors was not without great cost. The excessive celebrations of the battle at Rorke's Drift were intended to conceal the humiliating defeat of the British by the Zulus *on the same day* in the battle of Isandlwana, where the Zulus, despite heavy losses, defeated a British stronghold of more than 1,700 men. When the news arrived in Britain that spear-wielding savages had defeated the well-equipped and technically advanced British army, it was greeted with shock and disbelief. Some British historians rightly opined that contempt for the Zulu warriors was a factor in this momentous defeat of the empire.[39] In our time, the American empire, with all its technical wizardry—satellites, drones, predators, and other unmanned aerial vehicles—has suffered similar humiliations at the hands of the Afghan warriors, for whom it has an even greater measure of contempt.[40]

Wherein lies the capacity to see the mortal enemy as a human being who is as noble as oneself? What allowed the Zulus to serenade the British warriors, as if the latter were as noble or as brave as themselves? What allowed Homer to portray the Trojans as people very similar to the Greeks? What made Homer capable of seeing the political enemy as neither evil nor ugly, neither savage nor primitive? It may be argued that the Greeks in the *Iliad* knew that they were the aggressors, and were therefore not so smug or self-righteous. This explanation will not do. In our world, aggressors are inclined to justify their aggression by appeal to the wickedness or primitive savagery of their opponents, which supposedly threatens all of humanity. The Israelites were also the aggressors in their war against the Philistines; yet the Bible depicts their battle with the Philistines in the most moralistic and righteous terms. A better explanation is that the polytheistic mindset makes it possible to avoid dualism. When there is only one god, our god, who is the focal point of all goodness, then those who reject that god are by definition allied with the cosmic forces of evil, and therefore deserve destruction.

It may be objected that Plato made a point of not giving evil any metaphysical status, and some Christian philosophers have followed suit. All his efforts notwithstanding, Plato could not avoid dualism. Plato surmised that the cosmos must have a soul, which is the moving principle of all things. What else could account for the orderly movements of the sun, the moon, and the other planets? Anything as fantastic as a world soul would have to be divine, so Plato maintained.[41] However, having postulated that the world soul is goodness personified, and sensing that not all is well with the world, Plato had to invent an evil soul to accounts for the evil in the world.[42] In this way, dualism was born. This dualism contradicted his metaphysics in the *Republic*, where evil had no status in the hierarchy of being.[43] Clearly, Plato could not sustain this position. He went so far as to suggest that evil is more pervasive in the world than good, and that there is a "battle" between good and evil. Interestingly, he assumed that the gods and daemons are "our allies" in the battle.[44] He probably meant that the gods were the allies of humanity. What about people who reject the Socratic religion? What is to be done with the people who fail to recognize the divinity of the world soul? Since the latter is the focus of all goodness in the world, it follows that those who reject the world soul must be allied with evil. As we have seen, those who are not on the side of the religion of Socrates must be either converted or killed.

Unlike the Abrahamic religions, with which we continue to be cursed, the Homeric religion did not lead to the assumption that the enemy is the incarnation of evil that must be annihilated. It did not provide a moral justification for the extermination of the enemy; nor did it endorse self-righteousness in the massacre, conquest, and oppression of others. The sac of Troy in the *Iliad* was nothing more than a gigantic butchering and looting expedition. But it was never presented as a morally self-righteous act intended to "crush the wicked and humble the proud," as St. Augustine described the wars against unbelievers.[45] Homer did not consider the Trojans to be either wicked or uncivilized.

Being accustomed to the Biblical narrative in which God is always on our side, and we are "his people," and our enemies are the enemies of God, and hence opponents of the good and just, Homer's narrative is a breath of fresh air. Even though the *Iliad* is an epic about a war between the Greeks and the Trojans, who were by definition barbarians from Asia Minor, the term barbarian had no negative connotations for Homer.[46] However, in the period after the defeat of the Persian invasions of Darius in 490 BCE and his son Xerxes in 480 BCE (i.e., the Classical Age of the fifth century), the Greeks acquired a pan-Hellenistic identity that made them feel distinct and superior to non-Greeks. As a result, the term *barbaros* acquired a more nationalistic, racial, and imperialistic connotation. Athens promoted pan-Hellenism to unite the Greeks and strengthen her anti-Persian empire. The excesses of the Athenian empire (under the auspices of the Delian League) eventually led to the defeat of Athens in the Peloponnesian War. Nevertheless, Homer's capacity to regard the enemy as human beings like ourselves was echoed by Aeschylus in the *Persians*, Euripides in the *Trojan Women, Hecabe, and Andromache*. It was also evident in the treatment of the Persians by Herodotus in the *Histories*.[47] None of these authors were deluded self-righteous fanatics.

The Socratic alliance of religion and morality fosters the moral self-righteousness that is the hallmark of monotheism—even though Socrates was not the first monotheist.[48] Unhappily, the unitary conception of deity (understood in moral terms as goodness) leaves no grey areas—no incommensurable goods, no tragic conflicts, and no plurality where the good is concerned. By insisting on the unitary and singular goodness of the divine, the Socratic position invites dualism, self-righteous fanaticism, and the demise of plurality and mutual tolerance.

4 Religion Without Cosmic Justice

Plato objected to the idea that the gods inflict "misfortunes and a miserable life upon many good men." He thought that the gods must be the source of good only, and great lovers of justice and righteousness in human beings.[49] Thanks to Socrates, we tend to assume an intimate connection between religion and morality, but for Homer, they are two different things. Morality is about the relation of human beings with one another, while religion is about the relationship of human beings with the forces of nature.[50] The gods are manifestations of nature, and do not guarantee justice in this world or the next.

Achilles expressed the motto of the Homeric world when he said that "god is in his heaven and nothing is well with the world."[51] Sophocles expressed a similar sentiment when he said that no man could escape the grasping hand of misfortune.[52] This was the lot of humanity regardless of merit. Homer accepted this state of affairs, but the tragic poets—Aeschylus, Sophocles, and Euripides—highlighted the callous indifference to morality displayed by the gods and the world. They retold the stories of Homer in a way that underscored the violence, vanity, and injustice of the gods. Euripides expressed the matter even more starkly in *The Trojan Women* where the chorus asks: did Zeus betray Troy despite the magnificent temple built for him there with its altar fragrant with incense? The answer of the play is yes, Zeus betrayed Troy. All the tributes, libations, sacrifices, bribery, and flattery that are called prayers, did not work. The gods, like life itself, are unpredictable. They provide no protection from the brutality of existence—they *are* the brutality of existence.[53]

Nevertheless, the idea that the gods are upholders of justice or enforcers of morals was widespread, especially at the time that the *Odyssey* was written, assuming that it was written by Homer.[54] The idea is very seductive. It appeals to the human desire for justice. It is comforting to think that our sense of justice is at the core of the order of the world. It is tantalizing to think that we are a microcosm of the cosmos, and that we can understand the world merely by looking into ourselves. It is consoling to think that the world is ordered in a way that fits our inclinations and desires. It is tempting to think that justice will be done in the final analysis without any effort on our part.

The idea tempted Socrates; but it did not tempt Homer—not even in the *Odyssey*, which, unlike the *Iliad*, is widely considered to be a moralistic tale in which good triumphs over evil, and the wicked Suitors come to an ignominious end because of their villainy.⁵⁵ However, that is too simplistic an account of the epic for at least two reasons. In the first place, the massacre of *all* the Suitors at the end of the epic is unjust. Not all the Suitors were evil. Some were honest men who were genuinely seeking the hand of Penelope in marriage; and there is every indication that the long-suffering loyal wife led them on, and made them think she will remarry. Athena realized that some of the Suitors were good and others were not, but she made no effort to save any of them from the black hand of death.⁵⁶ The injustice involved opened the door to a cycle of revenge by the families of the suitors. This cycle of revenge was only averted by divine intervention at the end of the epic. Moreover, it is not the gods, but Odysseus and Telemachus, who determined the fate of the Suitors. Evil generally brings its own disaster, which even the gods cannot avert. Homer explains this at the very beginning of the epic.

The *Odyssey* begins with an assembly of the immortals in the palace of Zeus, where Zeus makes an eloquent speech on how lamentable it is for mortals to blame the gods for all their troubles, when it is their own misconduct and immorality that brings them so much suffering—suffering that was never intended by the gods to be their destiny.⁵⁷ Zeus uses Aegisthus as an example. After seducing Agamemnon's wife, Queen Clytemnestra, and killing Agamemnon upon his return from Troy, he was revenged for his treachery by Agamemnon's son, Orestes. As far as Zeus was concerned, the whole sordid mess had a logic of its own, which had nothing to do with the gods. Zeus went so far as to send Hermes to give Aegisthus some friendly advice, but he would not listen. The foolish man even thought that he could bribe the gods, and get away with murder! After his success in seducing Clytemnestra, he piled the holy alters with thighbones for sacrificial offerings for the gods, and covered the temple walls with fine fabrics and even gold.⁵⁸ Zeus thought his efforts were as stupid as they were hopeless—not because it is impossible to flatter the gods, but because the gods are powerless to stop human beings from retaliating against the injustices they suffer at the hands of their fellow mortals. It is not that the gods are lovers of justice; it is simply that justice and injustice have their own logic in the context of human affairs. The gods know that human beings are inclined to revenge the injustices against them, and are kind enough to warn them, as Zeus warned Aegisthus, that they are in no position to protect them from the wrath of their fellow mortals. That is the gist of Zeus's eloquent speech.

This great disclaimer at the beginning of the epic does not prevent the mortals in the epic from believing that the gods are in the business of punishing injustice. Telemachus is one of these mortals. In an impassioned speech to his fellow citizens, he complains that his mother's suitors are destroying his house, feasting on his provisions, and robbing him of his inheritance. He beseeches them not to sit idly by and allow this injustice to befall him, because the gods may be so outraged by such wickedness that their wrath may descend on the whole city.[59] The speech sounds naïve. However, such naiveté is to be excused in someone as young and as inexperienced as Telemachus—a boy who is approaching manhood without the advantage of a father—Odysseus being lost at sea. In such a weak and helpless position, Telemachus' best bet is to depend on the gods to avenge the injustice against him; but that is wishful thinking. Athena knows better. In order to help him, she must inspire him to grow up, take matters into his own hands, and avenge the injustice against him and his house. Taken as a whole, the *Odyssey* is an argument against waiting for divine justice. Relying on the gods inspires the kind of helplessness that Athena was determined to remedy in the young Telemachus.

At the end of the epic, the Suitors get their comeuppance, but not at the hands of Zeus and the immortals, but at the hands of Telemachus and his father—Odysseus, who finally makes it home. When Laertes, the aged father of Odysseus, finds out that his son has come home and has taken revenge on the Suitors, he concludes that the gods are still on Olympus, and the Suitors have paid the price for their insolence.[60] This is the faith of simpletons—a faith that is expressed again and again, but is not corroborated by the epic. On the contrary, the message of the epic is that those who wait idly for the wrath of the gods to descend on the iniquitous will be sorely disappointed. Unfortunately, the message is lost on the mortals in the *Odyssey*, who continue to claim that the wrath of the gods will descend on the unjust.

Odysseus, the central figure of the epic, is presented as a wily, inventive, scheming, and irrepressible intriguer. He is a cunning, resourceful, ingenious trickster. He is a man of nimble wits, a master of disguises, and a consummate liar, who is unsurpassed in subterfuge.[61] He is the architect of the Trojan horse, the infamous trick by which he succeeded in the sac of Troy and the massacre of its inhabitants. He is both a "sacker of cities" and a "favorite of the gods."[62] Being a "favorite of the gods" does not indicate moral virtue; it denotes high rank, good looks, wealth, and success in one's endeavors. It expresses the clearly observable fact that some people are lucky. Odysseus is lucky to have so many of the good things in life—wealth, rank, physical prowess, and success. He is also lucky to have survived when all his men perished; but all that luck is no reflection of his moral merits.

By the same token, we find Helen living in the lap of luxury, back in Sparta, reconciled with her husband Menelaus, her great beauty untarnished by the years—despite all the death and mayhem she has caused. Indeed, her palace was so opulent—gleaming with bronze, gold, silver, and ivory (treasures from plundering Troy) that the sight filled Telemachus with wonder![63] The gods are indeed the weavers of destiny,[64] but that destiny has little to do with moral rectitude. The favor of the gods is arbitrary, and not reflective of a moral meritocracy. Far from being a primitive perspective on the world, the Homeric view is more compatible with lived experience than the naïve assumption that the gods reward virtue and punish wickedness. This is not to deny that this naïve view is expressed again and again by characters in the *Odyssey*.

Even the worldly Odysseus, oblivious to his own iniquities, but enraged at the brutality of Polyphemus, the Cyclops, warns the brute that he will suffer retribution at the hands of the gods.[65] However, as the story makes clear, the reverse was the case. Odysseus was the one who suffered at the hands of the gods. Polyphemus was the son of Poseidon, who granted the Cyclops his wish that Odysseus should not get home, and if he does, it would be many years later, after losing all his comrades and his ships, and finding much trouble at home. In contrast, the only punishment that the Cyclops suffered was at the hands of Odysseus, who robbed him of his wits with wine, then blinded him. It is commonplace for mortals to think that the gods will punish injustice. It is indeed a tempting assumption, but it is one to which Homer did not succumb.

It has rightly been argued by Hugh Lloyd-Jones that even though the gods are not models of morality, they are not entirely indifferent to it.[66] As Lloyd-Jones explains, Zeus "is the protector of oaths (*Horkios*), protector of strangers and of the law of host and guest (*Xeinios*) and protector of suppliants (*Hikesios*)."[67] He is therefore compelled to punish offenses against these laws. This is an important point, but it should not lead us to moralize the gods of Homer by turning them into representatives of an eternal, unchanging, and immutable justice that transcends the flawed and limited justice of the world. As Lloyd-Jones readily admits, Zeus is defending the order over which he presides. Zeus upholds the *status quo* which secures his honor and supremacy, but that is not justice in the *de jure* sense of the term. At best, it is *his* justice—an extension of *his* power. It does not follow that justice and decency will prevail, because Zeus is not omnipotent and did not create the world.

As Alban Winspear points out, the role of Zeus is comparable to that of the *basileus*, the king or tribal chief. [68] The code over which Zeus presides is largely tribal.[69] Committing perjury, harming or disrespecting parents, or acting contrary to the rules of hospitality, were particularly egregious. In that context, justice is identical with custom, not with transcendent justice.[70] Like the tribal chief, Zeus is compelled to uphold the justice of his realm—it is his job. As long as he was in charge, he would preside over the rules of justice that define his reign. However, like the tribal chief, he did not have absolute power. The tribal chief could not act without the agreement of the council of elders. The latter could impose its will against him. By the same token, Zeus could not act in contravention to the wishes of his divine family, who could impose their will against him. So, Zeus was not always in a position to punish the transgression of his rules.

When it comes to the justice of Zeus, consider the fate of the Phaeacians in the *Odyssey*. These people were the model of generosity and hospitality. They rescued the shipwrecked Odysseus, provided him with lavish gifts, and used one of their own ships to take him all the way to Ithaca—his native land. How were they rewarded for their hospitality? On the way back from their kindly mission, Zeus allowed Poseidon to turn their ship into a stone, just as it approached the harbor. Why? Because Poseidon wanted to continue to punish Odysseus for killing the Cyclops, but Phaeacian generosity brought Odysseus's suffering to an end. So, Poseidon was eager to teach the Phaeacians not to be so kind to strangers. Needless to say, such a lesson undermines the law of hospitality, over which Zeus supposedly presided. Zeus allowed Poseidon to turn their ship into stone to assuage the latter's anger, but he managed to talk him out of surrounding their town with a ring of mountains.[71] In this way, Zeus avoided the alienation of Poseidon, and the destabilization of the order over which he presided. So, Zeus is not always in a position to enforce his rules, even when he wants to.[72]

The abduction of Helen by Paris can be interpreted as a classic contravention of the rules of hospitality.[73] Paris was a guest of Helen's husband, Menelaus; abducting the wife of one's host is unacceptable. So, the defeat of the Trojans can be construed as a punishment from Zeus for the transgression against the rules of hospitality. It follows that Zeus was concerned with justice after all.[74] In the first place, Helen was not abducted; all the evidence points to the conclusion that she went willingly with all her exquisite clothes and paraphernalia—a woman who was abducted could not possibly have had so much time to pack. Nevertheless, Paris did seduce her (with some help from Aphrodite). Seducing the wife of your host contravenes the rules of hospitality. So, Paris was definitely guilty—not only in the eyes of the Greeks, but also in the eyes of the Trojans, including his own family. So, Lloyd-Jones is right to point this out. Nevertheless, the Trojans were not defeated because of the conduct of Paris. There is nothing just about the price that the Trojans had to pay for Paris' transgression.

Contrary to what some scholars have maintained, the *Iliad* is not a tale in which the Greeks win the war because, being disciplined and organized, they deserve to win, while the Trojans, being glamorous and unruly, deserve to lose.[75] In truth, there are no winners in the epic.[76] After winning the war, most of the Greeks drowned on their way home, and lost much of their spoils from the sack of Troy. The whole venture was a futile enterprise filled with suffering and death. Homer does not valorize war as vanquishing evil. In contrast to Homer, the monotheists have bathed the violence of war with glory, since they think of it as a battle between absolute good and evil, in which the former is bound to triumph—in the long run. Homer had no such illusions. The *Iliad* is not a moralistic tale in which Troy is destroyed because Paris contravened the rules of hospitality. Besides, it would not be just for the city to be destroyed for the transgressions of one man.

There is no reason to follow Socrates by conflating religion with morality. It is fallacious to assume that only those who worship exactly as we do, can be trustworthy enough to marry our daughters, engage in business dealings, or run the government. In allying religion with morality we give it too much importance. As a result, minute differences take on gargantuan significance. Trifles lead to religious wars, which were rightly satirized by Jonathan Swift in *Gulliver's Travels*, where the "big endians" (those who break their eggs from the big end) were mortal enemies of the "little endians" (those who break their eggs from the little end). The outcome is endless orgies of slaughter that mirror the irrationality of the conflict between Catholics and Protestants in the sixteenth and seventeenth centuries, or Sunnis and Shiites in our time.

Plato worries that if the gods are indifferent to justice, if they cannot be bothered to punish the wicked and reward the good, then, what incentive will there be for people to be good and to treat their fellow human beings with fairness and respect? Plato himself provides one of the best answers to that question—namely, that righteousness is its own reward. However, Plato pushed the argument beyond reasonable limits; as a result, he doubted that everyone could appreciate the mutual dependence of justice and happiness. He concluded that rational considerations alone are not sufficient to inspire virtue. Fear of the gods and punishment in the beyond is necessary.

Unfortunately, the price in veracity that must be paid to provide this motivation is too great. It requires a colossal lie. It requires the myth of cosmic justice, which flies in the face of human experience. Everyone knows morally decadent, degenerate, and dishonest people who flourish, and honest ones who lead miserable lives, beset by every misfortune. Everyone knows of innocent children who are afflicted by frightful diseases that bring their short lives to an end in a torrent of pain and agony. To uphold the dogma of cosmic justice, Plato must insist on the myth of punishments and rewards beyond the grave. So much so that the myth of Er becomes the cornerstone of his moral teaching, meanwhile, the eudaimonistic ethos falls by the wayside. So, it is not accurate to say that Christianity is Plato for the masses, since Plato's doctrine is also designed for the masses. Like Christianity, it provides the priests with the dogma they will need, not to educate, enlighten, or ennoble the masses, but as an instrument of psychological terror and control.

5   The Hubris of Emulating the Gods

Plato objected to the gods of Homer on the ground that they fail to serve as moral models for humanity. He objected to the battle of the gods as described by Hesiod and Homer,[77] the castration of Ouranos by his son Cronus.[78] He complained that "these tales are harmful to those who hear them, for every man will be ready to excuse his own evil conduct if he believes these things are done" by either gods or close descendants of the gods.[79] If the gods and the heroes do not set a good example, the results will be a "considerable tolerance of evil."[80] It follows that gods should be good, moral, and upright. Plato is right to say that the conduct of the gods was scandalous and could not possibly provide a moral example for human emulation. However, the idea that the gods of Homer lead people astray by inspiring them to imitate the gods, as Euthyphro did, is preposterous. The gods of

Homer were not intended to be emulated. On the contrary, emulating them was *hubris,* which is the antithesis of piety. So, what is *hubris?*

There is a popular assumption that Greek literature involves a pattern of *koros-hubris-nemesis.* In other words, when prosperity and good fortune (*koros*) leads human beings to arrogance and over-reaching (*hubris*), the result is disaster, ruin, or divine retribution (*nemesis*).[81] But it does not follow that the *hubristai* deserve their fate. In punishing the *hubristai*, the gods are not punishing sin or wickedness. They are offended by the insolence of mere mortals and lash out against them. Nothing irks them more than mortals who think big; they do not like the idea that mere mortals could aspire to the sort of glory and splendor that belongs to the gods.

It is a mistake to assume that *hubris* is the Greek equivalent of sin and that *nemesis* is equivalent to divine retribution. Moralizing the Greek gods is the distorting product of Christianizing lenses, which are an obstacle to understanding the Homeric point of view. The gods did not create the world, and they were not in a position to make it just. If the gods play a role in bringing the *hubristai* down, that is not necessarily a tribute to the justice of the gods, but more often than not, to their jealousy, rage, conceit, and hypersensitivity to insults (especially from mortals). When Niobe, who had six sons and six daughters, bragged that she was more fruitful than the goddess Leto, mother of Apollo and Artemis, Leto sent Apollo to kill all her sons, and Artemis to kill all her daughters, then Zeus turned her into a stone statue.[82] There was no justice in that; Niobe did not harm anyone; she did nothing *morally* wrong. She was proud; but what she said about her fruitfulness was a matter of fact. When Archne, a mortal girl, boasted that she was better at weaving than Athena, the goddess turned the foolish girl into a spider destined to weave endless cobwebs. In Ovid's version of the story, the goddess challenged the girl to a weaving contest, and Archne beat the goddess fair and square. So, Archne's high estimation of her abilities might have been quite legitimate, but she was punished nevertheless. The same is true of Ajax in Homer's *Odyssey* (the so-called Lesser Ajax as opposed to the more famous one). On his way home from Troy, his boat was destroyed by a terrible storm in which all his companions perished, but Ajax managed to swim to shore and climb onto a rock. Then, he bragged that he was one that the sea could not drown; he believed that he had cheated death. His boasting angered Poseidon, the rock shattered, and he was swept out to sea and to his death.[83]

These are true myths. The true message of these tales is that all success in this world is precarious. However impressive our accomplishments may be, it is never justified to boast about them, because our good fortune can be reversed in a flash. Niobe's children can all be killed in an accident, and Archne could suffer from a stroke that paralyzes her weaving fingers. The point is that Niobe, Archne, and Ajax, were not guilty of villainy—but they were foolish enough to boast about their skills and good fortune in a world where good fortune is precarious. The gods serve as artistic substitutes of the afflictions that nature invariably has in store. It is foolhardy for mortals to think that they can escape the human condition, as Sisyphus did when he tried to trick Death.[84] In other words, *hubris* is an offense against the gods understood as the order of nature, which human beings must accept. N. R. E. Fisher has argued that *hubris* is violent, offensive, or humiliating acts directed at other people.[85] This is not an easy argument to make in light of the previous examples. Strictly speaking, Niobe, Archne, Ajax, and Sisyphus were not guilty of any criminal acts against other human beings. However, Fisher is not totally off the mark.

Even though *hubris* does not *necessarily* include immoral conduct against others, the arrogance associated with *hubris* is likely to lead to conduct that disregards the welfare or dignity of others. This is why *hubris* can lead to criminality on a grand scale. Aristotle clarifies the matter when he distinguishes between the criminality of great villains (*megaloponeroi*), and that of petty criminals (*mikroponeroi*).[86] As reflected in Greek usage, the former has its source in *hubris* and is generally associated with the rich and wellborn; while the latter, has its source in *kakourgia*—poverty or want.[87] In contrast to petty crime, which is motivated by material deprivation, great villainy aspires to honor, dominance, and a sense of superiority. In other words, great villainy is closely associated with *hubris* because it has its source in the arrogance that is often inspired by great wealth, good looks, noble birth, and good fortune—Alcibiades and Conrad Black come to mind. In that light, *hubris* is closely related to the crimes of the ruling classes, and is likely to involve assaults on the personal honor or the economic well-being of the lower classes.[88] So, it is not surprising that democratic Athens had a law against *hubris* to which the jury could attach any penalty, including death.[89]

There is a certain irony in the fact that those who are exceptionally blessed in society are also those most likely to display extremely antisocial conduct. In our time, bankers, who made gigantic personal profits while bringing the financial system to ruin in 2008, are a good example of *hubris;* so were the CEOs of the big American car companies with their private jets and their multimillion dollar bonuses who came to Washington to ask for a bailout of billions of dollars from the taxpayers who had lost their lifesavings and pensions. In Book IV of the *Politics*, Aristotle tells us that the lower classes will tolerate being excluded from political participation as long as they are not humiliated by acts of *hubris* by the ruling classes.[90] In a time of obscene accumulations of wealth and power in very few hands, it is instructive for us to be reminded of the significant role that *hubris* played in Aristotle's discussion of political unrest in Book V of the *Politics*.

Interestingly, Aristotle also reports that revolutionaries were described as *hubristai*—but only by the ruling classes. So, from the vantage of the elite, the revolutionaries were over-stepping the limits of their station. The upper classes are infuriated by the supposed insolence of the lower classes, just as the gods are outraged by the insolence of mortals. In other words, the concept of *hubris* is class sensitive. And no one is more sensitive to class than the gods. Recall how indignant Aphrodite was when Diomedes stabbed her and treated her with contempt for interfering in the battle at Troy.[91] Her bleeding wrist healed instantly; it was her pride that was the focal point of her injury. The trouble is that the ruling classes are inclined to behave as if they were gods among mere mortals; but so are radical revolutionaries who champion the cause of the people and promise a world free from all injustice and inequality. It follows that *hubris* is a vice that may be displayed by either the ruling classes or the revolutionary champions of the people. It accounts for a great deal of political instability and unrest.

The gods are not necessary to explain how success and good fortune can lead to vainglory, overconfidence, and outrageous political conduct, which is the source of ruin. In other words, the downfall of the *hubristai* follows naturally from their excesses. There is absolutely no reason to explain their failure by appealing to the idea of the just punishment of the gods. Understanding that *hubris* is a deplorable vice in human beings, has the effect of dampening the human propensity to act like a god. It has the effect of making human beings aware of their limitations; it urges them to moderate their ambitions and curb their excesses. It makes them realize that they cannot simply ignore the rules that they expect others to live by. It makes them realize that acting like gods among men is a recipe for disaster. Understanding morality as the imitation of the gods, or helping the gods in their projects, as Socrates understood piety, is bound to be disastrous, because it encourages *hubris*.

By moralizing the gods, Socrates and Plato hoped to make them into moral models worthy of human emulation. However, this is a fool's errand. No matter how hard we try to invent a picture of god or gods that are morally pure and perfect, *gods will always set a bad example*, as the case of Jesus illustrates. Even though he is routinely painted as meek and gentle, Jesus issued the most sinister threats when crossed—such as burning in hell to all eternity.[92] Morality cannot be the imitation of the gods, because no matter how hard they try, the gods are congenitally incapable of behaving themselves or being morally good. *Gods will be gods!*

6   Accepting Responsibility

Plato was convinced that Homer and the poets contribute to moral irresponsibility, which is one of the reasons he is eager to censor them in the *Republic*.[93] Plato's objection to Homer's myths is not only that they fail to get at the truth but also that they promote the worst kind of lie. Plato distinguishes between the ordinary lie and a much worse type of lie—the "lie in the soul."[94] Someone who dispenses ordinary lies knows the truth full well. However, the lie in the soul is more insidious. It is not an ordinary lie, but a form of self-deception where the liar is himself or herself unaware of the truth.

    According to Plato, Homer's myths lead people to blame the gods for all their iniquities, and this allows them to deny responsibility for their actions. This amounts to a colossal form of self-deception. On the whole, scholars have agreed with Plato that the psychic intervention of the gods makes people into puppets, and that this self-understanding is either primitive or delusional.[95] Why would gods drive people mad and make them do terrible things? This strange phenomenon of psychic intervention seems perverse. E. R. Dodds claims that belief in psychic intervention is a primitive way of thinking, which is superseded by a more sophisticated self-understanding introduced by Socrates and Plato. Dodds sides with Plato in thinking that belief in psychic intervention distances human beings from their wickedness, makes them feel innocent, and allows them to escape from responsibility. However, this is not accurate; the tragic heroes are free from guilt, but not from responsibility.

    Plato is right in claiming that Homer's characters tend to blame the gods for their iniquities, and in so doing, assert their freedom from guilt. For example, when Helen ran off with Paris and ignited the Trojan War, we were told that Aphrodite took hold of her mind and made her do it. When Heracles killed his children, we were told that Hera drove him mad and made him do it. When Agamemnon robed Achilles of his prize, he blamed the gods for what he did. However, implying that blaming the gods led them to deceive themselves about their responsibility is not true. Just because Helen, Heracles, or Agamemnon, blamed the gods for their actions, it does not follow that they were not willing to take responsibility for the evil they inflicted, and eager to make amends: far from it. They operated in a world of strict liability based on consequences, regardless of intentions; they had a more robust conception of responsibility that corresponded to the juridical view of early Greek law, which was oblivious to intention, focusing only on the act and its consequences.[96] Such a conception of responsibility is much more demanding than the view of responsibility that is linked to *mens rea* or a guilty mind (as is the case in modern criminal law). In the latter case, we are generally guilty only of the things we do intentionally, except where professional errors are involved—such as the pharmacist who dispenses the wrong prescription—in which case strict liability is the order of the day.

The gods may give agents reasons that lead them to act one way rather than another, but they do not rob them of their ability to deliberate, decide, and act intentionally. The decision to act is the agent's decision, even if the gods provide reasons why one course of action is preferable to another. As Bernard Williams has rightly argued, there is "no inconsistency between a divine intervention and the ordinary materials of psychological explanation," because, in the final analysis, it is mysterious why certain courses of action prevail over others, and a god's intervention is a way of representing the mystery.[97] In other words, there is more than one reason for action and more than one possible choice. The choice we make among a plurality of possibilities and reasons is the mystery at the heart of the deliberative process—a mystery signified by the gods.

In so far as action is not necessarily guided by deliberation, it may be argued that the gods are an artistic representation of our own passions.[98] If we interpret the gods in this way, then the plurality of gods is the plurality of our own conflicting passions. What makes one passion triumph over all others in a particular situation is unknown. Moreover, the passions that triumph may not be the passions that we expect, wish, or hope would triumph. Agamemnon and Helen are bewildered by the passions that led to their actions, which they regard as a temporary madness or delusion. However, they do not deny doing what they did. Nor do they consider their conduct involuntary; they acknowledge acting intentionally. They do not absolve themselves of responsibility, just because the gods rendered them temporarily insane. Nevertheless, they experience themselves as *innocent* in the sense that the evil they perpetrated does not spring from some inherent inner wickedness. This is not the same as refusing to accept responsibility. As Walter Kaufmann has rightly argued, the focus on guilt and punishment are counter-productive; it is much better to be future oriented and figure out how to make amends or compensate for the suffering one has caused.[99]

Helen of Troy is probably the best example of what Plato is worried about. In the *Iliad*, Helen recognizes the pernicious role that Aphrodite has played in her misfortunes, but that does not lead her to deny responsibility for her actions. She laments her foolishness; she wonders what could have possessed her to run off with Paris. She longs for her husband Menelaus; she calls herself a slut, and is generally disgusted with herself. She is on the right track, but does not go far enough; yes, Aphrodite tempted her to do what she did, but in the final analysis, she is the one who decided to do it. When Priam (the father of Paris and king of Troy who had more to lose by Helen's actions than anyone else) consoles her saying, it is not your fault my child—it is the gods, she knows it is not true. She knows she is responsible for her actions, but she is not willing to make amends. She does not have the courage to return to Menelaus on her own accord, beg his forgiveness, and submit to whatever penance he sees fit. In the *Odyssey*, we find Helen in Sparta living happily with Menelaus in her palace (in all its splendor) while others have paid dearly for her misdemeanors.

The Helen we encounter in Euripides's *The Trojan Women* is even more pathetic. In the play, Helen and Hecabe (the mother of Paris and queen of Troy) are pitted against each other, with Menelaus as the arbitrator. In making her case, Helen blames everyone but herself. She accepts no responsibility for her actions whatsoever. She blames the gods; she blames Hecabe for bearing such a beautiful son. She blames Priam for failing to have him successfully killed as a child when Hecabe's dream foretold the disasters he would bring on his city. She blames Paris for abducting her and taking her away by force. In short, the Helen we encounter in this play is a pitiful model of the kind of escapism that worried Plato. Her self-understanding is the paradigm of what Plato called the "lie in the soul" or self-deception. It is one of the reasons for Plato's indictment of Homer. There is no doubt that blaming the gods allows individuals to escape guilt, but there is no logical reason why this escape from blame would also involve a flight from responsibility. In *The Trojan Women*, Hecabe agrees with Helen that the gods are to blame, but she thinks that Helen nevertheless bears the final responsibility. She challenges Helen's claim that she was abducted and taken against her will by Paris

(Hecabe's son). Instead, Hecabe claims that Helen fell in love with her son's beauty. For Paris "glittered with gold in his oriental raiment," the likes of which Helen had never seen in her little world of Sparta (she stops short of calling it primitive).[100]

It is not only Hecabe who finds Helen guilty, but so does her husband Menelaus. As much as he would dearly love to believe that Helen was innocent, and abducted against her will, Menelaus finds her case without substance. In the play, he rules in favor of Hecabe and condemns Helen to death. In the end, Helen's hold on him is too powerful, and Menelaus is not able to carry out the sentence. The point is that even the man who loved Helen, the man who talked Agamemnon into amassing an army to bring her back from Troy, judged her to be a morally flawed person. It follows that Helen's escape from responsibility is a perversion of the Homeric ethos. Helen's moral faults are not the result of the Homeric worldview that Plato is so eager to censure. Nor does Euripides endorse her escape from responsibility, as his play illustrates.

The case of Agamemnon in Homer's *Iliad* also illustrates why blaming the gods does not lead to escape from responsibility. At the heart of the *Iliad* is the revolt of Achilles as a result of the injustice and humiliation he receives at the hands of Agamemnon. Achilles is furious that Agamemnon has taken his female captive, and so refuses to fight. He is determined to show Agamemnon and the other Greeks that they cannot win without him. Thetis, his goddess mother, prevails on Zeus to make sure that, in the absence of Achilles, the Greeks lose the battles to the Trojans. When Agamemnon finally realizes his mistake, he apologizes to Achilles for his unjust conduct. He blames Zeus for blinding his judgment.[101] He says he was not himself; he was in a temporary state of madness; he was in the grip of a delusion or *atē*. He blames Zeus for robbing him of his wits; but he does not deny doing what he did. He does not consider it an accident. He takes responsibility for his conduct and offers to make amends. He offers to return the girl to Achilles, along with rich and extravagant gifts by way of compensation.[102]

What is the point of blaming Zeus when he is going to take responsibility, right the wrong, and offer compensation? It may be argued that Agamemnon was simply trying to save face is a shame culture. That may be true, but there is more to it. Blaming Zeus allows Agamemnon to distance himself from the act. It allows him to separate the unjust act from his own character. By asserting a dissonance between his character and the act, he prevents this single act from defining him. Blaming Zeus for making him act in a way that he would not have acted, had he been in possession of his senses, allows him to disown the action as the definitive expression of his true self. It allows him to look at his transgression with horror; it allows him to be appalled by his conduct, remorseful for the harm inflicted, and eager to provide compensation, even though he did not intend the harm, and does not experience a debilitating guilt. In short, belief in psychic intervention (i.e., Zeus made him do it, or Aphrodite got hold of her head) is healthy, because it allows the Homeric Greeks to escape the paralyzing self-hatred induced by guilt.[103]

Blaming the gods does not lead to escape from responsibility, even when the harm done is totally accidental. For example, Herodotus tells the story of Adrastus, a Phrygian born to a royal family who accidentally killed his brother and was ostracized by his family. Croesus, King of Lydia, took him in and made him part of his family. Croesus had two sons; one was deaf and dumb and the other, Atys, was outstanding in all respects. One day, Croesus had a dream that Atys would be killed by a spear. So he tried to prevent Atys from going on expeditions, but to no avail. When Atys went on an expedition to hunt a huge monster boar that was threatening Mount Olympus, Croesus asked Adrastus to look out for him. When Adrastus fired a spear intended for the bear, it hit and killed the son he pledged to protect. When Croesus was presented with the body of his dead son, Adrastus prostrated himself before Croesus and declared that he deserved to die immediately. Despite his grief, Croesus responded that he was not to blame; he was but an "unwitting instrument" and the responsibility was with the gods (luck or fate).[104] But once it was quiet around the tomb, Adrastus took his own life at the graveside. So, the fact that the gods are blamed does not prevent human beings from taking responsibility and blaming themselves, *even when the act was accidental*. The tragedy of Adrastus is that his fate made it impossible either to distance himself from the events or to make amends.

When compared to the Orphic and the Christian approach to sin, the archaic Greek attitude to wrongdoing is constructive. The idea that sin is the logical byproduct of one's innate wickedness, or is integral to the corruption of the corporeal self, promotes hopelessness. Allowing the contemptible action to define oneself leads to self-loathing, which in turn results in guilt, expressed as a longing for punishment, self-immolation, and self-destruction. The result is a sense of helplessness, which comes from expecting the dreadful conduct to be repeated; and feeling at a loss when it comes to doing anything by way of either compensation or prevention. By blaming the gods, Agamemnon does not suffer from guilt and its attendant self-loathing, which would have been the result of regarding the unjust act as emanating from his inherent wickedness. Guilt and the desire for punishment accomplish nothing. It is much more constructive to distance oneself from the act, and figure out concrete ways of compensating for the damage done. Of course it is not always possible to do so, which explains why Adrastus killed himself. It follows that blaming the gods does not lead human beings to escape from responsibility.

Psychic intervention is more of a commentary on human nature than on responsibility. Attributing their evil deeds to the gods allows Homer's characters to see themselves as innocent. It means that evil is not integral to their nature. The Homeric emphasis on human innocence is more believable and more realistic than the emphasis on human wickedness, because most human evil is the byproduct of being blinded by the pursuit of some good or other, as Aristotle rightly surmised. Robbing a bank, warding off a threat, defeating a rival, are paradigmatic. Evil that has no purpose, evil that is gratuitous, evil that involves no tangible anticipation of some good or other is incomprehensible. Even though it is not unknown, it is extremely rare. When it happens, human beings react with shock, horror, and perplexity in the face of the senseless and grotesque. Gratuitous evil is anomalous. In contrast, the Homeric view of our humanity underscores the primacy of the good as the driving force of action. The Homeric emphasis on human innocence is not simpleminded or unsophisticated, it is objectionable simply because it is at odds with our Christian inclination to emphasize human wickedness.

The idea that psychic intervention is somehow "primitive" in the sense of having been transcended is not accurate. Psychic intervention is still with us. Christian writers, from Augustine to Luther, have merely inverted it. They attribute all human goodness to the descent of the Holy Spirit into the soul.[105] It follows that goodness belongs to God, and evil is integral to our fallen nature. Plato also believed that human beings were "corrupted at birth."[106] However, it is a mistake to assume that acknowledging our corrupted nature makes us inclined to take responsibility for our actions. On the contrary, it makes us wonder if we are responsible for our wickedness in view of the fact that we are not the authors of our nature. By assuming human nature to be innocent, Homeric men and women cannot blame their evil conduct on their fallen or perverse nature, and must therefore take responsibility for their actions for good and ill.

In other words, the assumption of human innocence is more conducive to taking responsibility than the assumption of human guilt.[107]

By defining the "greatest lie,"[108] the really despicable lie, as the "lie in the soul" or self-deception, Socrates gives license to all the deceitful, corrupt, and unprincipled liars whose intentional lies are exonerated on the ground that they are not true liars because they know the truth. In the *Lesser Hippias*, Socrates argues that the wily Odysseus, who excels in the deliberate manipulation of others, is superior to Achilles who thinks that those who say one thing and think another are as detestable as the "the gates of death."[109] Hippias (the Sophist in the discussion) disagrees strongly. He thinks that Achilles is the better man. Nevertheless, Socrates persists; he claims that Odysseus is the better man because he lies intentionally, and so, knows exactly what he is doing. In contrast, despite his avowed hatred of lies, Achilles says one thing to Odysseus and another to Ajax. He tells Odysseus that he will pack his ships up and leave, because he has no intention of helping Agamemnon any longer with his silly war, given the contempt with which he is being treated.[110] Then the next day, he tells Ajax that he will not budge from his tent and will not lift a finger, even if Hector comes all the way to the Greek ships and lights them on fire.[111] Hippias objects that Achilles is not being false, but expressing his passionate and contradictory feelings at different times, "in the innocence of his heart."[112] But Socrates insists that "voluntary liars" are better than involuntary ones.[113] It follows that the crude and cunning Odysseus is a better man than Achilles. Hippias is not convinced. Scholars have questioned the authenticity of the dialogue on the ground that its conclusion is morally scandalous and its argument is inferior to other dialogues. Nevertheless, the thesis of the dialogue is totally compatible with the distinction Socrates makes in the *Republic* between the voluntary lie and the lie in the soul.[114] By dismissing the immorality of the voluntary lie, Socrates invites a callous disregard for truth that is music to the ears of the unscrupulous.

7   THE MANLY VIRTUES

The triumph of Socrates in the history of the West is often hailed as a triumph of the "quiet virtues" over the manly virtues of Homer's noble warriors. Simply stated, the story is that Homer's warrior ethos was a celebration of the masculine virtues of prowess and display—valor, courage, strength, speed, and the ability to stand firm in the face of impending death. These competitive virtues placed the emphasis on results—in particular, success in war. On some accounts, the prevalence of these noisy, masculine, or competitive virtues all but drowned out the quiet, feminine, and cooperative virtues—the virtues of justice, temperance, and chastity. If success were all that mattered for excellence, if success is all that was needed to be held in high esteem as an individual of outstanding excellence (*agathos*) then, *any* means that led to success in the defense of the interests of oneself and one's clan, would do. As A. W. H. Adkins has argued, the seeds of the moral epidemic represented by the Sophists can be found in Homer.[115] Adkins writes: "Scratch Thrasymachus and you find King Agamemnon."[116] He thinks that Alcibiades represents the moral depravity that led to the betrayal and defeat of Athens.[117] In short, the Homeric values are the source of the moral crisis of the fifth century to which Socrates and Plato provide a solution by bringing to the fore the "quiet virtues" that are largely ignored by the competitive system of values found in Homer.[118]

The idea that the moral depravity manifested by the oligarchic coup of 404 BCE was the result of the selfish implications of Homeric values does not stand up to scrutiny. What makes this narrative preposterous is that it conveniently overlooks the fact that Alcibiades, Critias, and Charmides were friends and students of Socrates (not Thrasymachus, Protagoras, or any other Sophist). It was the students of Socrates who embodied the moral depravity associated with the defeat of Athens and the reign of terror that followed.

In rejecting the conventional narrative, I am not affirming the one propagated by Friedrich Nietzsche. According to the latter, the history of the West has been the history of the subversion of the manly virtues of prowess and display in favor of the quiet or feminine virtues of cooperation, purity of heart, and good intentions. In both the dominant narrative and its Nietzschean inverse, Socrates plays the pivotal role in the shift from one set of virtues to the other. The difference is that Nietzsche deplores the feminine virtues. Both narratives are equally flawed. The Nietzschean version of the story is as divorced from the historical facts as the traditional narrative. What is worse, Nietzsche celebrates a perverse version of the Homeric or masculine virtues, as I will explain.

Socrates has indeed been the focal point of a shift in values in the history of the West. It behooves us to look at this shift in values more critically. The shift from the competitive or masculine virtues to the cooperative or feminine ones is not unique to the West. It is a shift that every society, which moves from a state of impending danger to one of security, will undergo. Societies that live in a constant state of insecurity will naturally celebrate the masculine virtues of valor, strength, speed, and success; they will naturally praise the ability to stand firm in the face of danger and keep the enemy at bay. These virtues are useful, even necessary for the very survival of the community. Placing a primacy on these so-called masculine virtues is not a rejection of the feminine ones—the virtues of cooperation, mutual assistance, compassion, temperance, wisdom, and justice. The latter are equally necessary in maintaining the internal order, solidarity, and peace of the community, which are vital. However, in conditions of great danger and insecurity, the masculine virtues are bound to have priority. As the power of a society grows, and the external threats fade into the background, the masculine virtues recede. At that point, the quiet or cooperative virtues come to the fore. So, rather than a seismic historical shift, it is more accurate to describe the shift as a pendulum swing from emphasis on one set of virtues to emphasis on the other, depending on the historical circumstances.

Nevertheless, it is important not to misconstrue the masculine virtues. Whether it is celebrated or decried, the warrior ethos has been perverted. The masculine virtues are not beyond good and evil—they are not indifferent to justice; nor are they concerned with a narrow understanding of selfish interests. The claim made by Adkins that the moral epidemic of the fifth century was a function of the narrowing of the Homeric concern for kin to naked self-interest, makes no sense; because this amounts to abandoning the ethos altogether. The self-sacrifice of the warrior for the sake of the group is integral to the warrior ethos. Nor is the sacrifice understood by the warrior simply as self-sacrifice, but also as a personal quest for glory. In other words, the interests of the whole and the interests of the warrior are not at odds. Without the sacrifice of self for the group, there can be no glory for the warrior. Narrow self-interest does not begin to capture the situation at hand.

In Homer's *Iliad,* Sarpedon reminds a fellow warrior that they must be brave in the face of danger and even death, otherwise it makes no sense for them to be "singled out for honour,... with pride of place, the choicest meat and never empty cups" living on "great estates" with "lovely orchards and splendid fields of wheat" and being looked up to as if they were gods. Then he adds: "All this now obliges us to take our places in the front ranks...and fling ourselves into the flames of battle. Only then will our...men-at-arms say of us: 'Well! These are no dishonorable lords...that rule over us and eat fat sheep and drink the best sweet wine: they are indomitable and fight on the front'..."[119] The same could not be said of the French aristocrats of the *ancien regime* on the eve of the French Revolution.

It is also the case that the great warrior can sometimes get away with things that others cannot, just because of his success and valor. For example, Agamemnon assumed he would be able to get away with taking Briseis, the prize of Achilles. As a result of the injustice done to his honor, Achilles sulks in his tent for most of the epic. Since Achilles is without doubt the superstar warrior on the Greek side, the Greeks suffer heavy losses and are bested by the Trojans in the first part of the war. In this way, Homer makes it clear that the *agathos* cannot ignore justice and still hope to succeed.

It may be argued that this view makes justice valuable only for its effects—i.e., for prudential reasons. That is true; but its prudential reasons cannot be interpreted narrowly as selfish motives. Plato made a valiant effort to defend justice as an "end in itself," apart from any prudential value. Unfortunately, he succumbed to the seduction of the rewards and punishments of the afterlife. The preoccupation with personal salvation is a step backwards because it leads to selfishness and self-absorption—as Crito rightly points out in observing the behavior of Socrates after the trial.[120] When Crito fails to convince Socrates to escape, he rebukes him for being unmanly. The trial was a sham, the verdict was unjust, so how can he sit there and take it? How can he simply turn the other cheek? What kind of a man is he? What will his children think of him? Fathering them then leaving them with no heed to their upbringing or education? He has an opportunity to live well in Thessaly where he can bring up his boys among friends who will appreciate him. How can he turn that down and go passively to his death? Crito is justifiably perplexed and ashamed of such unmanly conduct.[121] Adkins dismisses Crito's position as a sign of the resilience of the manly or Homeric virtues that led to the narrow pursuit of self-interest, which were the hallmarks of the moral epidemic represented by the Sophists.

Anyone who is not totally bamboozled by Socrates is bound to see that Crito has a point. When compared to Hector, the prototype of the old

Homeric morality, Socrates is not only unmanly but also selfish. He chooses death, not reluctantly, but as the goal—the life-long quest of his philosophizing. Socrates is not risking his life for his city or his family; he is not dying for love of anyone. He is a martyr for an abstract idea—or an abstract god. Why? Surely, not because he believes that he has an obligation to Athens. It was not for love of his city that he was going quietly to his death. It was not for love of his family that he was willing to die. His love of death and martyrdom were motivated by a quest for personal salvation, and the promise of eternal life among the blessed. It was this narrow self-absorption that explains his unmanly choice. It was this narrow concern with self-salvation that made him a heartless father and husband.[122] It is worth noting that Jesus displayed the same disregard for family.

It may be argued that the world-transforming missions of men like Socrates and Jesus trumps the petty concerns of family life—but this is not the case. The callous disregard for others, including their nearest and dearest, is integral to their teaching. At the heart of the ethos they disseminate is the delusionary preoccupation with personal salvation or eternal life. The idea that Socrates represents an ethos that is higher than that of Hector is a testament to human gullibility, the cowardly rejection of the inevitability of death, and the seductive power of Socratic sophistry.

8   Savage Moralism Averted

Most of what we associate with religion—morality, guilt, faith, fasting, scripture, salvation, spirituality, and immortality, are absent in Homer's religion. That's what makes it so refreshing. It is a religion without lies, faith, morality, guilt, scriptures, sacred texts, or dogmas. It is a religion without salvation, or the need for redemption. It is a religion without spiritual oneness with the gods.[123] It is a religion without sacrifices, understood as self-mortification—fasting, celibacy, and the like.[124] Nothing but our self-congratulation leads us to assume that the absence of these elements makes Homeric religion somehow "primitive." On the contrary, fabrications about the fate of the soul in the beyond, the rewards and punishments of the afterlife, and the cosmic justice that rules the world—are elements that allow religion to contribute to human puerility, dualism, disregard for truth, *hubris*, and political fanaticism. These lies inspire evil on a grand scale and with a clear conscience.[125] I am not arguing that Homeric religion made people good. I believe that the search for the perfect, unadulterated, flawless, and pristine is part of the problematic legacy of Socratic thinking.

I have no intention of romanticizing ancient Greek religion. Its superstitious inclinations contain their own risks—flattering the gods with gifts and libations can turn into appeasing them with human sacrifices and other atrocities to escape their wrath.[126] Homer did his best to keep his gods as sunny as possible. The famous story of Agamemnon's sacrifice of Iphigenia so that favorable winds will blow to send the army off to Troy is not found in Homer. The only human sacrifice in the *Iliad* is the burning of the twelve Trojan boys on the funeral pyre of Patroclus. Homer rightly describes the event as Achilles' "murderous plan."[127] Plato is critical of Achilles' grief but not of the horror Achilles inflicts on these innocent boys. To Homer's credit, he does not conceal the ferocity of Greek warfare; nor is he tempted to sanctify it with the savage moralism that is the hallmark of the post-Socratic attitude to war.

NOTES

1. Augustine denounces the pagan gods as vile and malevolent "demons who teach depravity and rejoice in degradation." But thankfully, he adds, the blood of Christ has "set us free from their lies as well as their "demonic power." *City of God*, transl. by Henry Bettenson (London: Penguin Books, 1980), Bk. IV.27.
2. *Republic*, 386a ff.
3. Ibid, 377d.
4. Ibid, 389b. My italics.
5. Ibid.
6. Ibid, 414c.
7. *Phaedo*, 80d–81a; *Gorgias*, 523a ff. where he attributes this clearly Orphic myth to Homer; *Phaedrus*, 249a–b; *Meno*, 81b, ff.; *Republic*, 614b–621b; *Timaeus* 90c. See also *Alcibiades I*, 129c, in *The Dialogues of Plato* (Vol. I), translated by B. Jowett (London: Oxford University Press, 1931), 4 vols.
8. Taylor, *Socrates*, p. 51.
9. *Republic*, 364b–365a.
10. *Laws*, 908a–910d.
11. *Iliad*, Bk. 5.768; Bk. 5.355.
12. Walter F. Otto, *The Homeric Gods: The Spiritual Significance of Greek Religion*, transl. from the German by Moses Hadas (London: Thames and Hudson, 1954), p. 39: "The divinities become figures of reality in which the manifold being of nature finds its perfect and eternal expression."

13. Bernard Williams *Shame and Necessity* (Berkeley: University of California Press, 1993). As Williams explains: the gods are used to explain things that cannot be explained. For example, what makes a brave man run away? What makes an excellent shooter miss the mark?
14. I am indebted to my colleague, Ken Leyton-Brown for recognizing the important role played by luck in Greek religion. In my view, this is as true for the *Iliad* as much as the *Odyssey*. In *Homer on Life and Death* (Toronto: Clarendon Press, 1980), Jasper Griffin maintains that in the *Odyssey*, "there is no place for chance, and the poem cannot be understood unless that point is seen as important; and the divine is constantly at work; leading men and shaping their destiny—whether or not they are aware of it,"(p. 165). In contrast, Walter Kaufmann portrays the gods as identical with luck. See *Tragedy and Philosophy*, p. 144.
15. *Phaedo*, 80d–81a; *Gorgias*, 523a ff. where he shockingly attributes this Orphic myth to Homer; *Phaedrus*, 249a–b; *Meno*, 81b, ff.; *Republic*, 614b–621b; *Timaeus* 90c; *Alcibiades I*, 129c.
16. *Laws*, 908a–910d.
17. *Republic*, 386c; *Odyssey*, 11.488.
18. *Republic*, 386d.
19. *Phaedo*, 81a.
20. *Republic*, 387d–e.
21. Ibid, 387d–e.
22. This is the candid conclusion of Thomas C. Brickhouse and Nicholas D. Smith, *Plato's Socrates* (New York: Oxford University Press, 1994), p. 202.
23. *Phaedo*, 80d–81a; *Gorgias*, 523a ff.; *Phaedrus*, 249a–b; *Meno*, 81b, ff.; *Republic*, 614b–621b; *Timaeus* 90c.
24. *Iliad*, Bk. 14.346. See also Philip E. Slater, *The Glory of Hera: Greek Mythology and the Greek Family* (Boston: Beacon Press, 1968).
25. *Iliad*, Bk. I.469ff.; Bk. 2.420 ff.; *Odyssey*, Bk. 2.430.
26. *Republic*, 379d; *Iliad*, 24: 527.
27. *Republic*, 379c.
28. Ibid, 379c.
29. T.G. Rosenmeyer, "Drama," in M. I. Finley (ed.), *The Legacy of Greece: A New Appraisal* (New York: Oxford University Press, 1981), p. 142, n. 3.
30. *Iliad*, 17: 220.
31. Ibid, 3: 40–80.
32. Ibid, 15: 10.
33. Ibid, 22: 160ff.
34. Ibid, 24:30.
35. Ibid, 24: 405–423.
36. Ibid, 21: 270ff.
37. Ibid, 22:370.

38. Ibid, 24:630.
39. Saul David, "Zulu: The True Story," published by the BBC website, British History in-depth, November 5, 2009.
40. The case of the Americans is more complex, because their contempt of the Afghan warlords is tinged with envy, especially among American conservatives who admire and romanticize the ancient Greeks, and believe that America is the heir of Greek civilization; they know that the Afghans live in a world where manly courage is paramount. Understandably, these Americans are nostalgic for the glory that their war machines cannot deliver. See, for example, Robert D. Kaplan, *Soldiers of God* (Boston, Massachusetts: Houghton Mifflin Co., 1990).
41. *Phaedo*, 97b–98c; *Laws*, 966e.
42. *Laws*, 896e–897a, 89d, 904b.
43. *Republic*, 508e ff.
44. *Laws*, 906a.
45. Henry Poalucci (ed.), *The Political Writings of St. Augustine* (Chicago: Henry Regent Company, 1962), p. 165.
46. Arnold Toynbee, *Some Problems of Greek History*, (London: Oxford University Press, 1969), pp. 58–63; see also Helen H. Bacon, *Barbarians in Greek Tragedy* (New Haven: Yale University Press, 1961); Cartledge, *The Greeks* (New York: Oxford University Press, 1993), p. 38: says that "there is no trace of ethnocentric and derogatory stereo-typing of barbarians" in Homer.
47. So much so that some have cast doubt on the Greekness of Herodotus. Cartledge, *The Greeks*, pp. 37–38, surmises that Herodotus was not purely Hellenic, but of "mixed race." This supposedly explains his "tolerance of or even admiration for non-Greek barbarians."
48. A fragment form Xenophanes (570–475 BCE) indicates clearly that there is one god, mightiest of all, and not resembling mortals in thought or form. The fragment can be found in Sarah B. Pomeroy, et al., *Ancient Greece: A Political, Social, and Cultural History* (New York: Oxford University Press, 2012), p. 145.
49. *Republic*, 364b.
50. See E. R. Dodds, *The Greeks and the Irrational* (Berkeley, California: University of California Press, 1951), p. 31. See Bibliography for more details.
51. *Iliad*, Bk. 24. 530 ff., where Zeus had two jars—one filled with good gifts and the other with evil ones. To some men, he dispenses a mixture of good and evil fortune; but to other men he metes out an unmixed collection of bad luck. As to unmixed good fortune, that is reserved exclusively for the gods. See discussion by Dodds, *The Greeks and the Irrational*, pp. 29–32.
52. Sophocles, *The Theban Plays, Oedipus at Colonus*, transl. by E. F. Watling (Baltimore, MD: Penguin Classics, 1947), p. 122.

53. Euripides, *The Trojan Women*, 790.
54. Jasper Griffin, *Homer* (Toronto: Oxford University Press, 1980), sees significant differences between the two epics. In contrast, Walter F. Otto, *The Homeric Gods,* regards the two works as a unified and harmonious whole.
55. Griffin, *Homer on Life and Death*, takes this view of the epic.
56. *Odyssey*, 17.360.
57. Ibid, 1.30 ff.
58. Ibid, 3.270 ff.
59. Ibid, 2.60 ff.
60. Ibid, 24.351.
61. Ibid, 13.292.
62. Ibid, 8.2.
63. Ibid, 4.70.
64. Ibid, 11.130.
65. Ibid, 9.470 ff.
66. Hugh Lloyd-Jones, *The Justice of Zeus* (Berkeley, California: University of California Press, 1971). See Bibliography for details.
67. Lloyd-Jones, *The Justice of Zeus*, pp. 5, 8.
68. Alban Dewes Winspear, *The Genesis of Plato's Thought* (New York: The Dryden Press, 1940), p. 34.
69. Ibid, p. 35.
70. Ibid, p. 40.
71. *Odyssey,* 13.125 ff.
72. The irony of the matter is that when Odysseus wakes up on the shores of his native Ithaca, he thinks that he is somewhere else. So, he curses the Phaeacians, thinking they have deceived him, and prays to Zeus that they be punished for transgressing the laws of suppliants over which he presides. As readers, we know that he is indeed in Ithaca, and that the Phaeacians have been punished already, but not for any transgression.
73. Lloyd-Jones, *The Justice of Zeus*, pp. 5, 8.
74. Ibid.
75. Griffin, *Homer on Life and Death*, p. 4.
76. Simon Weil "The Iliad or the Poem of Force," in Simon Weil, *An Anthology*, edited and introduced by Siân Miles (London: Virago Press, 1986).
77. *Republic,* 390b–c.
78. Ibid, 377d.
79. Ibid, 391e–392a.
80. Ibid, 392a.
81. This view is represented by R. F. Walton, "Hybris," in *Theological Dictionary of the New Testament* (Grand Rapids, 1972) and Ninian Smart, *The Religious Experience of Mankind* (New York: Charles Scribner's Sons, 1969), p. 252, where Zeus is described as punishing the sinner. It has also

been popularized by Thomas Cahill, *Sailing the Wine-Dark Sea: Why the Greeks Matter* (New York: Random House, Inc., 2003), p. 122. This view is rightly challenged by Kaufman in *Tragedy and Philosophy* (Princeton, New Jersey: Princeton University Press, 1968). On *hubris* see N. R. E. Fisher, *Hybris: A study in the values of honor and shame in ancient Greece* (Warminster, England: Aris & Phillips, 1992), and E. R. Dodds, *The Greeks and the Irrational*. See Bibliography for details.
82. *Iliad*, 24: 610.
83. *Odyssey*, 4. 500.
84. The same is true for Tantalus who stole the food of the gods and gave it to mortals; like Sisyphus, he also thought that mortals might escape death. *Iliad*, 11.581 and 11.593.
85. Fisher is nevertheless right to say that *hubris* can and often involves offences directed at other people. Nevertheless, it remains the case that the gods do not punish the *hubristai* because they are interested in punishing wickedness.
86. Aristotle, *Politics*, Bk. IV, 1295b5–11, and Fisher, *Hybris*, p. 23.
87. Fisher, *Hybris*. pp. 7–35.
88. Contrasting the criminality of the rich with the criminality of the poor, gives Aristotle reason to recommend a polity that is dominated by the middle classes, who are neither so rich as to be tempted by great villainy, nor so poor as to be driven to petty crime. In his view, neither the very rich and well endowed nor the very poor and unfortunate are inclined to listen to reason. This is the basis of his defense of the middle class as the stabilizing factor in a decent political order. *Politics*, Bk. IV.
89. Fisher, *Hybris*, p. 36; O. Murray, "The Solonian Law of *Hubris*," in *Nomos: Essays in Athenian Law, Politics and Society*, edited by P. A. Cartledge, P. Millell, and S. C. Todd (Cambridge, 1990).
90. In discussing the Helots in Sparta, Aristotle suggests giving them a small amount of freedom so that they will not commit *hubris* by demanding equal rights with their masters. As the usage of Aristotle illustrates, the concept of *hubris* is very class-sensitive. This explains why Zeus cannot be accused of *hubris*. As Fisher points out in *Hybris*, from the point of view of Zeus, Prometheus's love for humanity is hubristic (p. 248); but all the indignities that Zeus inflicts on Prometheus are not hubristic.
91. *Iliad*, Bk. 5.330ff.
92. Inventing the cruel and sadistic concept of eternal damnation is testimony to the fact the New Testament was not an improvement on the Old Testament, Aquinas notwithstanding. See *Summa Theologica*, III, Q. 46, A. 2, Reply to Objection 3, and III, Q. 47, A. 3, Reply to Objection 1. See also my *Terror and Civilization: Christianity, Politics, and the Western Psyche* (New York: Palgrave Macmillan, 2004), Part I.

93. *Republic* 377 b ff.
94. *Republic*, 377e, 382a–d, G. M. A. Grube translation.
95. Bruno Snell, *Discovery of the Mind: The Greek Origins of European Thought*, transl. by T. G. Rosenmyer (New York: Harper & Row, 1960), see Bibliography for details.
96. Dodds, *The Greeks and the Irrational*, p. 3, claims that Homeric Greece was a *shame* rather than a *guilt* culture. Dodds thinks that blaming the gods was not so much a desire to shirk responsibility, as to save face in a shame culture. The distinction has also been made by Ruth Benedict, *The Chrysanthemum and the Sword: Patterns of Japanese Culture* (Rutland, Vermont: Charles E. Tuttle Co., 1946).
97. Bernard Williams, *Shame and Necessity* (Berkeley, California: University of California Press, 1993), pp. 31–32.
98. I owe this idea to my colleague, classicist Annabel Robinson. This fits with the naturalistic conception of the gods that makes sense to me.
99. Walter Kaufman, *Without Guilt and Justice* (New York: Peter H. Wyden, Inc., 1973).
100. Euripides, *The Trojan Women*, 1210ff.
101. *Iliad*, 19.88.
102. Ibid, 19.135–139.
103. This is why Nietzsche admired the Greeks, and found them much healthier than guilt-ridden Christians, which is one of the themes of his *Birth of Tragedy*.
104. Herodotus, *Histories*, Bk. I. 45.
105. For more on this matter, see my *Terror and Civilization*, Ch. 3, "Ethic of Love."
106. *Timaeus*, 90d.
107. In his effort to make certain that people did not take credit for their good deeds, Augustine ascribed them to the decent of the Holy Spirit in the soul. But if people cannot take credit for their good deeds, how can they take responsibility for their wickedness?
108. *Republic*, 377e.
109. *Lesser Hippias*, 370a ff.
110. Ibid, 370c.
111. Ibid.
112. Ibid, 371e.
113. Ibid, 371e.
114. *Republic*, 377e.
115. A.W.H. Adkins, *Merit and Responsibility: A Study in Greek Values* (London: Oxford University Press, 1962).
116. Ibid, p. 238.
117. Ibid, pp. 210, 242, note 16.

118. Ibid, pp. 259 ff.
119. *Iliad*, Bk. 12:310–320.
120. Adkins thinks that Crito represents the primitive Homeric morality that was destined to be superseded by the supposedly more advanced view of Socrates. But there is little in the way of reflection as to why the Socratic position constitutes an advance. *Merit and Responsibility*, p. 233.
121. *Crito*, 45c–e.
122. When his mother and brothers come to see him at the synagogue, Jesus fails to acknowledge them and points to his disciples as his real family (Mark: 3:31–35; Luke 8:19–21). When an admirer tells Jesus I will follow you, but first I must bury my father, Jesus replies, "follow me; and let the dead bury their dead" (Matthew 8:21–22).
123. Walter F. Otto, *The Homeric Gods: The Spiritual Significance of Greek Religion*, p. 3, says that the religion of Homer contains no "spiritual communion," or "soulful devotion" with the gods.
124. Jane Harrison, *Prolegomena to the Study of Greek Religion* (London: Merlin Press, 1962, 1980), pp. 3 ff. on the dual meaning of "sacrifices." Discussed in Bibliography.
125. See my *Terror and Civilization*, and *Aquinas and Modernity: The lost promise of Natural Law* (Lanham, Maryland: Rowman & Littlefield, 2008).
126. Harrison, *Prolegomena to the Study of Greek Religion*, p. 5.
127. *Iliad*, Bk. 23.175; this point is made by M. I. Finley, *The World of Odysseus* (New York: Penguin Books, 1979), p. 137.

CHAPTER 6

The Tragic Poets Defended

In the *Poetics*, Aristotle discusses the tragic poets in terms of plot, music, structure, and *catharsis*—a therapeutic good cry. Clearly, he does not take them seriously as a philosophical threat. In contrast, Plato regarded the poets as his intellectual opponents, and sets out to destroy them as independent purveyors of truth. With all his philosophical might, one would think he could have easily defeated them intellectually. Instead, he wanted them censored, robbed of their independence, and made into vehicles for the artistic dissemination of whatever might be "beneficial to orderly government."[1] There was something visceral about what Plato referred to as the "ancient quarrel between poetry and philosophy."[2] Plato presented the conflict as a dispute over the competing merits of reason and the emotions as the ruling principle of human life. So understood, there seems to be no contest. One would have to be entirely puerile to decide to follow one's emotions while renouncing reason. If the issue were that simple, there would be no need for Plato to censor the poets. Plato's desire to silence or co-opt them is an indication that they were intellectually powerful and difficult, if not impossible, to refute.

Plato disparages the poets by denying that they write so beautifully because they have a profound knowledge of their subject.[3] Instead, he claims that the poets are "third removed from reality" and are very capable of composing "without knowledge of the truth."[4] In Plato's view, reality is represented by the idea, form, or perfect concept. The craftsman imitates the eternal concept, but artists imitate the imitations, and have no knowledge of the eternal and unchanging; they have no contact with the truth, they merely imitate the fluctuating images in the world. Plato thinks that painting is particularly illustrative of what he means, and that what applies to painting also applies to poetry and tragedy. They are merely imitations without understanding.

Plato recognizes Homer to be the leader of the tragic poets.[5] He is certain that Homer writes about all sorts of things that he knows nothing about—generalship, war, the government of cities, education, and the like. As proof that he knows nothing about these things, Plato argues that we are entitled to ask him what war was ever won by his generalship? What government has he ever contributed to, as Lycurgus did for Sparta? (Notice that, he does not refer to what Solon did for Athens.) And, what education or special way of life did he leave to posterity, as Pythagoras did? (Notice that he singles out an Orphic mathematician as a paradigmatic educator.) Since Homer has bestowed none of these benefits on humanity, it follows that he has no knowledge of them.[6] This argument is not persuasive. People can understand things very well without being able to put them into practice. It is possible to understand the physics of a steam engine without being able to drive one, and vice versa. It is possible to define the concepts of courage or moderation without being either courageous or moderate, and vice versa. Homer was able to shed light on generalship by displaying the poor generalship of Agamemnon without being a general himself.

The idea that art is imitation without understanding is not true even for painting. As an amateur landscape artist, I would concede that art is imitation of the images in the world. But if that were all it was, then photography would have made painting obsolete. In truth, painting contains more than an imitation of the image—it contains also the feeling, mood, or response of the artist to the scene. What is true of painting is even truer of poetry and tragedy. The latter is not an imitation without knowledge. The setting and the characters are an imitation of life, but the whole play has a message. It is a work of intellect. That is precisely the source of Plato's antipathy to the poets. He has no objection to the art—he loves it, and is envious of its power.[7] He has no intention of banishing it; he would like to co-opt it for his own purposes.[8] It is not the messengers to whom he objects, it is the message. He objects to its anti-Socratic perspective—namely, that the soul is not immortal; justice does not prevail in the world; asceticism is nonsense; and death is anathema.

In this chapter, I will reject the Hegelian view of tragedy as the conflict between equally valid moral claims. I will also reject the related claim that

Socrates was a tragic figure. Even though I do not think that all the tragic plays can be subsumed by one formula, I agree with Nietzsche and Walter Kaufmann that tragedy highlights the arbitrary inhumanity of the world, and the ubiquity of innocent suffering.[9] Socrates and Plato reject this view of the world and insist that nothing bad can befall the just man. Sophocles begs to differ. I hope to show that, in the *Philoctetes*, Sophocles presents a portrait of the just man that is both morally and intellectually superior to what Socrates and Plato have to offer.

In general, I agree with Nietzsche that the success of Socratic ideas was the death knell of the tragic sensibility. However, by regarding Socrates as an icon of reason, Nietzsche perpetuates the legend of Plato. Moreover, by dethroning reason, Nietzsche cannot tell us why Socrates must be rejected. One of the reasons for rejecting Socrates is the *hubris* that his ideas encourage. Thanks to Socrates, Western moral thought has been dominated by the ideal of moral autonomy. By applying Bernard Williams' critique of moral autonomy to Socrates, we can see why Neoptolemus in Sophocles' *Philoctetes* provides a morally superior ideal of the just man than the Socratic model championed by Plato.

1   Tragedy as Innocent Suffering

Greek tragedy cannot be understood in terms of *hubris* and *nemesis*—if the latter are understood as crime and punishment, sin and divine retribution. If that is the case, and the suffering was the deserved penalty for sin, then there would be nothing tragic about tragedy. What makes these stories tragic is that admirable and principled men and women are the victims of the caprice of fate, the malice of the gods, the injustice of tyrants, or the callous indifference of the world to their merits. The ubiquity of innocent suffering is antithetical to the belief in cosmic justice. The tragic point of view does not assume that the world is made to suit human beings; it is based on the realization that the world is indifferent to what human beings value most—love, compassion, kindness, and justice.

The concept of innocent suffering is difficult to accept, even for a hard-nosed realist such as Aristotle. In Aristotle's view, tragedy is that distinctive art that is capable of both arousing *and* banishing the emotions of fear and pity—fear that what happened to the protagonist could easily happen to us; pity that the suffering experienced by the protagonist is undeserved; and relief that we have been spared the dreadful misfortunes of the protagonist.[10] As Aristotle rightly points out, there is nothing tragic about an evil man "falling from happiness into misery," since a man like that deserves his fate, he will fail to arouse either fear or pity.[11] This is why the protagonist must be good.[12] Without goodness, the action of the plot from happiness to misery would not be tragic; only undeserved misfortune can arouse pity. Nevertheless, Aristotle considered the suffering of a *totally* innocent person to be "odious." He claimed that we would be unlikely to identify with a perfectly innocent protagonist. So, to avoid the "odious" spectacle of innocent suffering, Aristotle surmised that the miserable fate of the protagonist must be brought about by *a flaw* in his or her character, or at the very least, a dreadful error in judgment.[13] Hence Aristotle's influential theory of the "tragic flaw." Supposedly, a tragic plot can only move us to fear or pity by presenting us with someone like ourselves—neither perfectly good nor totally evil. The trouble is that we would be hard pressed to find a "tragic flaw" in Oedipus, Antigone, Heracles, or Hippolytus.

Again and again, Aristotle appeals to Sophocles' *Oedipus* as a paradigmatic tragedy with a most artfully constructed plot. Oedipus is a young man of intelligence, courage, and integrity. Contrary to modern perceptions colored by Freud, Oedipus is not guilty of lusting after his mother or killing his father. When an oracle reveals what fate has in store for him, he is alarmed and dismayed. Believing that his adoptive parents were his biological parents, he leaves his home to make sure that he would never be in a position to transgress against the parents he loved. On his journey, he encounters a group of men who try to push him off the road. He fights back in self-defense and kills one of the men—who turns out to be the king of Thebes and his biological father. When he reaches Thebes, Oedipus solves the riddle of the Sphinx, and in so doing, frees the Thebans from the abject terror of a monster. He is made king of Thebes, and given the queen of the deceased king along with the kingdom. Unbeknown to him (or her) Jocasta is his biological mother. Oedipus is happy, wealthy, smart, and beloved by his people. When a plague descends on Thebes, an oracle maintains that the blight against Thebes would be lifted only when the murderer of the previous king is discovered, and duly punished. If Oedipus had a "tragic flaw" it was his love of truth and justice. He is determined to discover the truth and find out who the murderer was. He leaves no stone unturned, and even as the evidence begins to point to him as the murderer, he does not abandon the search. There were several opportunities in the play where Oedipus could have put an end to the search for the identity of the killer, but he does not. He goes so far as to threaten the herdsman (who knows the truth) with death for refusing to speak. Oedipus was determined to discover the truth no matter how dreadful, because he was certain that it was the only way to save Thebes from the pestilence. Jocasta, beginning to suspect the truth, tries to belittle the oracles and tells Oedipus that they are nonsense, which should be ignored. She is being very hypocritical, since she was the one who had ordered her newborn son fettered and left to die for fear of that fateful oracle so long ago. When Oedipus hears about the death of his beloved father who brought him up, he is grateful that he had nothing to do with his father's death; but he wonders if he did not indirectly cause his death by his departure. He longs to go home and see his mother and console her in her grief, but does not dare to do so for fear of the oracle. If there is a flaw in his character, it is his obsessive concern with oracles—a very common trait, if Herodotus is to be believed. The fact is that Oedipus was innocent, but he nevertheless took full responsibility for his conduct—and so did Jocasta. Oedipus blinds himself, and Jocasta kills herself. The upshot of the matter is that Oedipus did nothing to deserve this fate.[14] The chorus in the play wonders if the gods brought Oedipus down just because he was the darling of fortune. For the tragic poets, as for Homer, the gods are a reflection of life itself—ill fate easily befalls decent people.

Sophocles makes an elaborate case for Oedipus' innocence in *Oedipus at Colonus*, where Sophocles presents Oedipus after his banishment from Thebes by Polynices and Eteocles (his sons) and Creon (Jocasta's brother)—all hungry for sovereign power. Oedipus is blind, bitter, and in rags; he is an exile, and a suppliant cared for by his daughters, Antigone and Ismene in Athens, where Theseus, convinced of his innocence, gives him refuge. Again, Oedipus denies his guilt saying that none of these actions were of his choosing or devising, but does not shirk responsibility for his actions. He argues that he is the victim of malicious fortune and of the curse on his father's house—a curse that will continue to haunt his children. The injustice suffered by the noble Oedipus is so great, that even the gods are moved by it. So much so, that Athens, the city that prides itself on its love of justice, will be blessed for receiving Oedipus' request for sanctuary, instead of shunning him as a source of pollution. The gods also devised a special death for Oedipus—unlike that experienced by any other man. At the appointed time, a voice called him and led him to the appointed place where he died without a grave and without pain or suffering.

Sophocles' *Antigone* is another iconic tragedy in which the protagonist has no tragic flaw. The noble, pure, and devoted, Antigone suffers terrible injustice at the hands of Creon, the tyrant of Thebes. After Oedipus discovers the horror of his fate, his sons ally themselves with Creon (Jocasta's brother) to banish their father. Polynices, the elder brother takes the throne, but the younger brother, Eteocles, gets the support of Creon and the Theban people, banishes Polynices, and takes his place on the throne. The banished brother makes some friends among the Peloponnesians and returns to avenge himself against the usurper. In their fatal struggle over the Theban throne, the sons of Oedipus (and brothers of Antigone) kill one another. Instead of wisely laying this dark chapter of Theban history to rest, Creon decrees that the younger brother (Eteocles) is to be buried with honors as a patriotic defender of his city; meanwhile, the older brother (Polynices) is to be left unburied, a prey for dogs and vultures. Antigone cannot abide the dishonor to her brother and covers his body up with earth when the guards are napping—knowing that the penalty for disobedience to Creon's decree is death. When a messenger (one of the guards) tells Creon what happened, Creon rails against him and accuses him of having sold his soul for money and threatens him with death. The guards uncover the body once again and remain vigilant all night, staying out of the way and on a hill to avoid the stench. When Antigone returns to cover the body once again, she is arrested and brought to Creon, who condemns her to death.

Hegel regarded *Antigone* as the iconic tragedy. For Hegel, tragedy is a clash of two conflicting and incompatible claims where there is right on both sides. In the conflict between Creon and Antigone, Creon represents the claims of the city and its existing order, whereas Antigone represents the claims of the family.[15] There has been in contemporary studies of tragedy an inclination to follow Hegel in regarding tragedy as a clash of equally valid, but incommensurable moral claims—but without Hegel's optimistic dialectic, whereby the antagonists are eventually reconciled.[16] For example, Alasdair MacIntyre claims that *Antigone* is about the conflict between "the demands of the family and the demands of the *polis*."[17] For him, what is at issue is the conflict between the justice of the city (as represented by Creon) and filial obligation (as represented by Antigone). Antigone and Creon represent "rival moral truths," which cannot be reconciled. MacIntyre thinks that tragedy is about "different virtues" making rival and incompatible claims upon us. We have to recognize "the authority of both claims;" choosing one virtue over another does not "exempt me from the authority of the claim which I choose to go against."[18] Therein lies the tragedy: whatever I choose I do wrong.

This analysis does not ring true. The conflict between Creon and Antigone is calamitous, not because there is right on both sides, but because Creon is a tyrant in the classic sense of the term—an arbitrary ruler, who cares more about his power and authority than his city.[19] He claims that as head of state, he must be obeyed in all matters big and small, whether he is right or wrong; and he counts all disobedience to his commands as treason to the city. His patriotic claptrap equates love of Thebes with submission to his power.[20] Sophocles makes it clear that Antigone is innocent but Creon is not, because the painful remorse of Creon is at the heart of the play. In a flash of insight, he rushes to reverse his edicts by suspending the death sentence against Antigone and ordering a proper burial for her brother. Alas, his epiphany comes too late. At the end of the play, Creon recognizes that his pride and stubbornness have led to not only to the death of Antigone, but also to the death of his son (Antigone's fiancé), the suicide of his wife, and the contempt of his people. If Creon represented a virtue as valid as Antigone, then, it would not make sense for him to be repentant at the end of the play. In short, tragedy is not the clash of two equally just claims as Hegel, MacIntyre, and others claim. Nor is the tragic clash between Antigone and Creon a function of the historical disparity between the ideal and the actual that is destined to be overcome by history, as Hegel's optimistic dialectic would have it. The disparity is inescapable because history is not progressive, and tyranny invariably makes the disparity much worse than it has to be.

I am not denying that Antigone had a terrible choice, or that human beings are often confronted with terrible choices. However, the choices before her were not *morally* equal. The choice she made was morally admirable. The tragedy rests in the terrible death she had to endure as a result of her virtue. Tragic characters are also heroic when they know that the honorable choice will lead to their doom. They are heroic because they do not delude themselves into thinking that they will be rewarded in the beyond. What makes them heroic is that they face the harsh reality of existence and the finality of death with courage and without illusion.

The idea that tragedy is a conflict between equally valid moral claims does not stand up to scrutiny. What are the equally valid moral choices that Oedipus had to endure? His choice was between living with the harsh truth, or living a lie. He was too noble to live a lie; he chose the truth, and suffered the consequences. What about Agamemnon? Can we seriously believe that he was a tragic figure confronted by a terrible conflict between the personal and the political, between saving his daughter and sailing to Troy?[21] Was slaughtering his daughter the only route to glory in the Trojan War? Would it not have been more reasonable to keep the daughter and find a more honorable vehicle for glory than a war over an unfaithful wife? In short, none of these tragedies are about two choices that involve equal moral claims, or equal goods.[22]

2   HEGEL: WAS SOCRATES A TRAGIC FIGURE?

Nothing illustrates the Hegelian view of tragedy more clearly than Hegel's view of Socrates as a tragic figure. Hegel's defense of Socrates is ingenious because, unlike Plato's defense, it does not ignore the historical facts that made sense of the case for the prosecution. Hegel admitted that Socrates was the harbinger of the ruin inflicted on Athens by Alcibiades, Critias, and Charmides. Hegel set out to resolve the mystery of how this divinely inspired man, this towering figure in the history of the West, can be implicated in treachery and criminality writ large? Hegel concocted a defense of Socrates that is even more fanciful than Plato's enduring legend. He claimed that Socrates was a tragic figure. But the tragedy was not that of one man, it was the tragedy at the heart of the history of the West.

Hegel thought that Socrates pushed the conflict between individual conscience and the community to a dramatic new level.[23] The result was dreadful. Some of his students lost all connection with the conventional morality of their society. Liberated from the only morality they knew, the notorious students and intimate friends of Socrates— Alcibiades, Critias, and Charmides, wreaked havoc on their community. In this way, Socrates was "the ruin of Athens." In other words, when it came to corrupting the young, Hegel found Socrates guilty as charged. However, Hegel did not think that Socrates corrupted his students intentionally. He thought that Socrates discovered a universal morality that springs from the heart—a morality that surpasses not only the limits of the Athenian *Sittlichkeit*, or conventional morality, but also the limits of *any* conventional morality. Socrates discovered the voice of *conscience* that lay dormant in the face of the collective unconscious. He taught his students to question tradition and live by their own lights. Far from introducing an arbitrary or subjective morality, Hegel believed that Socrates discovered an "I" deep in his soul that was not just a private or personal voice.[24] It was the voice of the universal or transcendent. However, this universal Socratic "I" came into conflict with the Athenian "we." The two could not coexist, and Socrates was destroyed—but he was not silenced. Through his death, the West got a glimpse of the "universal Idea" or the "true good."[25] This is why Socrates was "the great historic turning point." So, how could the "true good" be the "ruin of Athens"?

Hegel's explanation is that Socrates had to destroy the old morality in order to introduce the new, universal morality—a higher morality that transcended the narrow parochialism of his city. However, by destroying the sentiments that held his students fast to their community, Socrates removed the only viable restraint on their conduct; he robbed them of the only morality they knew. Unfortunately, he did not succeed in inculcating the new morality into their hearts. He was unable to impress upon them the universal morality he had discovered. Bereft of the only morality they knew, they were sunk. This led them to behave like beasts with no moral restraints of any kind. In this way, Socrates unintentionally led them astray. Hegel's apology for Socrates amounts to saying that Socrates did not purposely corrupt them—he hoped to replace one morality with a higher morality, but could not finish the job. This is why Hegel considers Socrates a tragic figure who was both guilty and innocent at the same time. He was guilty because he was the ruin of Athens, and innocent because he did not intend the destruction he wrought.

Hegel's apology for Socrates is imaginative, but flawed. Why should introducing the higher morality require wiping the slate clean? Is it not more plausible for the higher morality to build on an existing foundation? How can the higher morality involve a dissent into lawless criminality? If the new morality leads to criminal anarchy in practice, then maybe it is not a higher morality after all. Nevertheless, Hegel insists on this scenario, which is a recurring theme in his philosophy of history.[26] For Hegel, this descent into criminality is not unique to the new morality introduced by Socrates, but is equally true of the higher moralities introduced by Christianity, the Enlightenment, and the French Revolution: every triumph of the higher, true, or universal morality soaks the world in blood.

Hegel admits that there is a flaw in this higher morality. He concedes that it is vulnerable to the seductions of a terrible subjectivity—a subjectivity that tends to absolutize itself and make private demands in the name of the universal. This is why it is the ruin of collective life and happiness. Hegel associates it not only with the ruin of Athens, but also with the Reign of Terror in the wake of the French Revolution. It is simply befuddling how every introduction of *Moralität*, this supposedly exalted universal morality, ends up sowing so much moral depravity. How can we continue to believe in the pure, pristine perfection of an idea when it manifestly causes so much harm? How can goodness be the source of so much evil? It is time to stop making excuses for the mayhem, authoritarianism, and imperialism that universalistic and monistic ideals invite.

The problem lies at the heart of the new morality itself. Hegel admits that the new morality brings bloodshed in its wake, but he refuses to contemplate the possibility that it is deeply flawed, and is therefore not a "higher" morality after all. The fact is that Hegel and Socrates share a radically autonomous or inward looking conception of morality that is rooted in solitary individuals who imagine themselves to be receptacles for the voice God. In the *Phaedrus*, Socrates claims to be divinely inspired.[27] He tells us that the soul of the philosopher "approaches to the full vision of the perfect mysteries, and he alone becomes truly perfect... and draws nigh to the divine, he is rebuked by the multitude as being out of his wits, for they know not that he is possessed by a deity."[28] Are there no limits to the self-righteousness of the divinely inspired? With all the violence and mayhem that this morality has caused, and continues to cause, it is time to question the limits of what philosophers call moral autonomy.

Hegel and Socrates are united in their obstinate denial of the grim flaws displayed by this new morality. How can Socrates know that the "I" deep in his soul represents the true and the just, despite the conduct of his students, and the outrage of his fellow citizens? What makes Hegel think that the "I" deep in the soul of Socrates is universal? How can the assertions of a solitary individual be declared universal when they leave his closest companions befuddled? How can such claims to universality be distinguished from mad delusions? Indeed, how can Socrates, the "vortex of Western civilization," be distinguished from a megalomaniac?

3   Sophocles: Why True Nobility is not Socratic

For Plato, Socrates was the paradigmatic model of the just man. In the *Philoctetes*, Sophocles presents Neoptolemus, the son of Achilles, as the classic exemplary of moral integrity. The question is: which portrait is more credible? And, who is more admirable, Neoptolemus or Socrates? I believe that there are good reasons for thinking that the portrait of the just man painted by Sophocles is not only more credible, but also more admirable than the Socratic one.

In contrast to Homer and the tragic poets, Socrates and Plato declared that it is impossible for a good man to suffer evil because the world has a deep moral structure, which ensures that justice will always triumph—in the final analysis. For Plato, the just man is the happy man, even if he were unjustly condemned to death. Like Socrates, Plato wanted the injustice of the world to be mitigated by the justice of the gods in the beyond. At the same time, he wanted justice to be chosen for its own sake, or for the effect it has in terms of the inner harmony and wellbeing of the soul, and not just for its consequences in terms of social honor and reputation, or rewards in the afterlife.

Plato managed to make a very convincing argument in the *Republic* about the inherent value of justice for the soul; his argument could have been successful if only it were qualified. What he should have said is that under normal circumstances, the just man is the happy man, and that justice is its own reward. However, politics, unanticipated circumstances, and bad luck, can make life hell. In these circumstances, justice has a cost; and the just man is the one willing to pay the cost. Had Plato been satisfied with this more realistic thesis, the argument in the *Republic* would have been more persuasive and the truth presented by the poets would not have been such a threat. For political reasons, Plato was determined to extinguish the fear of death, in order to create an invincible army. It did not occur to him that a plethora of such fighting forces would not be a boon to humanity. To support his argument, he had to link justice to rewards beyond the grave. If justice yields happiness, inner harmony, or psychic wellbeing, as well as rewards in the beyond, then it is indeed more profitable under any circumstances. It follows that there are *never* any circumstances in which there is a cost to pay or to suffer for being just. It follows that there are no tragedies where the noble option involves a terrible price. Sophocles begs to differ.

In the *Philoctetes*, Sophocles reveals that he has a richer, deeper, truer, and more authentic conception of the self and of the just man.[29] Philoctetes, a Greek warrior at Troy, beloved of Heracles, inheritor of his formidable bow (which never misses), accidentally steps into a sanctuary of a god and is viciously attacked by the terrifying snake that guards it. The result is a dreadful open wound on his leg that never heals, and produces endless and perpetual profusions of puss, whose stench is so intolerable to others that the Greeks decided to forgo the advantages of his unrivalled bow in the battle against Troy, and abandoned him on a remote and secluded island. There he lives alone in a cave, hunting for his food with the help of his bow, and enduring continual pain from his wounded leg. It is a classic example of tragedy understood as innocent suffering. Sophocles makes it clear that injustice is the natural state of affairs in which the gods are an integral component. While human beings decry this state of affairs, they also contribute to it, especially in war. As Neoptolemus says, "war spares the villain and dooms the decent man."[30] He adds that the gods are no help, since they "turn back hopelessly bad men from the mouth of hell but trample the righteous."[31]

In the play, a seer declares that the Greeks cannot win the battle against Troy without Philoctetes and his bow. So, the intrepid and shameless Odysseus, who initiated the exile and isolation of Philoctetes in the first place, convinces Neoptolemus, son of Achilles, to go with him to the island where Philoctetes was abandoned, and trick him into giving up his coveted bow or coming to Troy to insure the victory of the Greeks. Neoptolemus tells Odysseus that, like his father, he "loathes the smell of deceit" and would much rather deliver Philoctetes by force than fraud: he would rather "fail with honor than sink into victory."[32] In contrast, Odysseus is a man who wants to win at any cost.[33] He convinces Neoptolemus that neither force nor persuasion will work, and that deceit is the only stratagem. Neoptolemus succumbs to Odysseus' appeal to necessity. Having gained the trust of Philoctetes, Neoptolemus betrays him and takes his bow. After betraying Philoctetes, Neoptolemus is filled with self-loathing: "Everything's disgusting when a man denies his essential self, his acts violating his understanding."[34] He is tormented by his treachery. Unable to live with himself, he returns the bow and tries to convince Philoctetes to come to Troy. Eventually, he succeeds—but only with the help of Heracles.

What is interesting about the play is its focus on the self and its connection to justice—a theme that is generally associated with Socrates and Plato. In betraying Philoctetes, Neoptolemus feels that he has betrayed his true self, which is identical with acting honorably or justly. It is often believed that there is a difference between acting honorably and acting justly. Supposedly, the former belongs to a morality of shame, while the latter belongs to a morality of guilt. Scholars generally agree that Greek culture was a "shame-culture" as opposed to a "guilt-culture." On the whole, guilt is a matter of passing judgment on oneself, whereas shame fears the judgment of society. Guilt culture focuses on the inner world of intention, whereas shame culture focuses on the harm done to others. Guilt worries about character and temperament, whereas shame worries about reputation. Guilt is autonomous because the standard to which it adheres is understood either as the voice of reason or God, coming from within; it follows that the moral conclusions to which the agent arrives are independent of the opinions of others. In contrast, shame is heteronomous because it depends on the judgment of others in society. Shame does not rely on fear of divine punishment, or the punishment of one's conscience, but on social disgrace. In short, the morality of shame prizes honor, which is connected to public opinion, whereas the morality of guilt aspires to justice, which is independent of public opinion.

Scholars almost invariably regard guilt as a richer and more developed ethical sensibility, in contrast with which shame seems primitive. However, Bernard Williams has challenged this progressive account of human moral development.[35] He has argued that it is a mistake to believe that the Greek morality of shame is "crudely dependent on public opinion." As Williams explains, the "other" before whom one feels shame is not just any representative of public opinion, but an "internalized other." The latter is someone with whom one can identify, and whose opinion one shares, and respects. In other words, shame involves a complexity that transcends a shallow conventionalism. Moreover, shame does not merely look to the "outer world of harm and wrong;" it does not simply look to actions, but also to intentions, desires, and dispositions, because one can feel shame not only for harm done, but also for one's thoughts, desires, and inclinations. This means that shame does not concentrate only on the reactions of others, or on being found out, but also on one's "ethical identity."[36]

I believe that Sophocles' portrait of Neoptolemus is a good illustration of what Williams means. Neoptolemus is ashamed of himself for betraying Philoctetes. He feels that he has betrayed his true self. He cares about his honor, which includes his "ethical identity," as Williams would say. He is determined to regain his standing, not in the eyes of Odysseus, who praises him for his treachery, but in his own eyes—even if Odysseus and the rest of the Greek army condemn him. Neoptolemus becomes himself and reclaims his dignity when he finally turns against the seductive Odysseus and says: "You're a shrewd man Odysseus, but your words are foolish."[37] Then he adds, "It is better just than clever." Then he says: "I lied. I'm ashamed of that. I want to make amends." When Odysseus reminds him that the cost of his integrity will be the wrath of the Greek army, Neoptolemus says, "I'm more afraid of being unjust." Odysseus responds ominously, saying: "Your justice will face our power."[38] Neoptolemus understands that there is a *cost* to pay for his integrity, and he is willing to pay it. In other words, there are times when being just has a cost; and the honorable man is one who is willing to pay the cost. From that point on, the play changes, and Neoptolemus, not Odysseus, has the upper hand and leads the action. Now, he is true to himself, takes hold of his destiny, and becomes his father's son—the son of Achilles who hated lies more than death. Achilles (not Odysseus or the Greek army) is the "internalized other" before whom Neoptolemus could feel shame.

In classic Hegelian fashion, Alasdair MacIntyre regards the play as a tragic clash between the interests of the community (as represented by Odysseus) and the interests of the individual (as represented by Philoctetes).[39] He regards the tragedy as the conflict between two equal but incompatible goods. The assumption is that tragedy presupposes the anti-Socratic rejection of the unity of the virtues. However, this misses the mark.

There is no reason to think of the virtues as incompatible. Nothing prevents a person from being at once kind and fair, honest and moderate. Loyalty is the one problematic "virtue" that clashes with others. In the *Philoctetes*, Neoptolemus must choose between loyalty to the Greek troops at Troy, and his love of honesty and truthfulness. Loyalty has a spurious status among virtues. It is the highest virtue in the mafia. This is why it is not a *bona fide* human virtue, but is more often associated with dogs. In human beings, loyalty is a problem when those to whom we are loyal make unreasonable, unjust, or dishonorable demands—as Odysseus (and the Greek army he represented) made on Neoptolemus. The choice before Neoptolemus is not between two equal virtues. It is a choice between the treachery demanded by the troops on one hand, and honesty on the other. In choosing honesty over deceit, kindness over cruelty, Neoptolemus decides to be true to himself, and to his sense of honor, no matter what the cost. The play would have been tragic had the army killed him for his choice. As it turned out, Neoptolemus avoids tragedy only with the help of Heracles. Philoctetes is the tragic figure in the play, since he is the victim of innocent suffering.

Neoptolemus is not a tragic figure; he is a heroic figure because he accepts the fact that there are situations in which there is a high cost to pay for being just, and he is willing to pay the cost—the ultimate cost. Neoptolemus is his father's son; like his father, he knew what death meant. Achilles and his son did not romanticize death. In the *Odyssey*, when Achilles speaks with Odysseus in Hades, he asks about his beloved son. Odysseus details the exploits of his son—all the Trojans he has killed without suffering a scratch; he praises the valor, grandeur, and beauty of Neoptolemus.[40] In the *Philoctetes*, Sophocles provides an account of Neoptolemus that would have been even more satisfying to

Achilles, because Sophocles reveals that the son cared as much about his honor as did his father. For Achilles, that would have been more important than the number of Trojans who fell before Neoptolemus' sword. After all, the whole of the *Iliad* was driven by Achilles' injured sense of honor.

In Plato's *Apology*, Socrates compares himself to Achilles.[41] He says that like Achilles, he prefers death to dishonor. Some scholars have objected to the comparison on the ground that Achilles was concerned with honor, whereas Socrates was concerned with justice.[42] In other words, Achilles belonged to a shame morality, whereas Socrates represented the emergence of a guilt morality.[43] However, if Bernard Williams is correct, as I think he is, the difference between the appeal to honor and the appeal to justice is not mutually exclusive. Nevertheless, there is a significant difference between Socrates on one hand, and Achilles and Neoptolemus on the other. Unlike Socrates, Achilles and his son take death seriously. In contrast to Socrates, Achilles and Neoptolemus choose the honorable course in the absence of *any* reward. This is what makes them *heroic*.

Socrates is neither tragic nor heroic. He is not tragic because he was not an innocent victim with a dreadful plight he could not avoid—he was given every chance to get out of town, or to stop radicalizing young Athenians. He is not heroic because he does not take death seriously. On the contrary, he spoke confidently to his judges about his death, and the people whose company he hoped to enjoy in the afterlife. He bid his judges be cheerful about his death because he was confident that no evil can come to a good man, either in life or in death, since there will always be justice in the end. Socrates goes to his death serenely because he anticipates a reward for his righteousness. Socrates refuses to acknowledge that there is no guarantee that justice will always triumph. In other words, Socrates denies that there is ever a price to pay for justice. For him and Plato, justice is always the most profitable course of action. It follows that there are no difficult choices, let alone tragic ones. Sophocles knew better. His portrait of the just man is not only more realistic than Plato's, but also more admirable.

In the *Republic* Plato proposes a thought experiment in which he sets out to prove that a perfectly just man who has a reputation for injustice and is treated with contempt by others, will nevertheless be a happy man. This is not just a theoretical investigation, but also a portrait of Socrates as perceived by Plato.[44] What is true of the just man in Plato's thought experiment is true of Socrates. For Plato, the just man's estimation of himself is unshaken by the fact that others regard him as unjust and treat him with contempt. The opinion of others has no bearing whatsoever on his moral considerations because his moral sensibility has its source in an inner light:

> I think it better, ... that the majority of mankind should disagree with and oppose me, rather than that I, whom am but one man, should be out of tune with and contradict myself.[45]

It follows that his moral conclusions are totally independent, not only of public opinion in his society, but also the majority of mankind. On what grounds can we assume that his inner light is the light of truth? Plato expects us to accept Socrates' innocence in spite of public opinion. Yet, he gives us no reason why we should accept Socrates' view of himself and not that of others, especially when there is so much evidence that explains why others were distraught by his conduct. In discussing Plato's thought experiment, Bernard Williams rightly wonders how the just man of Plato's thought experiment can be distinguished from a "deluded crank."[46] Williams' observations apply to the real life of Socrates, even if he does not say so.

What makes Socrates a deluded crank is that his confidence in his righteousness remains unshaken, despite the evidence against his teaching, and the understandable ire of his fellow citizens. What makes Socrates a deluded crank is his crude self-satisfaction and lack of concern for the harmful effects of his teaching on others.[47] Williams rightly claims that the inward focus of a guilt ethic can be at odds with the "proper concern for others."[48] Williams' point is that this egoistic approach to the ethical life, which has been so highly praised in the history of moral consciousness, leaves much to be desired, because it is compatible with a callous indifference to the suffering of others. Although Williams does not mention Socrates, he is the paradigm of this heartless "withdrawal from humanity" that is the hallmark of the inward focus of the moral life and its egocentric pre-occupation with the self.

Socratic self-assurance, confidence in his inner light, is intimately connected to the conviction that the human psyche is the microcosm of the universe. How did Socrates and Plato arrive at this hypothesis? They developed seductive arguments that had the appearance of profundity. They surmised that by looking into the nature of the self, they could uncover the structure of the universe. In this way, they gave a new twist to the Greek dictum, "know thyself." In the traditional understanding, the dictum was a warning to human beings not to forget their limitations, and fall into *hubris*. At the hands of Socrates and Plato, the dictum was transformed into an elevation of humanity to the microcosm of the universe. In this way, looking into oneself would be the key to uncovering the secrets of the universe. Just as the rule of reason is the condition of justice and harmony in the soul, so the rule of the "world soul" insures that harmony and justice prevail in the cosmos. Unhappily, the idea that we can understand the cosmos by looking into ourselves is a form of self-assertion that can only hamper the search for truth.[49] Like the quest for dominance, self-assertion in philosophical speculation distorts the relationship between the knower and the world, and turns the philosophical quest into wishful thinking. In my view, Socrates' brazen assertions have neither served the philosophical quest for truth, nor the cause of morality.

In contrast to Socrates, Neoptolemus does not turn inward. He does not assume that his soul is the mirror of the universe. He does not focus merely on his own integrity; he is concerned about harm done to others. It is for the sake of Philoctetes, and for the sake of his honor, that Neoptolemus decides to confess his treachery, return the bow, and make amends. Neoptolemus is under no illusion that the gods reward the righteous and punish the wicked. He expects no reward either in this world or in the next. He knows that there are times when there is a cost to doing the honorable thing, and he thinks that the cost is worth paying, because he could not live with himself otherwise. For all these reasons, Sophocles presents a portrait of the just man that is both more realistic and more admirable than the one provided by Plato's legend of Socrates.

4   NIETZSCHE: DID SOCRATES DEFEAT TRAGEDY?

Friedrich Nietzsche is the first major philosopher in the history of the West to repudiate Socrates and declare him guilty—not for the treasonous conduct of Alcibiades or for the reign of terror led by Critias and Charmides, but for loving the truth. He dubbed him the "Pied Piper of Athens" and the "mystagogue of science" who led the whole of Western civilization to its ruin by seducing it into falling in love with truth and regarding its pursuit as the highest endeavor in the world.[50] By identifying Socrates with the Western devotion to truth, reason, and science, Nietzsche unwittingly contributed to the legend of Plato. However, Nietzsche was no friend of truth. He accused Socrates of shaking the confidence of the Homeric Greeks by robbing them of their instinctual vitality. Socrates took these heroic men of action and turned them into uncertain, confused, vacillating creatures, totally paralyzed by introspection. Such were the results of the defeat of instinct and the triumph of reason and science.[51]

Just how did the "Pied Piper of Athens" accomplish his sly feat of seduction? Nietzsche's answer is that Socrates convinced his fellow Athenians that he was in possession of the only true and rationally defensible morality. This was in stark contrast to their own inability to give any account of their ethos or way of life. Naturally, his claim was intriguing. But that's not all he promised. He also claimed that this rational morality was characterized by the identity of truth, beauty, and goodness. This was at odds with the tragic sensibility in which the real or true was the furthest thing from the human conception of the right, the good, or the beautiful, because the world was indifferent to what human beings held dear.

The upshot of the matter is that they were gullible enough to believe him. But in Nietzsche's estimation, what he promised them was impossible. Even Plato, with his prodigious philosophical talent could not prove the identity of the true, the good and the beautiful. And since there is a legend according to which Plato died with a copy of Aristophanes under his pillow, Nietzsche surmised that Plato died laughing, supposedly because he discovered that there was no such thing as a rationally defensible universal morality, and that the identity of truth, beauty, and goodness is an oxymoron. In other words, Plato died laughing at the swindle that Socrates managed to pull off. The loser in this grand jest was Western civilization, which was launched on an endless quest for knowledge that eventually became indistinguishable from faith in a universal morality and the worship of science.

Despite its radical facade, Nietzsche's portrait of Socrates is not a dramatic departure from the conventional view. It contains the same paradox. On one hand, Socrates is celebrated as the "vortex of Western civilization," a lover of truth, in the name of which he disrupted the stupor of convention, and sowed doubt with his questions and critical acumen.[52] On the other hand, Socrates opened the door to Christianity, which is far from being a champion of reason and science. Moreover, Nietzsche regarded Christianity as something sinister, and saw reason as something cold, calculating, and unlovely. So, how could someone who opened the door to Christianity (with all its irrational beliefs) be a "mystagogue of science"? The answer is: by a sleight of hand, intended to show that Christianity is devoted to truth.[53]

What sets Nietzsche's portrait apart from the conventional view is that Nietzsche was not a friend of truth or science. Long before the discovery of the atom bomb, Nietzsche anticipated that humanity's love affair with science would lead to disaster.[54] For Nietzsche, this was the fruit of Socratic culture, whose love of truth and worship of science knows no bounds. Nietzsche declared that the West has arrived at a fork in the road; it must choose between the deadly truth and the life-giving illusion. Nietzsche recommended the life-giving illusion on the ground that every living thing needs an atmosphere of myth and illusion in which to thrive.

Nietzsche was right to oppose a culture totally devoted to either science or religion. Unlike other "beguilements of culture",[55] such as art, literature, or music, science and religion, especially monotheistic religion, perceive themselves as being in possession of the one and only truth—the whole truth, and nothing but the truth. This makes them autocratic, intolerant, domineering, and destructive. As I will argue in the next section (7.6), it is not necessary to demonize reason and truth, as the postmoderns who followed Nietzsche have done. It suffices to maintain that reason cannot yield a single truth, because the latter is neither simple nor singular.

Even though Nietzsche is to be admired for having the courage to celebrate Homer and embrace the tragic perspective on life and the world, his response to the tragic reality of existence leaves much to be desired. As Albert Camus has pointed out in *The Rebel*, Nietzsche was in love with "the absurd," understood as the inhumanity of the world. He made a god out of it.[56] In contrast to Nietzsche's radical affirmation, Camus thought that the appropriate response was to revolt against the absurd, not to worship or imitate it. Like the tragic poets, Camus thought that human beings should define themselves in stark contrast to the cold inhumanity of the world. Like the tragic poets, Camus' advice is to forge ahead, because we cannot remain paralyzed by the fact that our fate is almost never in our hands. Like the tragic poets, Camus displayed a defiant spirit in the face of the injustice of the human condition.[57]

Finally, Nietzsche was right to declare that Socrates defeated the tragic point of view. However, that defeat was historical not intellectual. Plato could triumph over the poets only by silencing and censoring them. My quarrel with Nietzsche is that having dethroned reason, he could not explain why the Socratic world-view was inferior to the Homeric one, or any other one for that matter—apart from his personal preference.[58] He could not give us compelling reasons why Homer and the tragic poets are intellectually and morally superior to Socrates and Plato. Nietzsche was wrong to dethrone reason; he was wrong to underestimate the human need for truth. He was wrong to ally reason and truth only with science. He was wrong to ally science only with mastery and the disenchantment of the world. He was wrong to think that Socrates—a man who is famous for his trances, a man who communes with otherworldly beings—is a rationalist and a champion of reason, science, or truth.

5   Tragedy, the Bible, and Crime Fiction

Tragedy understood as innocent suffering is foreign to us because we are heirs of the Biblical tradition and therefore demand justice from God. When we suffer, we think like Job's friends, "you must have done something to deserve all this misery!" When Job proclaims his innocence and his righteousness, his "friends" balk. We are the friends of Job; we are the post-Homeric people who demand cosmic justice. So did Job; he learned his lesson the hard way. When, at the end of his trials and tribulations, he appealed to God asking him why he deserved so much suffering in view of his righteousness, God stormed out of the whirlwind saying, who do you think you are you little bit of nothing? Where were you when I "laid the foundations of the earth?" (Job: 38:4). Where were you when I made the morning stars sing, devised snow and hail, sea and land, darkness and light, life and death? And Job said, "Behold, I am vile; what shall I answer thee? I will lay my hand upon my mouth" (Job: 40:4). Job is silenced. He knows his friends are wrong, but he also knows there is nothing he can do to right the world. The innocent will suffer if it pleases God. Abject humility and resignation is the only correct posture in the face of this awesome power.

The book of Job is the most honest book in the Bible, because it is modeled on Homer's *Iliad* both in its wisdom and its structure. Like the *Iliad*, the action takes place on two levels—on earth and in heaven. As with Homer, we not only hear the conversation between Job and his friends on earth, we also hear the conversation between God and Satan in heaven. We know that God afflicts Job with the death of all his children, festering boils all over his body, and much more, for no other reason than to win a bet with Satan. So we know that Job has no vices, not even a "tragic flaw." We also know that there is no possibility of reconciliation between Job's claim ("I am innocent") and God's claim ("To hell with you; I am God.")

Christians are the friends of Job. In the face of Job's declaration of innocence they resort to all sorts of obfuscations to prove the justice of God ("everyone is guilty of something; we have no idea what God has in mind; we just can't fathom his infinite wisdom in view of our finitude; it must be for the best; etc."). In the Biblical narrative, knowledge, human wisdom, and understanding must be demoted and turned into the source of human arrogance and the root of evil. Eve is punished for her love of knowledge. Yet, Eve did nothing wrong; it is only natural for a creature with intelligence and curiosity to desire knowledge and understanding. It was God who was unjust in prohibiting her and Adam from the pursuit of knowledge. Being the friends of Job, Christians cannot bear to impute any injustice to God. A way out of the dilemma had to be found. The quest for knowledge had to be demonized if God's punishment of Adam and Eve was to be justified. Knowledge had to be associated with power (not with virtue) in order to make it sinister. Not surprisingly, the theme of "forbidden knowledge" has played a dominant role in the history of the West.[59]

It may be argued that the Socratic dictum that "virtue is knowledge" was transformed into the postmodern motto that "power is knowledge." In this way, the dilemma of *Genesis* is resolved. Eve's pursuit of knowledge is understood as a quest for power, and not the desire for understanding.[60] Once wickedness is attributed to Eve, the wickedness of God is avoided. By attributing evil to humanity, the unjust punishment of Adam and Eve becomes the manifestation of cosmic justice. However, from Socrates to Christianity the efforts to erase the tragic reality of existence are doomed to failure. The punishment of humanity for the "sin of Eve" is a classic manifestation of innocent suffering, and a testimony to the unassailability of the tragic point of view.[61] In other words, neither Socrates nor Christianity could erase the veracity of the tragic poets.

It is a testimony to the grandeur of ancient Athenian culture that tragedy was a popular literary genre. When Greek tragedies are contrasted with the popular crime dramas in books, films, and television in our time, we get a glimpse of the vast difference between our mentality and theirs. To grasp what is at issue, we need to ask the question that my colleague Nils Claussen asked: what does a popular literary genre such as Victorian crime fiction tell us about a society?[62] What does our addiction to crime fiction tell us about how we differ from the ancient Greeks? As a form of social entertainment, tragedy presents its audience with social, political, and religious criticisms of the world of men and gods. It confronts its audience with harsh realities, not bromides.

In contrast to tragedy, our popular crime genre caters to our longing for cosmic justice; since the police invariably catch the bad guys, crime fiction satisfies our desire to see evil punished; it gives us the satisfaction of knowing that God is in his heaven and all is well with the world. It reassures us that the juridical order of our society works in tandem with cosmic justice; even when the police fail to catch the villain, he somehow manages to fall off a cliff, or into a canyon. The result is a stupefying form of entertainment that lends support to the *status quo* as a replica of divine justice.

The two genres—tragedy and crime fiction—also contain different understandings of human guilt. Unlike Greek tragedy, our Christian civilization locates evil in human nature, not the world. Our fascination with crime fiction has something to do with the relief we are inclined to feel, not only for escaping the fate of those victimized by the ubiquity of crime, but also especially for our extreme good fortune in not being criminals ourselves. But for the grace of God, we could easily be the perpetrators of these terrible crimes. Therein rests the catharsis derived from crime fiction. In Greek tragedy, human wickedness is almost never gratuitous.

The anti-tragic perspective endorsed by Socrates betrays a puerile desire to escape from the terrors of existence. It indulges a Pollyannaish view of life. This view projects human desires onto the world. It refuses to accept the fact that the world was not designed to suit us. Distinguished classicists such as E. R. Dodds unquestioningly assume that the idea of cosmic justice "represents an advance on the old notion of purely arbitrary divine powers."[63] But why? Why is it more sophisticated to attribute innocent suffering to an almighty God who acts purposively, if incomprehensibly, than to attribute human suffering to an indifferent universe? The idea that the suffering will be for some grand divine purpose that will be revealed "in the end" does not make it any more palatable.

I am not suggesting that the tragic point of view prevents people form behaving badly—human beings have always been capable of that. I am claiming that the tragic sensibility prevents people from justifying their brutality in high-minded or moralistic terms, because they are doing the business of God. It prevents them from claiming that they are divinely inspired, and are acting in the name of the divine. It prevents human beings from being self-righteous about their cruelty, because they are improving humanity. It prevents them from conducting their savage wars and bloody insurrections with a clear conscience. It gives them a capacity for empathy with their enemies that is almost incomprehensible to modern men. It makes people painfully aware of the fickleness of fate and the vagaries of fortune. It encourages a realistic assessment of their conduct that allows them to acknowledge their crimes, repent, and make amends. These virtues have been eclipsed by Socratic religion, which is why it can hardly count as an advance in human self-understanding.

Notes

1. Plato, *Republic*, 607 d–e, transl. by G. M. A. Grube (Indianapolis: Hackett Publishing, 1974).
2. Ibid, 607b.
3. Ibid, 598e.
4. Ibid, 599a.
5. Ibid, 595c, 598d.
6. Ibid, 599c–600b.
7. Ibid, 607d.
8. Ibid, 607e.
9. I am indebted to Walter Kaufmann, *Tragedy and Philosophy* (Princeton, New Jersey: Princeton University Press, 1968). However, Kaufmann's view is much more complex and difficult to summarize, although I attempt to do so in the Bibliography.
10. Aristotle, *Poetics*, ch. 6, 1449b 25.
11. Ibid, ch. 13, 1453a 5.
12. Ibid, ch. 15, 1454a 20. This is the case even if the protagonist is "a woman or a slave," which Aristotle thinks is a challenge for the playwright because women are "inferior" and a slave is a "wholly worthless being."
13. Ibid, ch. 13, 1453a 9.
14. Kaufmann, *Tragedy and Philosophy*, p. 209.
15. Hegel, *Philosophy of Right*, transl. by T. M. Knox (New York: Oxford University Press, 1952), paragraph 166.
16. For example, Alasdair McIntyre, *After Virtue: A Study is Moral Theory* (Notre Dame, Indiana: University of Notre Dame Press, 1984); Martha Nussbaum, *The Fragility of Goodness* (New York: Cambridge University Press, 1986); and Peter Euben, *The Tragedy of Political Theory: The Road not Taken* (Princeton, New Jersey: Princeton University Press, 1990). See details in Bibliography.
17. MacIntyre, *After Virtue*, p. 132.
18. Ibid, p. 143.
19. In *The Fragility of Goodness*, Nussbaum follows Hegel's view of *Antigone* as a conflict of equally valid claims, or "spheres of value," she nevertheless admits that Antigone is the more sympathetic figure, pp. 67–68.
20. This might explain the effort on the part of ultraconservative interpreters to rehabilitate Creon and blame Antigone as a radical, headstrong girl with no understanding of statecraft. But Sophocles has already painted a picture of Antigone in *Oedipus at Colonus* that is the furthest thing from radical, or disobedient. She is selflessly devoted to her blind father, and advises him to abide by the customs and laws of the land in which they are exiles.
21. Euben, *The Tragedy of Political Theory*, p. 274.

22. MacIntyre, *After Virtue*, pp. 142–143. Sometimes, MacIntyre confuses a clash of virtues with a clash of goods. In my view, these are different things. While a clash of virtues is most unlikely (except where loyalty is concerned, as I argue later), a clash of goods is commonplace. However, it is not tragic—most are trivial: eggs or cereal for breakfast? More significant is a choice between work that provides more money, or more fulfillment. Luckily, not all the goods in life clash.
23. Hegel, *Lectures on the History of Philosophy*, 1840, 3 vols., translated by E. S. Haldane (London: Routledge and Kegan Paul Ltd., 1892, 1955), Vol. I.
24. Ibid, p. 385.
25. Ibid, p. 402.
26. Georg Wilhelm Friedrich Hegel, *The Philosophy of History* (1822), transl. by James Sibree (New York: Prometheus Books, 1999), pp. 223, 241. When Hegel speaks about the Greeks as the defenders of Western liberty, he means the Athenians; Hegel was no friend of Sparta. He was rightly critical of its severity and coarseness. He abhorred its treatment of the Helots (the indigenous people who were enslaved to work the land).
27. *Phaedrus*, 238c, 244a–c, transl. by R. Hackforth, in *The Collected Dialogues of Plato*, edited by Edith Hamilton and Huntington Cairns (Princeton, New Jersey: Princeton University Press, 1961).
28. *Phaedrus*, 249c–d.
29. Sophocles, *Philoctetes*, transl. by Armand Schwerner, in *Sophocles I*, edited by David R. Slavitt and Palmer Bovie (Philadelphia: University of Pennsylvania Press, 1998).
30. *Philoctetes*, 341.
31. Ibid, 350.
32. Ibid, 70 ff.
33. In Plato's *Lesser Hippias*, 369c ff., transl. Benjamin Jowett, in *The Collected Dialogues of Plato*, op. cit.
34. *Philoctetes*, 715.
35. Bernard Williams, *Shame and Necessity* (Berkeley: University of California Press, 1993), pp. 92–93.
36. Ibid, p. 96.
37. *Philoctetes*, 1003.
38. Ibid, 1013.
39. MacIntyre, *After Virtue*, pp.144–45.
40. *Odyssey*, 11.539.
41. Plato, *Apology*, 28 b–d, transl. by G. M. A Grube, in *Plato: Five Dialogues* (Indianapolis: Hackett Publishing Co., 2002).
42. Euben, *The Tragedy of Political Theory*, p. 219, does not discuss the distinction between a shame and a guilt morality, but implies it by insisting on the distinction between honor and justice.

43. It is worth noting that Plato never abandons the importance of shame, which plays a large role in the *Laws*, as a way of regulating the moral conduct of ordinary people.
44. *Republic* 361a–c.
45. *Gorgias*, 482c, transl. by W. D. Woodhead, in *The Collected Dialogues of Plato*, op. cit.
46. Williams, *Shame and Necessity*, p. 99.
47. I have argued elsewhere that this cold indifference to the suffering of others has been a feature of the Christian preoccupation with self-salvation. See my discussion of John Bunyan, in *Terror and Civilization* (New York: St. Martin's Press, 2004), Part I.7.
48. Williams, *Shame and* Necessity, p. 97.
49. It may be argued that the Socratic position does not differ substantially from the claim that man is the measure of all things, as attributed to Protagoras. However, as asserted by Protagoras, this claim is compatible with the tragic view of existence, because it suggests that man alone has a sense of right and wrong, good and evil. It does not involve the fallacy of imputing to the universe our own characteristics. In contrast, the Socratic view entails the sort of self-absorption that is an obstacle to the search for truth. In *The Problems of Philosophy* (New York: Oxford University Press, 1959), Bertrand Russell attributes to Protagoras the self-assertiveness that I attribute to Socrates—see ch. xv, "The Value of Philosophy." I am sympathetic with his sentiment, but I have no idea why he does not apply it to Socrates.
50. Friedrich Nietzsche, *The Birth of Tragedy and The Genealogy of Morals*, translated by Francis Golfing (New York: Doubleday & Co., 1956), p. 93.
51. Nietzsche, *Birth of Tragedy*, pp. 84–85.
52. Ibid, p. 94.
53. This sleight of hand was perfected by Thomas Aquinas' claim to have reconciled the Bible with the Greek philosophy of Aristotle. See my *Aquinas and Modernity: The Lost Promise of Natural Law* (New York: Rowman & Littlefield Publishers, Inc., 2008), ch. 2.
54. Nietzsche, *Birth of Tragedy*, p. 94.
55. Ibid, p. 109.
56. Albert Camus, *The Rebel*, translated by Anthony Bower (New York: Vintage Books, 1956), p. 76.
57. This defiant attitude is in stark contrast to the inclination to "surrender" to the will of the almighty and incomprehensible God, which is the response of Judaism, Christianity, and Islam.
58. Nietzsche's attempt to abandon truth and dethrone reason undermines his own insights. Nevertheless, this is the reading of Nietzsche that is popular among the postmoderns. For an excellent articulation of it, see Alexander Nehamas, *Nietzsche: Life as Literature* (Cambridge, Mass.: Harvard University Press, 1985).

59. Roger Shattuck, *Forbidden Knowledge: From Prometheus to Pornography* (New York: St. Martin's Press. 1996).
60. Oswald Spengler, *The Decline of the West* transl. by Charles Francis Atkinson (New York: Alfred A. Knopf), 2 vols., vol. 2, p. 309. Spengler wrongly believed that the decline of Magian culture (i.e., Christianity) leads to the Faustian inclination to replace the Socratic "Knowledge is Virtue" with "Knowledge is Power." For Spengler, the latter is the motto of the civilization of the West in its condition of decline. In my view, Spengler is wrong; Christianity involves the demotion of knowledge through its association with sin, pride, and the quest for power, which were all attributed to Eve, just for her intellectual curiosity.
61. Christianity makes the doctrine of cosmic justice its official view—but this should not be taken too seriously. Nietzsche made the mistake of taking it seriously, which led him to conclude that Christianity destroyed tragedy. Contrary to Nietzsche, I argue in my *Terror and Civilization*, op.cit., that Christianity does not succeed in destroying tragedy. On the contrary, attention to the texts reveals that Christianity is rich in tragic gloom.
62. Nils Clausson, "Crime, Criminality and Class in Three Sherlock Holmes Stories," a paper delivered at the *International Conan Doyle Symposium* at the University of Regina, November 8–10, 2008.
63. Dodds, *The Greeks and the Irrational*, p. 34.

CHAPTER 7

Socratic Mischief

Scholars from Hegel to Gregory Vlastos and John Burnet have regarded the Socratic conception of the divine as a significant "advance" in the history of human thought.[1] The new conception of the divine endorsed by Socrates and developed by Plato did indeed pave the way for the triumph of the Abrahamic religions in general, and Christianity in particular. However, the triumph of Christianity over the pagan religions of Greece and Rome was no boon to human civilization. It did not inaugurate an age of peace, freedom, or tolerance—not to mention Enlightenment. The dreary signs were already visible in the Socratic conception of the divine, which became the cornerstone of Plato's dystopia. In this chapter, I catalogue the bleak implications of Socratic religion, which continue to plague humanity. The irreproachable character of the divine cannot account for innocent suffering. It can only contribute to the exponential growth in the burden of human guilt. Moreover, the valorization of an irrational faith accounts for the emergence of a dark and menacing authoritarianism. And the confusion of *hubris* with piety fuels political extremism. Together, all these elements have made (and continue to make) politics more radical, self-righteous, intolerant, and war mongering. As if all this is not enough, the monism of Socratic thought has inspired the nihilism of postmodernity. I argue that for all its shortcomings, postmodernity is the justified awareness that there is something rotten at the heart of Western thought. I defend a pluralistic conception of the right and the good—which should be distinguished from multiculturalism.

1   The Burden of Guilt

In changing the nature of the gods, Socrates changes human self-understanding, especially in relation to evil. Homer's gods were manifestations of the natural world and shared the latter's cold indifference to questions of morality. Once the gods are turned into paragons of virtue, evil can no longer be attributed to them. The unassailable goodness of the gods robs human beings of their innocence. As a result, people begin to see themselves in a new light. They can no longer regard wrongdoing as a temporary lapse in judgment. Instead, they must regard their unjust acts as a direct product of the congenital defectiveness of their humanity—evil must be rooted in human nature. By following Socrates in demanding the absolute and inviolable goodness of the gods, Plato attributed to humanity more than its share of evil in the world. As a result, humanity must bear a colossal burden of guilt. This emphasis on human wickedness undermines the eudaimonistic ethos, which was supposed to be the hallmark of Plato's philosophy. Instead, the terrors of Orphism become the foundations of morality. Moreover, exagerrated conceptions of guilt encourage feelings of pollution and impurity, and the corresponding need for catharsis and purification. The ubiquity of such feelings creates a social atmosphere in which priests, shamans, and other swindlers assume positions of power and importance. They promise absolution from guilt, magical potions, and other indulgences to circumvent the punishments of the afterlife—for a fee of course.

Plato managed to escape the difficulties of the Christian problem of evil, but he did not avoid the doctrine of original sin. In the *Timaeus*, Plato opines that the origin of the world as we know it is likely to have been the product of the Demiurge or master-craftsman. The latter does not create the world *ex nihilo;* he arrives on the scene to find a primal chaos that he orders according to the principles of reason—the ideas or forms. The Demiurge is benevolent and wise, but he cannot create a perfect world due to the limitations of matter.[2] Unlike the god of *Genesis*, he is not omnipotent, and is therefore not mired in the perplexing problem of evil.[3] Nevertheless, human beings get the short-end of the deal. The Demiurge shapes the souls of the new (Socratic) gods from the light and lovely stuff at the top of the celestial bowl. But when it comes to shaping the souls of mortals, all he has left is the sludge at the bottom of the bowl. So, the moral shortcomings of humanity are a function of the limitations of the inferior matter from which they are made. In this way, something akin to the fiction of original sin is born.

1 THE BURDEN OF GUILT

Why is the fiction of original sin so grotesque? After all, is it not a true myth? Is it not a truthful account of the human propensity to evil? Not really. The idea of original sin robs human beings of the freedom to choose between good and evil because it deems them fallen, or created from the ashes of the Titans, or made from the sludge at the bottom of the celestial bowl, or some such tale. This allows them to escape from responsibility. It perpetuates the "lie in the soul" that Plato accused Homer of promoting. It is a lie that leads people to believe (as Christians from Augustine to Martin Luther have believed) that human beings are "in bondage to sin." This has the effect of undermining morality rather than supporting it. Besides, it flies in the face of the doctrine of cosmic justice that it was intended to uphold. If human beings cannot help being wicked, then it can hardly be just to punish them. Moreover, the focus on human depravity leads to an obsession with the evil within. No one understood the cost of this perpetual introspection as well as Hegel. As much as he appreciated the deepening of the soul that Christian introspection involved, Hegel also recognized that it was not without its dangers. Indeed, he acknowledged that it allows Satan to triumph in the world.[4] Hegel did not explain what he meant, but it seems to me that one can only brood over the evil within for so long, then an external source of evil must be found, confronted, and if possible, destroyed.

Muslims must have recognized the need to vent their hostility against this psychic tormentor when they created a theme park where pilgrims at the Hajj in Mecca can stone Satan to their heart's content. Since it is only make-believe, it is not likely to be satisfying to everyone. This is why the focus on the evil within is invariably transformed into a struggle against Satan's representatives in the world. In Christianity, the result was the torture of heretics, the burning of witches, and the killing of pagans, Jews, scientists, women, and freethinkers. The history of Islam was somewhat more moderate, but in our time it has become more radical and horrific. Those who defend Islam today by claiming that *jihad* is a struggle against the evil within, and not the killing of infidels, fail to recognize the intimate connection between the introspective focus on the evil within and the need to destroy the representatives of Satan in the world. Ironically, the preoccupation with the evil in the soul allows evil to triumph in the world. Yet, the former Pope Benedict XVI emphasized the importance of focusing on introspection understood as recognition of evil within the heart as the key to human piety and goodness.[5]

My criticism of introspection is not a rejection of the reflective life. It is a rejection of the brooding, self-immolating focus on the ubiquity and power of evil, that penetrates the soul, and from which there can be no escape—at least not without divine intervention. This dark psychic self-understanding is likely to create a sense of entrapment, hopelessness, and despair that are deleterious to the self-confidence required to act well in the world and to make amends for our injustice. In other words, the conviction that wrongdoing springs directly out of one's innermost self has a crippling effect. By taking responsibility for the consequences of our wrongdoing without assuming that the act is a manifestation of our insurmountable inner wickedness, the Homeric point of view prevents a collapse into a paralyzing self-hatred, which may hinder the ability to compensate for our misdeeds. Besides, if good conduct is antithetical to our nature, then education in virtue is a process of despoiling, domesticating, and denaturing—it is a process against which we must rebel if we are to be true to ourselves. This could easily lead to developing an attachment to evil as the mark of our authentic identity. Signs of this pathology are evident in Sigmund Freud, Friedrich Nietzsche, and others, as I have argued at greater length elsewhere.[6]

2   AUTHORITARIANISM UNHINGED

The loss of innocence is intimately connected to a shockingly radical authoritarianism, which is intended as a remedy for our congenitally flawed humanity. The apparently paradoxical claim that virtue is knowledge but cannot be taught is the cornerstone of this authoritarianism. I have argued that the Socratic paradox is not all that paradoxical. When the virtue of the many is distinguished from the virtue of the few and the latter is allied with wisdom and presented as a special gift of the gods, the paradox evaporates. Virtue is knowledge that cannot be taught because it is a gift of the gods that is given only to the few.

Plato, Alcibiades, Phaedrus, and others thought that Socrates was "divinely inspired."[7] Socrates promoted the idea with his long and legendary trances in which he supposedly received divine messages.[8] He regarded his own philosophical mission as a "service to the gods."[9] He had a special "divine sign" that was decisive in guiding his conduct. For example, he appealed to the silence of the voice during his trial to confirm his conviction that his defiance and his choice of death over exile were right.[10] All these eccentricities were integral to his authority.

Socrates had the honor of sharing in divine wisdom, which is necessary for genuine virtue. Once virtue is understood as a divine gift, then it makes sense to say that it cannot be taught—at least not indiscriminately to anyone, even someone with sufficient rationality. Yet, Plato and Socrates maintained human beings cannot live well together unless those who are privy to divine wisdom get to rule. They alone are fit to guide their fellow human beings—not by persuasion and consent, as Pericles guided his fellow Athenians—but in a style devoid of understanding—a style akin to the way that parents guide their children. The latter follow the parents not because of *what* they say, but because of *who* they are. The inferior submits to the authority and wisdom of the superior as one submits to a god. That was Plato's dream society as outlined in the *Republic*. In the *Laws*, citizens were taught to believe that the laws were established by the gods. In fairness, Plato also emphasized the importance of a preamble to every law, explaining what good it aims to achieve and what evil it aims to avoid, but this is no substitute for persuasion. The laws themselves were not a matter of deliberation.

This unhinged authoritarianism is at the heart of the supreme puzzle of the career of Socrates: How could someone who devoted himself to the "care of the soul," fail so spectacularly with his closest associates? I have argued against giving the "care of the soul" a purely moralistic, liberal, and individualistic gloss. On the contrary, the care of the soul is first and foremost a political program of hitherto unimaginable authoritarianism. It is the care of inferior souls by the divinely inspired. This authoritarianism belongs as much to Socrates as to Plato. It is as integral to the early dialogues as to the late ones. It is the sort of doctrine that flatters those who think that they are chosen to guide humanity to its proper destination. It is very likely that the evils of Critias and Charmides and the treachery of Alcibiades were ideologically inspired. Socrates taught them to think of themselves as having the true knowledge of the political craft, and therefore destined to guide the inferior many to their proper end.

The fact that the inferior ones had no appreciation of the gift being bestowed on them by the superior few is par for the course. Their opinion is irrelevant. Politics requires specialized knowledge. The Socratics knew what was best for others. Their expertise was comparable to that of a physician—they were physicians of the soul. The gulf between them and ordinary humanity was akin to the gulf between a shepherd and his sheep, or the doctor and the patient. As we have seen (1.6 and 3.7), the doctor has the right to amputate an arm or a leg to save the patient, even against the latter's will. Moreover, this special knowledge is a divine gift, which cannot be taught.

It is time to recognize that Socrates was no liberator of the mind, but quite the contrary—he was the architect of a frightful authoritarianism, which became a reality in the Christianized Platonism that engulfed

Europe during the nightmarish reign of the Catholic Church.[11] A direct pipeline to divine wisdom is at the heart of the Socratic conception of political authority. This close alliance between the divine and those who wield political power has been a popular trope of Abrahamic religions. From Moses and St. Paul to the Catholic popes and the Ayatollah Khomeini, all these pretenders have followed Socrates in appealing to the divine source of their wisdom as the basis of their moral and political authority. Endowing political authority with divine sanction makes it as unquestionable as it is intrusive. The Socratic understanding of politics as the "care of the soul" allows the most private aspects of the lives of citizens to become the business of the state. The result is Plato's dystopia as imagined in the *Laws*, where the law deals, not only with concrete injuries and injustices that ought to be redressed, but also with private matters that include sodomy, extra-marital sex, adultery, homosexuality, and the like.[12] Plato's assault on private life is the logical result of the Socratic understanding of political authority as the "care of the soul." Interestingly, this intrusive conception of politics is with us still—not only in devout Muslim countries, but also in the United States, which imagines itself to be a beacon of freedom and modernity.

3   Turning Hubris into Piety

As we have seen (5.5), *hubris* is boastful arrogance that leads people to be oblivious to their limitations, compare themselves with the gods, and imitate or act like gods among mortals. In contrast, piety consists of knowing one's place, eschewing grandiose ambitions, extremism, and excess. Piety is the opposite of *hubris*. Socrates transforms the concept of piety when he turns the gods into moral models for human emulation (2.4). He thinks that this alliance of religion and morality will lend the latter some formidable support. Unhappily, the result of this alliance has been the opposite of what Socrates anticipated. Far from dampening the human propensity to *hubris*, the moralization of the divine encourages a conception of piety as sharing in the projects of the gods (2.5). In this way, mortals identify their own projects, plans, and goals with rendering service to the deity. This allows them to fancy themselves as the instruments of the divine on the Earth. Socrates made it clear to the jury that he saw his own mission in that light.[13] In the face of the most gargantuan obstacles, catastrophes, hostility, and opposition, such men are undeterred. Come what may, they are brimming with resolute conviction and self-righteousness. They make a virtue out of their arrogance and call it piety.

The Socratic redefinition of *hubris* as piety is a recipe for political disaster. It encourages the kind of *hubris* that leads to great villainy because it allows those who believe that they have a special intimacy with the divine—which is to say, people like Socrates and his students, to behave like gods among men. It invites them to imitate the Master Craftsman of the cosmos in shaping and ordering the human world according to the ideas to which they alone have access—as if other human beings were mere stuff to be shaped, manipulated, and organized according to a single vision.[14] At the hands of Socrates, such *hubris* acquires the aura of benevolent righteousness and loses its association with grand villainy.

Ever since Socrates, religion has justified its existence in terms of lending support to morality. The opposite has been the case. Once the divine is characterized by unassailable goodness, those who presume to know the divine are tempted to do its bidding. Judaism, Christianity, and Islam are belligerent religions because they act for God and fight his battles. We continue to live in the grip of the militant zealotry of these religions. In contrast, polytheism made no moral claims. To its credit, it did not confuse *hubris* with piety; as a result, it did not pervert morality, or endorse the senseless slaughter of unbelievers or heretics. In contrast, monotheism, which is the dark flower of Socratic religion, has soaked the earth in blood. What it has inspired is not ordinary wickedness filled with shame and self-loathing—but villainy cloaked in self-righteous moralism.

4 Socrates, Enlightenment, and Imperialism

The mischief of Socratic religion became manifest in Europe when the Catholic Inquisition transformed Plato's dystopia into historical reality. When the arrogance, injustice, and lies, could be endured no longer, the system imploded from within. The wars of religion that tore Europe apart in the sixteenth and seventeenth centuries finally led to the recognition by the Enlightenment thinkers that Christianity has played a very pernicious role in the politics of Europe. They realized that religion thrives on ignorance and fear, so they celebrated reason in the hope that reason will lead to a better society. Naturally, they took a strong stand against priestly power; and managed to rid Europe of priestly tyranny. So, there is no doubt that the Enlightenment was spectacularly liberating on the domestic front. It was no mean achievement to end the gloom of theocratic rule. Nevertheless, Enlightenment philosophers made a critical error. They made a god out of reason and science; they assumed that scientific rationality was the single, supreme good, and that nothing evil could come from it. They failed to anticipate the war machines, the death factories, and the atomic bomb. They thought that reason could bring political order, freedom, and peace based on rational concord. They ignored the limits of rational consensus. They dreamed of a world without enemies. They dreamed of hegemonic power that excludes legitimate alternatives. They moralized politics, and turned all political conflicts into conflicts of good and evil, just as Christianity had done before them.

It is a mistake to compare the European Enlightenment with the Greek enlightenment in the middle of the fifth century, when the Sophists emerged on the scene. The latter taught that the traditions, morals, and myths that we inherit from previous generations are not eternal, unchanging verities that are cast in stone. They are something to be examined, criticized, rejected, or modified. The Greek Enlightenment opened up possibilities. By declaring that "man is the measure," they sent the message that there were untapped prospects, opportunities, and potentialities. According to Plato, Socrates was confused with the Sophists, and became a scapegoat for the champions of the traditional norms and conventions. Like the Sophists, Socrates was a critic of Athenian politics and religion. Like the Sophists, he distinguished between nature and convention. But unlike the Sophists, he believed that, being divinely inspired, he had access to the one true rational moral and political order that is in accordance with nature. The European Enlightenment was the heir of Socrates.

Instead of allowing reason to serve a plurality of human possibilities, the Enlightenment philosophers followed Socrates in thinking that the right and the good is singular and that those who are rational will come to the same conclusions and pursue the same ends. By positing the singularity of the good, they reproduced the Socratic and Christian traditions in secular form. They displayed the same evangelical spirit, and the same crusading proclivities. Not surprisingly, the Enlightenment did not dampen the appetite for conquest or colonialism.[15] It did not transcend the singular conception of truth that would continue to be the basis of the desire to rule the world. On the contrary, the West became convinced that it must rule the world, not in the name of divine revelation, but in the name of reason. This explains why the age of Enlightenment was also the age of European colonialism.[16] The latter was euphemistically understood as the "white man's burden." The idea that the West is obligated to spread its superior culture to all mankind continues to inspire American foreign policy.

It is time to loosen the grip of Socratic delusions on the self-understanding of the West. It is time to abandon the understanding of the history of the West in terms of a glorious trajectory that begins with the magnificence of Hellenism and proceeds to the sublimity of Christianity as a marvelous blend of Hellenism and Hebraism, Athens and Jerusalem.[17] This supposed blending is a fiction, because Hebraism is not the completion or perfection of Hellenism, but its demise. It would be more accurate to say that the values of the West have their origin in Socrates, were brought to their logical conclusions by Plato, radicalized by Christianity, and endowed with an aura of respectability by the Enlightenment. Unhappily, the Enlightenment failed to transcend Socratic authoritarianism because it failed to make a sufficiently radical break with his monism and universalism. In short, it was a valiant effort that liberated the West from priestly rule—an accomplishment that cannot be underestimated—but its benefits to the rest of humanity have been negligible, if not altogether destructive.

5   Postmodern Nihilism

All its shortcomings notwithstanding, postmodernism is the recognition that there is something deeply flawed at the heart of Western civilization—in particular, its moral chauvinism, universalism, and absolutism invite colonialism. I am sympathetic to the anticolonial spirit of postmodernism, even if I cannot endorse its nihilism. For all its apparent radicalism, postmodernism has not transcended the universality of the Socratic tradition, because it imagines its nihilism to be a universal and final truth. Moreover, this nihilism is itself a byproduct of Socratic culture, as I will explain.

As we have seen, the religion of Homer did not revolve around dogmas, beliefs, or faith. It was fanciful, but it did not require belief in the miraculous, irrational, or impossible. It did not require faith in all sorts of supernatural phenomena that are antithetical to lived experience. In contrast, the religion of Socrates—with its insistence on the immortality of the soul, release from the cycle of re-birth and death, and the rewards and punishments of the afterlife—depended on beliefs that had no connection to lived experience. Socrates bequeathed to us a culture in which faith is paramount. However, a culture that depends on faith is precarious. When people no longer believe in the dogmas that tax credulity, the edifice collapses, because there is nothing other than faith in the indemonstrable to keep it alive. When a culture puts all its eggs in the basket of faith, and the basket is revealed to be a worthless mirage, the culture is left destitute. Christian culture is a case in point. No one understood this better than Nietzsche. When God is dead, when faith is destroyed by unbelief, the faithful are left with nihilism, which is not to be confused with atheism. It is possible to be an atheist without being a nihilist. Nihilism is born of disenchantment. A nihilist is someone whose whole life revolved around faith in God; and when that faith is shattered, life becomes tasteless, insipid, worthless, and without purpose or meaning.

Nietzsche wanted desperately to affirm life and avoid nihilism despite the death of God. Ironically, it is the postmodern disciples of Nietzsche who manifest this nihilism most vividly in our time. Postmodernism has a nihilistic streak because it is born of disenchantment with modernity—understood as the Enlightenment project with its faith in reason, truth, science and human progress. Kant defined modernity as a "task" to lift humanity out of puerility and superstition toward freedom, rationality, self-understanding, and self-reliance. Following Michel Foucault, postmodernists are disenchanted with this modernist project. They do not believe in progress. They doubt that there is such a thing as free agency; they suspect that the free and rational individual is a fiction of the liberal imagination; they regard the self as shaped by power. They are not enchanted by reason; they are convinced that it is a scam of power that lends the latter hitherto unsurpassed authority.

Postmodernists should not be confused with the neo-Marxists or Critical Theorists of the Frankfurt School—Theodore Adorno, Max Horkheimer, Herbert Marcuse, and Jürgen Habermas. The latter claim that the Enlightenment project was noble in its inception, but has gone astray, or has been highjacked by nefarious capitalist forces. In contrast, postmodernism questions the soundness of the project itself. It rightly rejects the historical trajectory toward a single universal human order as a ploy of colonialism and oppression. However, it goes too far in adopting Nietzsche's rejection of truth and reason in favor of myth and illusion. Nietzsche thought that Socratic culture, by which he meant a culture steeped in the virtues of reason and science, has brought us to the brink of self-annihilation. As mentioned earlier, we are at a fork in the road and must choose between the deadly truth on one hand, and the life-giving illusion on the other. Nietzsche bids us choose the life-giving illusion. The question is: Which illusions are life-giving?

Nietzsche preferred Homeric to Socratic culture. He thought of cultures as the creation of extraordinarily creative individuals. Their appearance is a function of the "will to power." So, when the postmodern followers of Nietzsche ask: What is truth? Their answer is that there is no truth independent of "will to power" and the triumphant myths that people believe at any given point in history. Of course, the "will to power" is notoriously ambiguous. It may refer to military might, or it may refer to the seduction of ideas through literature, philosophy, religion, or even science. For Nietzsche, Socratic culture is seduced exclusively by science and scientific rationality. Following Nietzsche, postmodernists repudiate scientific rationality.

One of the most candid versions of this postmodern posture appears in Paul Veyne's book, *Did the Greeks Believe in Their Myths?* His answer to this question is: of course they did, because every age believes in its myths since there is no truth outside or apart from the myths of any given society. Veyne tells us that the myths of every society are inseparable from their "interests" and "programs." Since there is a plurality of interests, programs, forces, or powers, there is also a plurality of truths in history.[18] For Veyne, these programs emerge spontaneously out of the "constitutive imagination," which builds "successive dream palaces, all of which have passed for truth."[19] Every age has its myths or its reality, in which it naturally believes. The Greeks believed in their myths as much as we believe in ours. For Veyne, one "program" is not truer, or more just than any other. They are simply different programs with different interests. He goes so far as to say that there is no difference between the Nazis and any other form of imperialism. Moreover, it is useless, hopeless, and meaningless to fight against any of these programs because they are like earthquakes, and it makes no sense to fight against nature.[20] He assures us that every program will "go on creating as many victims as the ideologies that exclusively rouse our indignation."[21] He tells us that his dog does not wonder what he ought to do, and that we should not wonder either. There are lots of questions that he does not want us to ask—such as, how can we be happy? How can we organize our society to make it more just? Unlike Veyne's dog, people ask these questions, and they are willing to go hungry to achieve intangible things such as justice and freedom.

Veyne does not want us to think. The trouble is that we are thinking beings; so asking us not to think is fighting against our nature. We are nothing like his dog. Veyne does not agree. He thinks that "most times have not exhibited self-doubt and have not asked such questions."[22] Nietzsche also thought that before Socrates came along and corrupted them, the Greeks did not ask such questions. Veyne is echoing Nietzsche who thought that, prior to Socrates, the Greeks believed in their heroes and their myths; they had no self-doubt. Apparently, they were real men, which, in Nietzsche's estimation, are men of action, not thought. This is a widely held assumption, even by the admirers of Socrates who have no use for Nietzsche. The assumption is that Socrates introduced the Greeks to the quest for truth and the radical questions it involves. Supposedly, it was Socrates who taught them how to think. I beg to differ. The Greeks did not need Socrates to teach them how to think. Euripides was much more critical of Greek society than Socrates and his fawning aristocratic admirers. Unlike Euripides, Socrates was not critical of slavery, or of the savage wars of the Greeks.

Veyne tells us that the Greeks believed in their myths to the extent that they served their "interest."[23] Veyne denies that "programs" can ever be divorced from or come into conflict with the "interests" they serve.[24] Why not? Because he declares by fiat that "truth" or "ideology" mean the same thing as "interest" and therefore the two cannot come into conflict with one another. This is the position that Plato attributes to Thrasymachus in the *Republic*—namely, that there is no such thing as justice independent of power. Those in power make the laws that further their own interests, or the interests of their class or group; and that is what passes for justice. As Socrates rightly points out, those in power are not always successful in furthering the interests of their group. As Socrates maintains, injustice "causes factions and hatred," whereas "justice brings a sense of common purpose and friendship."[25] In this way, it is possible to distinguish between better and worse policies, even if we do not share Plato's view that there is one order of society that is perfectly just or completely free of injustice.

As dark, offensive, and nihilistic as it all sounds, there is nevertheless a grain of truth in the postmodern posture. It has the value of challenging the singular, monistic, universalistic, and autocratic conception of truth. It also reminds us of our hypocrisy. Veyne is right to remind us that everyone believes in their own gods, it is the gods of others that they deem worthless.[26] In saying this Veyne thinks that he is saying something universally true—namely, that this hypocrisy is the universal condition of humanity—but that is not the case. It was not the attitude of the pagans who respected and even adopted the gods of others. It was certainly not the attitude of the pagan gods who tolerated each other in the same sanctuary. What Veyne is saying about the gods is particularly applicable to the monotheistic tradition. I am not suggesting that polytheistic cultures were free from hypocrisy, vanity, or self-congratulation; only that the old religion did not give these vices a moral sanction.

Thanks to Socrates, the old myths were replaced with new myths about the immortality of the soul, and the rewards of the afterlife. It follows that nothing bad can happen to a good man. These new myths tax credulity; this is why Plato had to make *belief* in them mandatory on pain of death. In the nihilistic darkness of the postmodern world, there is no sense in preferring the old gods of Homer to the new gods of Socrates. One "regime of truth" will surely follow another as night follows day. In truth, these myths or "regimes of truth," are not like earthquakes; there is nothing inevitable about them. Veyne concedes this when he describes them as "palaces of the imagination." However, they cannot be simultaneously "palaces of the imagination" and "earthquakes." Palaces are human creations, but earthquakes are not. To overcome the conflict, Veyne adds that the palaces built by the "constitutive imagination" are somehow "spontaneous." Veyne thinks he has uncovered some eternal truth about the mysterious birth of human cultures and societies. It is an echo of the "spontaneous order" of Friedrich Hayek. As I have argued at greater length elsewhere, postmodernity is not the leftist movement it often pretends to be.[27]

Postmodernism is as nihilistic as it is radical. This nihilistic radicalism can manifest itself in one of two ways—in the conservatism of Veyne or the revolutionary spirit of Foucault. Veyne's conservatism mirrors the relativism of old. If every regime is as good or as true as any other, then we might as well embrace the regime in which we find ourselves. There is certainly no reason for overthrowing any regime, regardless of its character. There is not even any reason for troubling ourselves to make small incremental changes intended to resolve particular injustices. However, postmodern nihilism need not necessarily manifest itself in this ultraconservative manner.

Foucault represents the revolutionary tendency in postmodernism. Both Foucault and Veyne are equally nihilistic; the difference is what they decide to do with their nihilism. Veyne tells us to accept the world as it is, believe in the myths of our time, stop dithering in a state of intellectual paralysis, forget all these philosophical questions that have no answers of any worth, and become manly enough to act on our beliefs, like Nietzsche's imaginary Greeks.

Foucault rejects this conservative posture. When asked if his philosophical position leads to political apathy, he denies this in no uncertain terms. Instead, he claims that his philosophical position leads to "hyper- and pessimistic activism."[28] Foucault recommends deconstructing the beliefs of our time in order to reveal that (despite their claims to truth) they are but the disguised manifestations of the will to power. Once we have exposed the façade, and totally discredited them, they will crumble. However, we should not expect them to be replaced by anything better. The fact that this hyper-pessimistic activism will not accomplish anything is no reason to disparage it. The struggle, the *jihad*, is itself the end.

This is not a new idea. It was given its classic expression in Jean-Paul Sartre's "existential Marxism."[29] It is a political philosophy born of nostalgia for a revolutionary activism after the belief in the revolutionary transfiguration of the world has waned. The true believers thought that the revolution would bring an end to tyranny, injustice, and oppression for all time. When faith evaporates and nihilism sets in, then apathy becomes a clear and present danger. The goal is to sustain the dedication, the passion, the excitement, and the hyper-activity of true believers—even after the faith is dead. Simulating the fervor of faith is the key. The point is to valorize the struggle itself. Make no mistake; it is a *jihad* without hope or end. It is a *jihad* where nothing can be achieved; and this hopelessness is known to the *jihadists* in advance.

Terry Eagleton, a Christian Marxist, has recommended the same hopeless hyperactivity.[30] Eagleton has no faith in the revolution, since the world is hopelessly and incurably decrepit, humanity is the scum of the earth, and the transfiguration of the world is impossible. Nevertheless, like Foucault, Eagleton is bent on a hopeless and endless struggle. The Christian Marxism of Eagleton echoes the repudiation of life and the quest for martyrdom that is characteristic of Christianity. Socrates anticipated this antipathy to life when he surmised that the body was the prison of the soul, when he chose death as a release, and when he redefined piety as service to the projects of the gods—whatever they may be.

When the dogmas defy reality, and faith evaporates, the result is the nihilism that pervades the Christian Marxism of Eagleton, the atheistic Marxism of Sartre, and the hyperactive pessimism of Foucault. All of them are products of the Socratic culture of belief. Farfetched myths, which promise transfiguration, can only be sustained by a leap of faith. When that faith evaporates, nihilism looms large. To avoid collapsing into despair, the purposeful struggle to transform the world must be maintained—without hope or illusion.

My criticism of postmodernity notwithstanding, I must nevertheless praise it. Why? Because it involves a clear recognition that there can be no single regime of truth, and no social order that surpasses all others in goodness and justice. This insight has led Veyne to assume that these powers, programs, or regimes of truth, follow one another spontaneously as night follows day, and that they represent the "palaces" built by the imagination of different epochs, as if they follow one another in a sequence.

The world is not that simple. More often than not, these regimes exist simultaneously. If there is no common denominator that can be the basis of diplomacy, then the only alternative is war. If enemies represent the forces of evil, then diplomacy becomes proof of weakness, and compromise becomes capitulation to evil. The result is biblical wars of extermination. The American War on Terror is a case in point. What can postmodernism tell us about it? Paul Veyne would tell us to embrace it because it is as inescapable as an earthquake. It is our myth, our truth. So, let's not overthink it. Michel Foucault would bid us to deconstruct the idea of the War on Terror, and reveal that it is the disguised manifestations of the will to power. Once defeated, expect another equally hypocritical and mendacious "regime of truth" to replace it. None of this is helpful. Postmodern nihilism is but the realization that there is something rotten at the heart of Western philosophy.

When Homer's Greeks launched their war against Troy, they did not fool themselves into thinking that their goal was to defeat evil—they were after the loot. No doubt, Menelaus thought his honor was at stake; but not too many of the warriors gave that much thought. Those who know they are fighting for loot will not be foolish enough to fight when the task at hand is hopeless. In contrast, the War on Terror is paradigmatic of Socratic culture, with its astonishing self-deception. Those who delude themselves into thinking that they are fighting for the true, the right, and the good, are inclined to fight endlessly and martyr themselves needlessly. The effect is the moralization of war and the exaltation of violence.

6 Debunking the Socratic Legend

Debunking the fictitious but formidable portrait of Socrates created by Plato is a step toward a self-understanding of the West that is more modest and less extravagant. There is reason to think, along with Nietzsche, Walter Kaufman, and Bernard Williams, that the tragic sensibility has much to offer. It is my contention that Homer and the tragic poets would have provided a more truthful, genuine, and generous, self-understanding for the West that is superior to the Socratic, Christian, and Kantian traditions to which we are heir. Traditions are not a matter of fate; it is up to us to decide what aspects of the past we choose to valorize. If we can see Socrates more objectively, it may be possible to make better choices when it comes to defining our "traditions."

It is time to make a clean break with the Socratic singularity and universality of the good—and its pretentious self-righteousness. It is time for a more pluralistic approach—an approach that recognizes the plurality of the good. The trouble is that every assault on the universalistic inclinations of the West is regarded as a collapse into a morass of relativism. This need not be the case. There is an important difference between relativism on one hand and pluralism on the other. While relativism is intellectually self-defeating, pluralism is not. Indeed, most political conflicts are conflicts between genuine and legitimate goods. There is a plurality of goods that are not necessarily commensurable, and as a result, cannot be captured in a single regime—not even in a multicultural regime. Pluralism is not to be confused with multiculturalism, which is the illusion that a multiplicity of incommensurable goods can be simultaneously celebrated by one society.

The pluralistic approach to politics does not assume that all good things come in one package or political program, while all the evils come in another. For example, the West, led by the United States, is eager to spread freedom and democracy around the world. However, freedom and democracy are not necessarily compatible. In cases where the United States has toppled dictatorships, and replaced them with democracies, there has been less freedom and even less security. This leaves the Americans mystified because they assume that with democracy, all sorts of other good things automatically follow. Yet, liberty and democracy do not necessarily go together, as the Arab Spring has made amply clear. If all good things came in the same package or were mutually compatible, then politics would not exist—everyone would choose the good package, and there would be no conflict.

The pluralistic approach does not assume that the ideals and aspirations of the West are those of humanity. The War on Terror is puerile because the project of defeating evil is endless, irrational, and unattainable—especially when evil is defined so broadly that it includes everything that does not conform to the ideals and even the interests of the West. The result is endless war. Realistically speaking, it is impossible to live in a world without enemies; it is impossible to live in a world in which everyone endorses our ideals, plans, and aspirations. The War on Terror is ill conceived, not because there is no such thing as reason, truth, or goodness, but because the West is not the sole embodiment of the right and the good. There is more than one right way, and more than one set of ideals and aspirations. Unless the West abandons its Socratic hangover, it will remain indistinguishable from its most lethal enemy—the self-styled "Islamic State," whose motto is (with a menacing index finger lifted to the heavens) one God, one truth, one path!

It is time to forsake the Socratic faith in the singularity of the good. It is time to recognize that every choice has its threats, hazards, and inherent vices. It is impossible to aspire to world peace under the auspices of a single order without the sort of global tyranny into which the United States has stumbled. It is time to realize that the absolute and unimpeded rule of the custodians of truth is impossible without grotesque crimes, akin to those of Critias and Charmides. Trying to impose a single order on the world is bound to lead to eternal struggle. It is time for the West to stop echoing the arrogance, self-righteousness, and self-importance of Socrates. It is time for the West to abandon the idea that it is the sole custodian of a universal truth, applicable to all humanity. It is time for the West to tame its *hubris*, instead of mimicking Socrates by denouncing its enemies for having an aversion to its wisdom, goodness, and justice.

Finally, it is important not to lament the loss of the Socratic legend, as if destroying it would rob the world of something glorious and sublime. In truth, the very opposite is the case. The intellectual effort required to unravel Plato's fanciful portrait is as liberating as it is edifying. Debunking the legend of Socrates might open the door to a more pluralistic vision. In this way, we might abandon the baseless conviction that there is one true god, one right way, and one set of values applicable to all humanity at all times and places. We might relinquish the delusion that we must defend our values in every corner of the globe. We might abandon the idea that every challenge to our values is a mortal threat that must be exterminated. We might come to understand that there are competing goods that cannot be simultaneously enjoyed. We might begin to recognize that there is no single, pure, pristine, and incorruptible vision, religion, worldview, or way of life that encompasses all the good things that are worthy of our humanity.

NOTES

1. Gregory Vlastos, "The Paradox of Socrates," in Vlastos (ed.), *The Philosophy of Socrates: A Collection of Critical Essays* (Notre Dame, Indiana: University of Notre Dame Press, 1980); John Burnet, "The Socratic Doctrine of the Soul," *Proceedings of the British Academy*, Vol. VII (January 26, 1916), p. 13.
2. Plato, *Timaeus*, 28a, in *The Collected Dialogues of Plato*, Edith Hamilton and Huntington Cairns (eds.) (Princeton, New Jersey: Princeton University Press, 1961).
3. For my brief account of the problem of evil, see "The problem of Evil, Part I" and "The problem of Evil, Part II" in *Free Inquiry* (October/November 2011), pp. 13, 50–55, and (December 2011/January 2012), pp. 14, 54–55.
4. Hegel, *Philosophy of History* (1822), transl. by J. Sibree (New York: Prometheus Books, 1991), "Modern Age" p. 425.
5. Benedict XVI, *Spe Salvi* (On Christian Hope, 2007).
6. See *Terror and Civilization* (New York: St. Martin's Press, 2004), Part III, "Inner State of Siege," Part IV, "Promethean Revolt" and "Romanticizing Evil."
7. *Phaedrus*, 238c, 244a–c.
8. *Symposium*, 215b.
9. *Apology*, 23b.
10. Ibid, 40a.
11. On the Catholic Inquisition see my *Aquinas and Modernity: The Lost Promise of Natural Law* (New York: Rowman & Littlefield Publishers Inc., 2008).
12. See for example, Plato, *Laws*, 841 d (prohibition of extra-marital sex and sodomy), 836 c–d (prohibition of homosexuality), and 942 c–d (the "emancipation" of women as the representatives of private life).
13. *Apology*, 30a.
14. Hannah Arendt has rightly criticized Plato for turning politics into what she calls "making" as opposed to "acting." The former is appropriate for the crafts, whereas the latter is appropriate for politics. Turning politics into a craft is disregarding the reality and plurality of other human beings with goals and ends of their own. See Hannah Arendt, *The Human Condition* (Chicago: University of Chicago Press, 1958).
15. In our time, some of the staunchest defenders of Western superiority, dominance, and conquest are stalwart secularists such as Christopher Hitchens, Sam Harris, and Paul Berman.
16. To be fair, not all Enlightenment philosophers were colonialists at heart—then or now. Johann Gottfried Herder was a pluralist and Denis Diderot thought that exporting the hypocrisy and corruption

of his society made no sense. See Sanka Muthu, *Enlightenment Against Empire* (Princeton: Princeton University Press, 2003).
17. Mathew Arnold, "Hellenism and Hebraism," in *Culture and Anarchy* (New York: Oxford University Press, 1932, 2007).
18. Paul Veyne, *Did the Greeks Believe in their Myths? An essay on the constitutive imagination*, transl. by Paula Wissing (Chicago: University of Chicago Press: 1988), p. 90.
19. Ibid, pp. 117, 122.
20. Ibid, p. 128.
21. Ibid, p. 126.
22. Ibid, p. 126.
23. Ibid, p. 85.
24. Ibid, pp. 85, 84.
25. Plato, *Republic,* 351d and 352 c.
26. Veyne, *Did the Greeks Believe in their Myths?* p. 114.
27. See *Alexandre Kojève: The Roots of Postmodern Politics* (New York: St. Martin's Press, 1994).
28. Paul Rabinow (ed.), *The Foucault Reader* (New York: Pantheon Books, 1984), p. 343.
29. Jean-Paul Sartre, *Critique of Dialectical Reason*, translated by Quintin Hoare (New York: Verso, 1991).
30. Terry Eagleton in *Reason, Faith & Revolution: Reflections on the God Debate* (New Haven: Yale University Press, 2009). See my critique of Eagleton in "Re-Inventing Christianity," *Free Inquiry,* (August/September, 2010) pp. 12 & 44.

Annotated Bibliography

Adkins, A.W.H. *Merit and Responsibility: A Study in Greek Values.* London: Oxford University Press, 1962.

Adkins considers Homeric values to be the source of the moral epidemic of the fifth century to which Socrates and Plato provide a solution. The latter is a matter of bringing to the fore the "quiet virtues" of justice and temperance—virtues that are largely ignored by the competitive system of values found in Homer. See my disagreement with Adkins (5.7).

Aristophanes. *The Birds.* New York: Dover Publications Inc., 1999.

In this satirical comedy, two Athenians abandon the city, its democracy, its litigiousness, and its gods in favor of establishing a new city where the birds are the new gods. The idea is to dethrone the gods in favor of the birds, on the grounds that the birds eat insects, mark the seasons, and do all sorts of other things that are more useful to humanity than anything that the gods have ever done. The all out war against the gods is easily won, because Prometheus is a traitor and Heracles is a glutton. But in the end, the new regime recreates all the grandeur and pomposity of the gods. So, the idiocy, conceit, and self-glorification continue. It is worth noting that lampooning the gods did not lead to a charge of impiety against Aristophanes. So, there is more to impiety than ideas, as I argue in Section 2.

Arnold, Matthew. *Culture and Anarchy,* edited by J. Dover Wilson. Cambridge, England: University of Cambridge Press, 1957.

Arnold describes Hellenism in the most rhapsodic terms, as the "unclouded clearness of mind," the "unimpeded play of thought," and the "spontaneity of consciousness" (p. 132). It has "a kind of aërial ease, clearness, and radiancy," and is full of "what we call sweetness and light" (p. 134). Unfortunately, the Hellenic vision of life appeared pre-maturely, and man was not yet ready to live by it; "centuries of probation and discipline were needed to bring us to it" (p. 136). Then the bright light of Hellenism faded and Hebraism ruled the world. Hebraism was dark, morbid, obsessed with sin, self-conquest, self-sacrifice, and blind obedience to the will of God. It provided man with an extensive network of prescriptions that envelop all of life. Nevertheless, Arnold thought that Hebraism was necessary to allow human culture to move toward perfection and re-claim the liberty that made its pre-mature appearance in the Hellenic age. This is the same motif used by Hegel to explain the darkest periods in the history of the West—as the necessary prelude to the progress in store for humanity.

Bacon, Helen H. *Barbarians in Greek Tragedy.* New Haven: Yale University Press, 1961.

Bacon identifies three senses of the Greek word, *barbaros:* (i) unintelligible, (ii) foreign or non-Greek, (iii) foreign and inferior. She claims that neither Aeschylus nor Sophocles use the term in a pejorative sense, but Euripides uses it to mean intrinsic moral inferiority (p. 12). In the plays of Euripides, the term often "loses all reference to nationality and means *only* savage, evil, cruel, etc. Bacon shows that even though all three meanings were current at the same time, the prevalence of the third sense of the word "coincides with the intensification of national consciousness, and the corresponding hostility towards outsiders that arose during the struggle with Persia" (p. 11, note 8). Even though Euripides uses the term in the pejorative sense in which it was understood by his audience, I think that he avoided the dualism that inclines toward the demonization of the enemy. See Section 5.3. Indeed, he challenges the Pan-Hellenic conviction in the superiority of Greeks in plays such as *The Trojan Women, Hecabe,* and *Andromache.*

Brickhouse, Thomas C. and Smith, Nicholas D. *Plato's Socrates.* New York: Oxford University Press, 1994.

Brickhouse and Smith provide the best recent apology for Socrates that I have read, because they do not whitewash the historical, political, or religious facts, but confront them. Why did Socrates associate with such unsavory characters? Brickhouse and Smith maintain that he sought out the worst of the worst—the men that he thought could make the most terrible mistakes (p. 171). He tried to make them wise, but did not succeed. They argue that Plato presents Socrates in conversation with all sorts of people such as Thrasymachus, Protagoras, and Callicles, with whom he disagreed very strongly. The conclusions of Brickhouse and Smith echo the Platonic legend of Socrates as a pious man who was unjustly convicted in a case that amounted to "guilt by association" (p. 166). Having dismissed the centrality of the political charge, Brickhouse and Smith focus on the religious charge. They claim that the Socratic moralization of the gods was not objectionable in the least (p. 182). However, his personal divine "sign" was a source of concern (p. 189). Nevertheless, they argue that it was compatible with traditional beliefs in general and the practice of divination in particular (pp.196, 198–99). It follows that the charge of the "first accusers" (*Apology,* 18a), namely Aristophanes and those who assume that Socrates is one of the Sophists, is at the heart of the matter—a charge that is clearly false.

I find their argument unconvincing. After all, Socrates knew Alcibiades from his youth, and they were clearly lovers, until Socrates became an ascetic, at least that is what I believe is implied by Plato's *Symposium.* Socrates also knew Charmides as a very young man, and was physically attracted to him, as he tells us in Plato's *Charmides.* Whatever *we* may think of pederasty, it was not meant to be simply a way for mature men to satisfy their sexual appetites; it was also intended to be a nurturing relationship for younger men. In other words, Alcibiades and Charmides were nurtured by Socrates from their youth, which is why he must bear some responsibility for how they turned out. Critias was older, but was part of the Socratic circle, as presented in Plato's dialogues. Unlike the relationship of Protagoras, Callicles, or Thrasymachus, to Socrates, the relationships of Alcibiades, Charmides, and Critias to Socrates, as presented in Plato's dialogues, were not intellectually adversarial.

Like other efforts to defend Socrates, Brickhouse and Smith distance Socrates from the later dialogues of Plato by treating Socrates as being above the political fray, not allied with the oligarchs, or particularly hostile to democracy (p.157). In contrast, I argue that Plato's hostility to democracy was greater under the spell of Socrates than it was in his maturity, when the influence of Socrates had waned (Section 1.5). Brickhouse and Smith can divorce Socrates from Plato's middle and late dialogues only by ignoring the logical connection between the religious innovations of Socrates and the later dialogues of Plato. I provide reasons why I do not endorse the separation of the early from the middle and late dialogues in Section 4.

On the question of impiety, I share what Brickhouse and Smith call their "constructive view" of the Euthyphro as a dialogue that does indeed provide us with an account of the Socratic conception of piety as serving the gods in their great work (pp. 64ff). They lament that Socrates does not tell us what that work is (p. 66), but they surmise that he is serving the gods by trying to make men wise and good through philosophical reflection (pp. 66, 178). In contrast to Brickhouse and Smith, I think that the ambiguity of the divine task is what makes this brand of piety particularly dangerous, see Section 2.5. In my view, the Socratic mission is not as innocuous as it appears, for reasons I provide in Sections 4.3 and 4.5.

Burnet, John. "Socrates," in *Hastings Encyclopedia of Religion and Ethics*. New York: Charles Scribner's Sons, 1928, Vol. xi.

Rightly regards Socrates as a precursor to Christianity.

———, "The Socratic Concept of the Soul," *Proceedings of the British Academy*. London: Oxford University Press, Vol. viii, pp. 235–60. Elaborates on the essay above.

Burnyeat, M. F. "Cracking the Socrates Case." *The New York Review* (March 31, 1988), pp. 12–18.

> In this review of I. F. Stone's book, *The Trial of Socrates,* Burnyeat recognizes the brilliance of Stone's work. Nevertheless, he echoes the traditional view of Socrates as a teacher of virtue. He claims that the conflict between Stone and Socrates is a conflict between two totally uncompromising idealists: Stone's career has been a diligent and valiant fight for freedom and democracy, while Socrates devoted himself to the pursuit of virtue. Burnyeat implies that the conflict between them is analogous to the conflict between virtue and freedom—a conflict that Burnyeat does not discuss. In my view, this conflict is politically treacherous. It is impossible to make virtue politically supreme without trespassing over freedom; and it is not possible to make freedom supreme without tolerating a certain degree of vice. Burnyeat implies that the two ideals are equal. But they are not—at least not in the political realm. This means that the two "idealists" are not politically equal. Virtue is lovely as a personal ideal, but as a political ideal, it is monstrous. If Socrates were indeed concerned with the personal quest for virtue, as Burnyeat and most other scholars maintain, then there would be no conflict between freedom and virtue, Stone and Socrates. In Section 4, I argue that the "care of the soul" to which Socrates was dedicated, was not a mission to entreat every individual to seek virtue; it was a profoundly political endeavor—because individuals are not capable of doing it on their own. The result is a terrifying, quasi-theocratic authoritarianism.

Burnyeat, F. M. "The Impiety of Socrates." Thomas C. Brickhouse and Nicholas D. Smith (eds.). *The Trial and Execution of Socrates: Sources and Controversies.* New York: Oxford University Press, 2002, originally in *Ancient Philosophy*, Vol. 17 (1997), pp. 1–12.

In this clear and refreshing essay, Burnyeat narrates his experience asking his audience if Socrates was unjustly condemned. Audiences believe this is the case by overwhelming margins. Then, he quotes from the *Euthyphro*, and asks his audience to decide if Socrates was guilty of not believing in the gods of the city. The audience has a change of heart; they overwhelmingly believe that Socrates was guilty of impiety. Of course, this is not a historical understanding of impiety, nor does Burnyeat pretend it is. I agree with Burnyeat that the dialogue shows clearly that the religious ideas of Socrates differed from those of his contemporaries, but I disagree with Burnyeat that Euthyphro represents the traditional view; so, it does not follows that by defeating Euthyphro, the dialogue succeeds in defeating the Homeric or traditional conception of religion, as I show in Section 2.3.

Cartledge, Paul. *The Greeks*. New York: Oxford University Press, 1993.

Cartledge argues that the Greeks were very preoccupied with their distinctiveness and superiority *vis à vis* other people. Like Edith Hall, he thinks that the Greeks defined their identity as the opposite of the barbarians in a form of negative stereotyping known as "orientalism." For Cartledge as for Hall, the polarity of Greek and barbarian was central to the Greek way of thinking. This binary opposition is the basis of the polarity of Jews and gentiles, Europeans and Orientals, males and females. These are not simple opposites, but a hierarchy of superior and inferior. Since Greeks were superior to barbarians and half the Greeks were female, and females were inferior to males, it follows that all the barbarians had to be depicted as effeminate, which by implication gives Greeks a monopoly on manliness (p. 12). What is admirable about the book is that it tries to make the Greeks strange and foreign instead of being our familiar ancestors. The thesis makes sense when applied to Aristotle, but I do not believe that it succeeds when applied to Homer, Aeschylus, Euripides, or Herodotus.

De Ste. Croix, G. E. M. *Athenian Democratic Origins and Other Essays*. New York: Oxford University Press, 2004.

The discussion of the Athenian practice of Ostracism is particularly illuminating. De Ste. Croix argues that the practice is not as ridiculous as it is often portrayed. He agrees with Aristotle that it was intended to get rid of individuals who possessed exceptional political power and influence. But he disagrees with Aristotle's claim that it was intended to avoid tyranny by these powerful individuals. After all, if the individual was extremely popular and influential, it was unlikely that he could be ostracized. Instead, De Ste. Croix modifies Aristotle's account by arguing that the point of the institution was to get rid of a very powerful and influential politician who was advocating a policy that was contrary to the will of the majority. So, the reason for ostracizing such a man is to protect the state from serious divisions that would weaken the state or even lead to civil war (stasis) or treachery and the betrayal of the city to a foreign foe. Unlike exile (a punishment often inflicted on the surviving leaders of the losing side of a civil war, p. 206), which involved a permanent loss of civic status and the confiscation of one's property, ostracism involved no loss of property and had no direct deleterious effect on the family of the ostracized. After ten years he could return not only to the city, but to political power and prominence, as several examples testify. In this way, a deep division that would have weakened the city is averted at the expense of ten years out of a politician's career. De Ste. Croix uses examples of several ostracized politicians to show that this was in fact the effect of the policy. He also surmises that the men ostracized in the 480s were likely to have been politicians who were soft on Persia—it is not that they were pro-Persian, it is more likely that they thought that "without Persian overlordship, Athens would be likely to fall under Spartan domination" (p. 202). This made them a threat to the dominant faction that was led by Themistocles, who believed in an unqualified resistance to Persia without a hint of "appeasement." De Ste. Croix concludes that the practice was therefore not only very democratic, but also strengthened Athens in her effort to resist Persian domination. He admits that the practice was liable to abuse, and that was the reason it was abandoned after the ostracophoria of 417 BCE, where Alcibiades and Nicias, the two leading politicians of the day on opposite sides of the invasion of Syracuse, conspired to have their supporters vote for the ostracism of a third party. De Ste. Croix's account is quite impressive and convincing, but there is no reason that the ostracism could not have been used for more than one purpose—to rid the city of threatening divisions *and* of individuals who had the inclination and sufficient support to overthrow the democracy and establish a tyranny, as was suspected of Alcibiades. On the political career of Alcibiades, see Section 1.1.

Dee, James H. "Critias of Athens." *Free Inquiry*, Vol. 32, No. 2 (February/March 2012), pp. 48–49.

In this interesting essay, Dee celebrates Critias as one of the "Great Minds" in being among the founding father of atheism, because Critias expressed his hard-core atheism so openly in the extant excerpt of his play, *Sisyphus*—a phenomenon that Dee assumes was extremely rare in antiquity. Dee is aware that Critias was the notorious leader of the Thirty Tyrants and one of the followers of Socrates. See my discussion of Critias in Sections 1.2 and 1.6.

Dodds, E. R. *The Greeks and the Irrational*. Berkeley, California: University of California Press, 1951.

In this celebrated book, Dodds tells the story of the failure of Greek rationalism. He associates rationalism with reason, science, Socrates, and the Sophists. He also thinks that they had important predecessors, such as Heraclitus and others. The Greek Enlightenment introduced ideas that Dodds counts as an advance over the archaic ideas of the past. Most important among these is a new conception of the human psyche. Supposedly, the ancient Greeks understood human wickedness in terms of psychic intervention whereby *ate*, or the irrational, takes over the mind and leads human beings to do things that they would never have done if they were in possession of their faculties. According to Dodds, belief in psychic intervention was superseded by the more sophisticated psychology of Socrates and Plato, who emphasized personal responsibility. I argue against this position in Section 5.6.

Dodds also thinks that the Greek Enlightenment introduced the more advanced conception of cosmic justice to replace the capriciousness of the Greek gods. He laments the failure of Greek rationalism and the rise of superstition, which Plato tried unsuccessfully to tame. The point of the book is that Greek rationalism failed—and that the defeat eventually created the atmosphere in which Christianity was able to thrive. So, what explains that defeat? Dodds compares the Greek case to the America of his time (i.e., the McCarthy Era), and finds that there is a certain "fear of freedom" as Eric Fromm's *Escape from Freedom* testifies. Dodds thinks that economic hardship, war, and suffering have something to do with the fear of freedom, but ultimately, he thinks that the archaic concept of *ate*, as the representative of the irrational, takes over and wins out. Besides, the fear of freedom is not imaginary, but quite real. For, when freedom leads to the rational questioning of collective beliefs, and these collective beliefs are swept away, self-assertion and lawlessness are likely to be the result. So, it is only natural for society to revolt against Enlightenment. This revolt supposedly manifested itself in Athens with the persecution of intellectuals—Socrates, Anaxagoras, Protagoras, and others. Dodds ends by invoking the image of the horse and rider; the latter represents humanity coming to the edge and about to jump out of the irrational and embrace the opportunity, the freedom, and the exhilaration that the rational presents, but turns back. Dodds hopes that humanity is merely hesitating before the jump, and not in full flight or retreat. He wonders if it is the rider or the horse. He suspects that it is the horse, which is his metaphor for the unconscious. He thinks that by fathoming the unconscious, psychoanalysis will help us triumph over the irrational and its corresponding fear of freedom. At the very least, psychoanalysis will not allow the irrational and its fear of freedom to dominate us. Like Freud, he regards Christianity as a neurosis in which the irrational reaches unprecedented heights.

Even though I agree with Dodds about Christianity, I find his position disturbingly Freudian. As I have argued elsewhere, far from being a liberator, Freud popularizes Christian ideas in a pseudoscientific guise; and is plagued by the irrationalism and neurosis that was the legacy of Christianity (*Terror and Civilization*, New York: Palgrave Macmillan, 2004, Part IV). Dodds shares Freud's view of himself as a champion of reason and science. Like Freud, Dodds associates the progress of civilization with rationalism and science; he is not sensitive enough to the barbarism that science is nevertheless capable of unleashing.

I side with Bernard Williams in rejecting Dodds' view that the ancient Greek understanding of wickedness in terms of psychic intervention is a primitive notion that was superseded by the more sophisticated views of Socrates and Plato (Sections 5.6 and 6.3). I dissent from Dodds' claim that the concept of cosmic justice is "an advance" when compared to the tragic point of view (Section 5.4). I also reject Dodds' view of Socrates as a thinker on the forefront of the Greek Enlightenment. Contrary to Dodds, I think that Socrates played a significant role in the defeat of Greek rationalism. Socrates adopted a politically disastrous religion, which Plato institutionalized in the *Laws*—a dystopia that anticipates the totalitarianism of the Catholic Church (Sections 4.3 and 4.5).

Euben, J. Peter. ed. *Greek Tragedy and Political Theory.* Berkeley, California: University of California Press, 1986.

The essay by Euben "Political Corruption in Euripides' *Orestes*," is of particular interest. Even though it is a thoughtful and scholarly analysis of the tragedy, his effort to distance Euripides from Aeschylus and Sophocles and ally him with Socrates is unconvincing. It is true that both Euripides and Socrates were critical of Athenian politics and society. However, this similarity is superficial in comparison to the differences in their worldview. Euripides provides a critique not only of political corruption, but also of the gods. Socrates is a divinely inspired man who is eager to put the gods on a moral pedestal that neither Homer nor the tragic poets would consider. Moreover, Euben takes seriously the idea that Socrates did not consider himself in possession of the truth. He suggests that Socrates thought that "dialogue" is the closest that human beings could get to the truth because our natural partiality could only be mitigated by the presence of the perspectives of others. While Euben's sentiment is eloquent, Socrates can hardly be the poster boy for such intellectual humility. Euben's position rests on distancing Socrates from the mature Plato—a position that I argue against in Section 4.

Euben, J. Peter. *The Tragedy of Political Theory: The Road not Taken.* Princeton, New Jersey: Princeton University Press, 1990.

> Euben argues that the conflict between Socrates and Athens is a metaphor for the conflict between philosophy and politics. In his estimation, philosophy and politics, Socrates and Athens, need each other to thrive. The reason is that they share something in common that is essential to their very being—both require others, without whom they are partial, deluded, and unjust. So, unless they are reconciled, philosophy will withdraw from the public space and become irrelevant; and politics will become partial and unjust. Euben takes the Socratic "dialogue" seriously as an open-ended discussion where diverse views are explored with mutual respect, and not just a monologue punctuated by yes-men. By the same token, Euben also takes seriously the idea that Socratic philosophy rests on the recognition of its own ignorance. He tells us that Socratic philosophy comes closest to the truth only in dialogue, without which it is arrogant and dogmatic—he is clearly blind to its authoritarian conceit. Euben thinks that the modesty of Socratic philosophy makes it akin to politics properly understood, which requires the recognition of its partiality. This is why politics needs philosophy and Athens needs Socrates. It follows that the prosecution and conviction of Socrates represents the tragic alienation of philosophy and politics to the detriment of both. Euben concludes that Socrates is deeply and profoundly "democratic," is dedicated to Athens, and "rooted" in her democratic culture, which explains why he preferred death to exile. Euben believes that Socrates is also "democratic" in another sense: by teaching the care of the soul, he makes his fellow citizens fit for democracy, since the latter requires virtue. By putting philosophy on trial, Athens acted in a self-destructive manner that accounts for its injustice and corruption

(p. 218). In other words, Socrates is indeed the gift of the gods to Athens, as he imagined himself to be.

What does all this have to do with tragedy? Euben rightly points out that the performance of tragedies in honor of Dionysus was an Athenian political institution that was integral to its democratic culture; in educating citizens, it makes them less partial and more open-minded, and therefore more fit for democracy (pp.55–56). Socrates supposedly continues in this Athenian tradition of educating his fellow citizens. This similarity notwithstanding, the differences between Homer and the tragic poets on one hand, and Socrates and Plato on the other, are staggering as I show in Sections 5 and 6. Euben begs to differ. In his view, "Socrates" and "Plato" represent two tragic and mutually incommensurate choices. Socrates represents perpetual questioning that reveals the shortcomings of all choices, which lead to chaos if not confusion. Plato stands for making a choice, taking a stand, even if it leads to partiality, "normalization," and the tyranny of reason. Even though Euben does not put it so bluntly, he thinks that Plato and Athens take a stand against Socrates. At the same time, Euben thinks that Plato recognized what he was giving up—he understood reason's potential for tyranny as much as Michel Foucault. Plato realized what a difficult choice is involved in doing political theory; he understood that political theory involved a tragic choice between order and open inquiry.

In the final analysis, Euben's view of Socrates echoes Plato's legend of the innocent sage who is unjustly silenced by the mob. Euben's analysis is divorced from the reign of terror inflicted on Athens by Critias and Charmides, because he does not believe that Socrates had any "pupils" (p. 218). Like all those who adore Socrates, Euben is eager to separate him from the authoritarian politics of Plato, and ally him with his own democratic idealism. Indeed, Euben suggests that the philosophical quest for order, definition, and clarity is itself tyrannical—a tragic reality that Plato was fully cognizant of. Supposedly, Socrates avoided the special "affinity" between philosophy and tyranny, to which Plato succumbed—in spite of himself, and in full knowledge of the tragic choice involved—(pp. 248–249, 274). For Euben, the tragedy of political theory is that the road on which Socrates embarked has not been taken. This is why Socrates must be killed or banished in the ideal city described in the *Republic* (p. 264) not to mention the *Laws*. In other words, Plato had to create a world in which his beloved Socrates is condemned once again, because he must have recognized, as did Athens, that human beings cannot live in the state of perpetual questioning and intellectual openness represented by Socrates. They need answers—and with answers we get partiality, the closed society, and that dreaded thing—"normalization."

Euben's book represents an eloquent articulation of the romantic, democratic, liberal leftists in North America who are influenced by Michel Foucault. I have argued elsewhere that in the European context, postmodernism is not necessarily leftist (*Alexandre Kojève: The Roots of Postmodern Politics*, New York: St. Martin's Press, 1994). Euben insists that politics needs a nondogmatic philosophy that does not aspire to knowledge of truth, but realizes with Socrates that such knowledge is unattainable, and that all claims to truth are manifestations of will to power. It is clear that a philosophy that rejects every quest for order as tyranny could be of no help to politics. At best, it would paralyze the decision-making process; at worst, it would foment endless upheaval and insurgency. Even though he does not express it this way, Euben implies that the choice between liberty and order is a tragic one. In my view, he exaggerates the ubiquity of tragic choices. I think that aspiring to ordered liberty is not impossible. Moreover, excluding values that are in conflict with such ordered liberty is hardly tragic; it is certainly a far cry from tyranny.

In contrast to Euben, I am not inclined to see democracy as an open-ended philosophical conversation; I am as wary of it as Socrates and Plato. Nor am I inclined to see Socrates as the open-minded, undogmatic, endlessly playful, self-refuting, antiauthoritarian maverick that Euben imagines him to be. Instead, I argue that Plato's mature political philosophy is the logical byproduct of the philosophical premises of Socrates. So much so, that the dystopia presented in the *Laws*, is one where the religion of Socrates is backed by the sanctions of the state on pain of death (Section 4).

Fisher, N. R. E. *Hybris: A study in the values of honor and shame in ancient Greece.* Warminster, England: Aris & Phillips, 1992.

This is a fascinating and exhaustive study of *hybris* (*hubris* in recent spelling) to which I am deeply indebted. Fisher argues that *hubris* is primarily an offense against human beings that is not motivated by the desire for wealth, love of luxury, or sexual excess, but springs from the desire for superiority over those who are humiliated or otherwise abused. Rape and murder are examples. Fisher is critical of the religious view of *hubris* as an offense against the gods that is punished by *nemesis*. He rightly argues that the view that *nemesis* automatically follows *hubris* cannot be used to explain tragedy. In his view, hubristic characters are not tragic: Oedipus is a tragic figure because he was not hubristic. In the *Oresteia,* neither Agamemnon nor Clytemnestra is a tragic figure. Agamemnon is callous in killing his daughter Iphigenia, and Clytemnestra is callous in killing her husband. The most tragic figure is Orestes, even though he commits an act of "horror and impiety" by killing his mother, his motives are pure, because he was forced to avenge the murder of his father. It follows that Orestes does not commit the heinous act (*ate*) in *hubris*. This leads Fisher to the very interesting conclusion that motives matter even in a world where they are supposed to be irrelevant (p. 295). Fisher is not denying that there is a dominant pattern in Greek literature: excessive good fortune and prosperity (*koros*) leads to a mentality of excessive arrogance, ambition, and over-reaching (*hubris*), which results in horrible atrocities and dreadful crimes (*ate*). Fisher is simply denying that this pattern can be used to explain tragedy in literature or history. For Fisher, the downfall of Athens as described by Thucydides is the result of her prosperity or *koros*, which leads to *hubris, ate,* and disaster (pp. 391ff). His point is that these patterns are not tragic. To be tragic, the errors of the victims of *nemesis* or disaster (sometimes mistakenly understood as divine retribution) must be human and pardonable, not monstrous, bestial, or terrifying.

Fisher makes an interesting point regarding the status of Aristotle's "irritating paragon, the 'great-souled man' (the *megalopsychos*) of the *Nicomachean Ethics*" (p. 12). The *megalopsychos* displays an abundance of arrogance and a harsh contempt for his inferiors. Fisher claims that he could be considered hubristic, except that in the eyes of Aristotle, his arrogance is justified. Aristotle's point is that those who have his wealth and privilege, but lack his virtue, are not likely to bear their good fortune appropriately, so are inclined to *hubris* (p. 12).

Gay, Peter. *The Enlightenment: The Rise of Modern Paganism*. New York: W. W. Norton & Co., 1966.

Gay thinks that the philosophers of the Enlightenment regarded Socrates as the best that Greek civilization had to offer (p. 81). Unlike Socrates, they did not wish to turn away from nature in order to focus on self-knowledge. Instead, they were committed to the scientific revolution of their age, which they "hoped would become the prelude, and even the servant of moral and political improvement" (p. 82). The real significance of Socrates for the Enlightenment was through his death, which Condorcet described as "the first crime announcing the war between philosophy and superstition, which still continues today" (p. 82). Their vision of Socrates as a rational stalwart against superstition flies in the face of his faith in the immortality of the soul, the rewards and punishments of the afterlife, and his asceticism. While I admire the Enlightenment's achievements, I think it echoes Socrates in thinking of the right and the good in singular terms, which makes it vulnerable to universalistic imperial conceits (Section 7.4).

Griffin, Jasper. *Homer on Life and Death*. Oxford: Clarendon Press, 1980.

Griffin argues that the greatness as well as the insignificance of human life is highlighted by the fact that it is observed by the gods. The epic allows us to observe human life from the perspective of the gods, and in so doing, see both its greatness and its insignificance. Moreover, the contrast between men and gods illuminates the nature of human life and death because the gods are deathless, have no cares, and do not suffer. In contrast, human life is one of suffering and death. He claims that the Homeric perspective in which the gods serve as an audience for human activities proved to be difficult to maintain outside of the *Iliad*: "the divine onlooker, if he does not intervene for justice, tends either to be criticized as immoral, or to become detached altogether from human life in Epicurean idleness" (p. 203). In the *Odyssey*, they "observe human sin and righteousness moving among men in disguise, an unambiguously moral idea..." (p. 203). Despite the detachment of the gods in the *Iliad*, Griffin considers the epic to be also a moralistic tale. He thinks that Paris is the "archetypal Trojan," in which case all of Troy is implicated in the sin of Paris (p. 5). It follows that the Trojans started the war and deserve to lose. They also lose because they are glamorous, frivolous, and undisciplined, while the Greeks are grim, orderly, serious, and disciplined (p. 4). I argue against the moralization of Homer's epics in Section 5.

Hall, Edith. *Inventing the Barbarian: Greek Self-Definition through Tragedy*. Oxford: Clarendon Press, 1989.

Hall maintains that the tragic poets "invented" the conception of the barbarian as the despicable "other" in contrast to which the Greeks defined themselves. Supposedly, the other tragic poets follow Aeschylus in thinking that the Greeks were manly, courageous, pious, moderate, wise, law-abiding, rational, egalitarian, and democratic. On the other hand, barbarians were effeminate, complacent, cowardly, cruel, cunning, unjust, impious, and despotic. In this way, the portrayal of the enemy was a form of self-praise. Hall argues that this binary opposition of Greeks and barbarians is the earliest example of "Orientalism" in the classic sense as used by Edward Said (*Orientalism*, 1978). She goes so far as to claim that this was the most influential idea that the Greeks bequeathed to Western civilization (pp.70, 73, 99, 110). Hall also Christianizes the tragic poets by claiming that in *The Persians*, Aeschylus not only celebrates the triumph of the culturally superior over the culturally inferior, but also regards the defeat of the Persians as proof that the gods punish the "transgressors" for their iniquity (p. 70, n.54). Nevertheless, Hall succeeds in showing that the term *barbaros*, which she admits was not used pejoratively in Homer, has come to have a pejorative connotation in the fifth century, due to the rise of pan-Hellenic identity after the defeat of the Persian invasion headed by Xerxes. However, from this fact, it does not follow that the tragic poets were on a poetic mission to uphold and idealize democratic Athens and its empire. I find the claim that Aeschylus intended *The Persians* as a celebration of the superiority of the Greeks unconvincing, since his portrait of the Persians is as sympathetic as Homer's portrait of the Trojans. On the latter point, see Section 5.3.

Hamilton, Edith. *The Greek Way*. New York: W. Norton & Co., Inc., 1930.

The book is written with passion and clarity. Hamilton regards Socrates, St. Paul, and modern science as the culmination of the Greek spirit that defines the West. In her account of the Greek way and its distinctiveness from other ancient civilizations, Hamilton emphasizes Greek curiosity about the natural world, and contrasts that to the "oriental" spirit of the ancient Egyptians and their priestly aristocracy. Hamilton is delightfully anticlerical, but she fails to see any similarity between the sinister power of the Egyptian priesthood and the power of the Catholic priesthood in the Middle Ages. Her blindness to the darkest aspects of Western civilization makes her a classic example of "Orientalism," which can be defined in biblical terms as the ability to see the speck in one's brother's eye but not the plank in one's own eye.

————-. *Mythology*. New York: Back Bay Books, 1942.

This book is delightful in its artful retelling of the classic myths. However, Hamilton's romantic view of the Greeks does not stand up to scrutiny. She is convinced that the Greeks are just like us and that "Nothing we learn about them is alien to ourselves" (p. 7). She goes so far as to claim that the Hebrew Bible is very Greek because, like the Greeks, it is "pre-occupied with the visible," and like the Greeks, the Hebrews found the "satisfaction of their desires in what was actually in the world around them" (p. 8). St. Paul supposedly shared the same perspective when he declared that the invisible must be understood by reference to the visible (p. 8). Hamilton seems to forget that the Hebrew God was not all that visible, not even to the select few, who acted as his mouthpiece. And when it comes to the Christians, they are notorious for regarding the visible world as worthless and destined to be destroyed by God in the very near future. Hamilton tells us that the Greeks were at ease with their gods and even "free to laugh at them." This does not support her case, since the Biblical God was formidable, awe-inspiring, and totally other, and no one dared to laugh at *him*. Even Jesus, does not succeed in humanizing him; he only makes him more vengeful and terrifying with all his threats of eternal hellfire. When it comes to priests, Hamilton thinks that in Greek mythology, "the priest is rarely seen and is never of importance," p.11. Nevertheless, it was a priest of Artemis who demanded the sacrifice of Iphigenia so that favorable winds will blow, allowing the Greek ships to sail to Troy. The *Iliad* begins with a plague suffered by the Greek warriors and a priest of Apollo who tells Agamemnon that he can lift the plague only if Agamemnon returns his captive Chryseis (the priests' daughter). Hamilton is right in thinking that the Greeks had little regard for priests as indicated by the case in which a priest and a poet fall on their knees before Odysseus and beg him to spare their lives. Odysseus kills the priest without a thought, but spares the poet (p. 11). Homer claims that the hero was in awe of the poet because the latter learns his art from the gods. The implication is that the poet is nearer to the gods than the priest. Greek religion had no professional priesthood. This is one more reason that the Hebrew Bible, of which we are the heirs, is not Greek. In the Hebrew Bible, priests rule as the mouthpieces of God, and even when the Hebrews decide to have kings, the priests are the king makers—witness how they destroy Saul in favor of the usurper, David. No one has documented the malevolent role that was played by priests in the history of the ancient Hebrews better than Stefan Heym in *The King David Report* (Evanston, Illinois: North Western University Press, 1972), which is both a novel and an astute biblical analysis of the role of the priesthood in the Old Testament.

Hamilton is closer to the mark when she observes that the "terrifying irrational has no place in classical mythology... the demonic wizards and the hideous old witches who haunted Europe and America up to quite recent years, play no part at all in the stories. Circe and Medea are the only witches, and they are young and of surpassing beauty—delightful not horrible" (p. 10). She surmises that Heracles might be an "allegory of Greece herself" because he freed the world from the monsters that were supreme over humanity. I think the admiration for ancient Greece among scholars such as Hamilton has its source in the fact that the absence of magic, witches, and demons makes the Greeks seem very modern. Nevertheless, identifying them with modernity is a mistake, because they were far too superstitious, and modernity is far more Christian (for good and ill) than it likes to admit. In the final analysis, Hamilton, sees the Greeks as setting the stage for the higher civilization of Christianity. Zeus is gradually transformed; instead of being thunder and lightening, he becomes the "Universal Father" and giver of all good things, like the "civilized" God of the Christians (pp. 14–15). In my view, the very reverse is the case—Zeus as portrayed in the *Iliad* was a genuine father from the start, in contrast to the Biblical God, who is a small, tribal, and inferior deity (Section 5.3).

Hamilton is unwittingly condescending when she says that the gods had a good and a bad side. For her, there are two antithetical ideas (good and evil) fighting to define the characters of the gods—with the noble side struggling to emerge as the dominant trait. So understood, the Homeric gods are a prelude to the understanding of the divine as the incarnation of goodness—a view of deity that she assumes to be advanced, and destined to make its historical debut. She wrongly assumes that a religion that is intimately connected with morality is superior to a religion that is not; as a result, she regards the moralization of the gods as an advance. I argue against this view in Section 5.

Hans, James S. *Socrates and the Irrational.* Charlottesville, VA: University of Virginia Press, 2006.

An illustration that the sentimental idealization of Socrates shows no sign of waning. See my review of the book in *Dialogue: Canadian Philosophical Review*, Vol. 47, No. 1 (Fall 2008), pp. 196–198.

Harrison, Jane Ellen. *Prolegomena to the Study of Greek Religion.* London: Merlin Press, 1962, 1980.

In this important work, Harrison affirms the sunny disposition of Homer's religion. She does not think that this sunny disposition is simply part of the "splendid unreality of the heroic saga," since Thucydides, a decidedly sober writer, expresses the same view of religion. In the Funeral Oration of Pericles, the latter boasts that Athens provides its inhabitant with plenty of opportunity for celebration, recreation, and sacrifices. In other words, there are plenty of religious festivals celebrated in Athens. As Harrison points out, what was meant by "sacrifices" is the antithesis of anything that we generally associate with religion: "In Homer sacrifice is but, as it were, the signal of a banquet of abundant roast flesh and sweet wine; we hear nothing of fasting, of cleansing, and atonement" (pp.1-2). In other words, the Homeric religion was a joyous affair; it was an opportunity for feasting, recreation, and relaxation. Harrison agrees with Socrates that Greek religion was a transaction between men and gods—an exchange for mutual benefit—a *quid pro quo*. In exchange for burnt offerings and libations in honor of the gods, the gods might smile on the endeavors of humanity. However, Harrison thinks that this sunny attitude characteristic of Homer is difficult to sustain, and that it is easy to slide from this *quid pro quo* of "servicing" the gods in order to win their favor to "appeasing" the gods in order to escape their wrath. The result is fear and superstition, which lead people to revile and flatter the gods simultaneously (p.5). In her view, Greek religion hovered between these two dispositions. She brings forth evidence that the classical age recognized two different types of rituals—the rites of "service," "ministration," or "tendance" directed at the Olympians, in which there was no fear. On the other hand, there were rituals of "riddance" or "aversion" directed at totally alien spirits (pp. 3, 7). The distinction is between *do ut des* (I give that you may give) and *do ut abeas* (I give that you may go and keep away). Harrison quotes Isocrates saying that there are two kinds of gods and ceremonies: the Olympians are served by sacrifices and burnt offerings, on alters and temples of the state as well as of private individuals, whereas the dark spirits are the subjects of ceremonies of riddance; so, we have two different types of gods with diverse natures and different ceremonies (p. 8). The ceremonies dedicated to the Olympians are a "meal shared," and there was no "holocaust," as Harrison describes the gloomy ceremonies in which the entire animal was sacrificed to the gods as a burnt offering, with nothing left for humans to feast on. Harrison thinks "the real religion of the main bulk of the people in the sixth and even the fifth century" is not the cheerful religion Homer, but the religion of fear (pp. 7–8, 10–12).

The distinction that Harrison makes between the cheerful religion and the religion of fear is an important insight, because the second type of ritual is what is generally associated with the superstition, decadence, and intellectual atrophy for which Socrates supposedly provides a cure. Harrison thinks, "Socrates put his finger on the weak spot of Greek religion" as a transaction (p. 3). In my view, Socrates did not put his finger on the problem at all. In fact, Socrates fails to make the distinction that Harrison makes between the sunny and the dark ceremonies. If he had, he would have focused on the dark religion of fear and superstition, in which case, Homer would not have been his target.

Ironically, Harrison objects to the cheerful religion of Homer on the grounds that "it had in it no seeds of spiritual development" (p. 6) and that it needed to be superseded since it had done its job for civilization. She does not tell us exactly what that job is, and why it is no longer necessary. Even though Harrison thinks that the religion of fear is "primitive," she is in sympathy with it because she thinks that it contains a kernel of truth —namely, the reality of evil (p. 6). Like Harrison, Socrates was decidedly on the dark side. Orphic elements in his thinking made him sensitive to the ubiquity of sin and the fate of the soul after death. The malevolence of his gods manifests itself in the beyond; nor can they be appeased by ceremonial offerings. They require personal purification, and commitment to an ascetic life of self-abnegation, which is altogether antithetical to the Homeric spirit. In Section 2.5, I show how Socrates replaces the cheerful Homeric conception of piety with a politically volatile conception of piety that anticipates radical Christian and Muslim inclinations to act on behalf of the divine.

Havelock, Eric A. *The Liberal Tradition in Greek Politics.* New Haven: Yale University Press, 1957.

> An account of the deadly process by which Plato not only defeated his intellectual opponents, but concealed their very existence from posterity by an artful process of appropriation and subversion. Sophocles, Euripides, Protagoras, and others were the victims. As a result, the stupor inflicted on the scientific understanding of human anthropology began to lift only with the advent of Darwinian thought.

Herder, Johann Gottfried von. *Reflections on the Philosophy of History of Mankind* (1784–91), edited by Frank E. Manuel. Chicago: University of Chicago Press, 1968.

> This is a classic example of the romaticization of the Greeks. Even their vices—such as the treatment of women—are excused as necessary in view of the effect of the climate. Unlike the German climate, the Greek climate is, according to Herder, more conducive to women's ability to exercise their wiles on men. The romanticization of the Greeks continued to be a professional hazard among German philosophers—witness Hegel, Martin Heidegger and Hannah Arendt. I discuss Hegel's view of Socrates and the Greeks in Section 6.2.

Herman, Gabriel. *Ritualized Friendship and the Greek City.* New York: Cambridge University Press, 1987.

> This is an excellent account of the institution of *xenia* or guest-friendship. This institution is important in understanding the unwillingness of Socrates to escape as presented in Plato's *Crito.* See Section 3.5.

Hornblower, Simon. *Mausolus.* Oxford: Clarendon Press, 1982.

> The book focuses on the role played by Mausolus and his family in the spread of Greek culture in the Persian satrapy (province) of Karia in Asia Minor (modern south-west Turkey) in the fourth century BCE. The author shows that contrary to popular belief,

the Hellenization of the Greek east began long before the conquests of Alexander. Halikarnassos, Herodotus's city, joined the Delian League under Athens from the beginning (at least as early as 454 BCE), without necessarily breaking with Persia (p.26). The author surmises that intermarriage was common and thinks that this explains why it was easy for Herodotus to be "*philobarbaros*," as Plutarch maintains (p. 25, note 154). The assumption is that a Greek could not look sympathetically on the barbarians unless he was part barbarian himself.

Johnson, Curtis N. *Socrates and the Immoralists.* Lanham, Maryland: Lexington Books, 2005.

This is a scholarly account of the Socratic conception of justice as a condition of health in the soul. Johnson understands the Socratic mission as a craft that rids the soul of falsehood to make it ready for true beliefs (p. 26), which can "withstand elenctic scrutiny" (p. 216). Ridding the soul of false beliefs makes it ready for justice. Johnson maintains that the craftsman is not necessarily responsible for his failure, because the material on which he works may not be ideal. Critias, Charmides, and Alcibiades are not mentioned.

Kaufmann, Walter. *Tragedy and Philosophy.* Princeton, New Jersey. Princeton University Press, 1968.

This is a work to which I am deeply indebted. Kaufmann challenges the dominant views of tragedy from Aristotle to Nietzsche. His criticism of Aristotle's *Poetics* is devastating. Contrary to Aristotle's theory of the "tragic flaw," Kaufmann rightly argues that Greek tragedy must be understood in terms of innocent suffering. I echo his views in Section 6.1. Kaufmann also objects to Nietzsche's claim that tragedy died of optimism—that is, faith in reason and progress. Instead, he claims that tragedy is not possible in the wake of Auschwitz and Nagasaki. In a world of such hopelessness, comedy, including black comedy, is preferable. Tragedy is a heroic way of dealing with human suffering, which is impossible in the face of such radical despair. Nevertheless, Kaufmann is not altogether without hope since he sincerely believes that the creation of the state of Israel is the solution to Auschwitz.

Knox, Bernard. *Word and Action: Essays on the Ancient Theatre.* Baltimore, Maryland: The Johns Hopkins University Press, 1979.

In his review of the film, *Iphigenia* by Michael Cacoyannis, Knox suggests that the film provides an interpretation of Euripides' *Iphigenia at Aulis* that focuses on the priest. The oracle had nothing to do with the goddess; it was invented by the priest, Calchas, to satisfy his *philotimia*, or lust for power. The wind starts to blow before the sacrifice; Agamemnon dashes to save his daughter, but it is too late.

MacIntyre, Alasdair. *After Virtue: A Study in Moral Theory.* Notre Dame, Indiana: University of Notre Dame Press, 1984.

The book is more caricature than history or philosophy. Every epoch is described in a way that makes it incomprehensible to the next. MacIntyre paints Homer's characters as flat, unreflective automatons—products of a social world that they never question (Ch. 10: "The Virtues in Heroic Society"). Yet, he rightly adds that what makes these individuals "heroic" is their willingness to fulfill that role even if it leads to their death. This suggests that they are fully cognizant of what they have undertaken. In other words, they cannot be heroic or admirable if they are unreflective automatons.

MacIntyre thinks that with Sophocles, tragedy begins to question the norms of society and reveal the conflicts imbedded within. In particular, he regards tragedy as "the conflict of good with good" (p. 163). For example, *Antigone* is about the conflict between "the demands of the family and the demands of the *polis*" (p. 132). For him, Antigone and Creon represent "rival moral truths," which cannot be reconciled. Likewise, Sophocles' *Philoctetes* is about the conflict between the interests of the community (as represented by Odysseus) and the interests of the individual (as represented by Philoctetes) pp. 144–45. MacIntyre thinks that tragedy is about "different virtues" making rival and incompatible claims upon us. I question this Hegelian view of tragedy for reasons I provide in Sections 6.1 and 6.2.

McPherran, Mark L. *The Religion of Socrates*. University Park, Pennsylvania: Pennsylvania State University Press, 1996.

In this very detailed work, McPherran takes the religious charges against Socrates seriously; he does not regard them simply as a cover for political concerns. When it comes to the charge of impiety, defined as not recognizing the gods of the city and inventing new gods, McPherran thinks that Socrates was not guilty. He examines two aspects of the distinctly Socratic view of the divine and maintains that they are not at odds, or at least do not threaten, the gods of the city. The first is the peculiar *daimonion* that Socrates was known to have an intimate connection with. On the face of it, this private intimacy with the deity may seem threatening. However, McPherran argues it is not a threat because its communications were purely negative, merely preventing Socrates from doing certain things, but not prescribing anything. Moreover, the idea of communing with a deity is not all that peculiar and can be assimilated with other "diviners" (p. 136). I find the argument convincing where the daimonion is concerned.

The second distinctive aspect of the Socratic conception of the divine is the moralization of the gods—the insistence on the absolutely impeccable moral status of the gods and their love of human virtue. McPherran argues that this moralization of the gods was compatible with the gods of the state, even if it was not compatible with the warring gods of Homer. After all, the state depended on invoking the gods to punish perjurers, contract-breakers, and those who spoke in the Assembly as a result of bribery or with the intention to deceive (p. 23). In that light, the amoral gods of Homer would not be useful as gods of the state. He concludes that the Socratic moralization of the gods, is not totally novel, but is quite compatible with the role they played in the civil order (pp. 142, 143). I do not find this argument convincing. There is a world of difference between the "moral" gods of the city and the "moral" gods of Socrates. The gods of the city uphold the morality of the city, whereas the gods of Socrates uphold an absolute morality that transcends the justice of the city and even passes judgment on it. Moreover, the Socratic moralization of the gods prohibits curses, as McPherran readily admits (p. 150). So, how can the state function with such upright gods? How can it function with gods that cannot be invoked to retaliate against its enemies? In the absence of the vengeful *lex talionis* (the law of retaliation), in the absence of the material reciprocity involved in the *do ut des* ("I give that you may give") aspect of religious sacrifices, it is not clear how the gods, as understood by Socrates, could be of use to the city. McPherran hedges somewhat by acknowledging that the Socratic conception of piety may have been the source of some anxieties. But on the whole, he does not think that these anxieties are warranted because he thinks that the Socratic view of piety is the genuine article, the "real universal piety" (p. 27) that transcends that of his contemporaries.

In his careful analysis of the *Euthyphro*, McPherran rightly asserts that the dialogue provides a conception of piety as "that part of justice that is a service of humans to gods in their work (ergon), a work that produces some good results" (p. 54). He further maintains that Socrates' philosophical mission was itself an act of piety, whereby Socrates believed he was serving the gods in their work (p. 56). I have no disagreements with McPherran's reading of the dialogue. I take issue with this acceptance of the Socratic conception of piety as true or superior to the traditional view (p. 27). I think the Socratic view turns piety into *hubris* by allowing self-proclaimed, divinely inspired men to attribute their projects to the deity, and to maintain that they are acting on behalf of the divine. In the Homeric world, men took ownership of their projects, and implored the gods for help in achieving their ends, and not the other way around. I have argued in Section 2.5 that the Socratic conception of piety is radical and dangerous.

Even though he admires the Socratic conception of piety, McPherran suspects that it might be liable to abuse. So, he proceeds to interpret Socratic piety in a way that undermines these objections. He acknowledges that the Socratic understanding of piety would require identifying what the work (*ergon*) of the gods is, but thinks that the "specification of that *ergon*" cannot be known with "completeness or certainty" by mortals (pp. 66–67, 71). Socrates says nothing of the sort in the

Euthyphro or anywhere else. McPherran simply deduces this from Socrates' "frequent disavowals of wisdom" (p. 69), which McPherran takes seriously. Nevertheless, all the disavowals of ignorance notwithstanding, it remains the case that Socrates was certain that his own project of improving the souls of others was a divine mission—something that McPherran does not deny. So, in view of the fact that Socrates thought democracy and democratic politicians corrupted their citizens, and were therefore at odds with divine objectives, it is easy to see how some of the students of Socrates would feel free in transforming Athenian democracy by any means, no matter how violent, if they were convinced that they are serving the divine cause of improving the souls of their fellow human beings. McPherran tries to take the sting out of the Socratic project of improving the soul by claiming that it is a purely philosophical project that is simply intended by its "destructive mode" to eliminate "the epistemological conceit possessed by most humans" (pp. 80–81); and that it is Plato who "storm(s) the heavens with an erotically passionate, epistemic optimism that Socrates would have found intolerably hubristic" (p. 299). Now, it may well be that the Socratic elenchus would lead to a desirable humility where knowledge of the gods and their projects are concerned, but this humility was not on display in the dialogues of Plato or Xenophon. McPherran's recognition of Plato's deification of the philosopher (pp. 297, 300) is in my view, a logical consequence of the Socratic position. McPherran laments the Platonic view as having "outstripped the agnostic limitations at the heart of Socratic piety" (p. 301). I think that this radical separation of Socrates from Plato is a product of wishful thinking, which ignores the seamless continuity of the early and late dialogues. It is telling that McPherran hardly mentions the violent dictatorship of the Thirty, and when he does, he describes it as part of a list of misfortunes that befell Athens, and even credits the Thirty with tolerating religious "deviances" that were not tolerated by the democracy where Socrates was prosecuted (p. 170–171). It remains a mystery how the philosopher who refused to "storm the heavens" for lack of "epistemological conceit" could have inspired these political radicals.

Meier, Christian. *The Greek Discovery of Politics.* Transl. by David McLintock. Cambridge, Mass.: Harvard University Press, 1990.

> Even though the book is unclear and ambiguous in style, the chapter on "The *Eumenides* of Aeschylus and the Rise of the Political" makes the interesting point that the conflict in the play between the old gods and the new gods mirrors the conflict between the old aristocratic order and the new democratic order. Meier suggests that the most significant shift toward the democratic regime was not the reforms of Cleisthenes, which gave the people more power to defend themselves against the nobility, but the complete removal of the power of the nobility upon the destruction of the Areopagus (the traditional body of nobles that ruled the city). Meier claims that this is the political background of the play, and that the compromise between old and new at the end of the play is the compromise that Athens needed to stave off civil war, especially after the murder of Ephialtes, who proposed the elimination of the Areopagus in the Assembly. He also suggests that the shift from the old gods—primitive, hideous, savage, implacable—to the new gods was a renunciation of the spirit of vengeance. Meier thinks that the Areopagus is "the instrument for breaking the chain of vengeance and counter-vengeance, the curse that lies upon the house of Atreus" (p. 91).

Moore, Clifford Herschel. *Ancient Beliefs in the Immortality of the Soul.* New York: Longmans, Green, & Co., 1931.

> Moore regards Orphism as the earliest spiritual religious movement to posit the immortality of the soul. He thinks that Orphism grew out of the Bacchic or Dionysiac mysteries. Inspired by wild music and dancing, the devotees transcend the consciousness of their body and indulge in the frenzy of tearing apart a living creature (usually a bull) and devouring its raw flesh (p. 7). Moore links Orphism with the Eleusinian mysteries (pp. 12–13). The latter were developed in the seventh century BCE and were practiced until 396 CE when Alaric the Goth destroyed the sanctuaries at Eleusis (p. 13). He thinks these mysteries took life after death for granted (p. 13). Those who were initiated in the

rites of Demeter were assured not only prosperity in this life but also freedom from the ills associated with existence beyond the grave. Other scholars maintain that the Eleusinian mysteries were not connected to Orphic ideas of immortality, but solidly integral to the ritualistic polis religion (see Erwin Rohde, *Psyche: The Cult of Souls and Belief in Immortality among the Greeks*, in this Bibliography).

Murray, Gilbert. *Hellenism and the Modern World*. London: George Allen & Unwin Ltd., 1953.

Murray argues that Hellenism is integral to the European heritage, which he regards as a mixture of Athens, Rome, and Jerusalem. Judaism has a great book, but it is narrow and exclusive—only the children of Abraham can be a part of it, while the uncircumcised are abhorred. Rome had a great capacity for governance and a sense of justice, but little in the way of imagination. It is the Hellenic heritage that is the real glory of the West. Hellenism has its source in Athens, and its ideals are embodied in Pericles' Funeral Oration as described by Thucydides. Of course, the ideal is not identical with reality. Nevertheless, the freedom, art, poetry, philosophy, skepticism, respect for law, equality of citizens, and the absence of superstition, excessive cruelty, torture, prostration before the Great King, arbitrary rule, execution without trial, human sacrifices, and all the ugly things that Murray associates with barbarians, makes Hellenism seem "modern" in the best sense of the term. Following Thucydides, Murray tells us that all was destroyed by *Arche*— which Murray understands as the lust for power. This evil mistress got hold of Athens and destroyed her. The beautiful city that represented civilization, the city that set itself up as the antithesis barbarism, behaved in ways that were much worse than anything that the barbarians were capable of. Why? It decided to impose itself on others by force because it could not tolerate the rejection of its gifts. Nevertheless, Hellenism was not altogether extinguished. It was passed on by Alexander to a much larger world—hence the Hellenistic Age. Eventually, Macedonia was overtaken by Rome, but Hellenism was still not extinguished. Even when Rome fell, Hellenism, understood as the Athenian spark that defines Western civilization, was not destroyed. The nations of Europe inherited the Hellenic culture. Murray compares the nations of Europe to the Greek city-states. What happened to Athens happened to them. The lust for power in the form of colonialism and Nazism destroyed their civilization. Murray claimed that after being lured, bewitched, and destroyed by *Arche*, after being devastated by war, Europe was no longer fit to carry the Hellenic legacy. That legacy has been passed on to America, which is the new heir of the Hellenic spirit. Murray was convinced that thanks to the United States, the West has just embarked on a new Hellenic Age. In my view, this may have been plausible in 1953, but unhappily, the seductress *Arche* has been at it again. America is running amuck in the world with one outrage after the next, and can hardly be the poster child of the Hellenic spirit as understood by Murray. This is a nice story and there might be some truth in it if Hellenism were understood as an ideal that has inspired the West on more than one occasion. The most implausible part of Murray's narrative is the claim that this Hellenic heritage was fused with the Judaic one to create the brilliant hybrid of Hellenism and Judaism in Christianity. In this book, I argue that there is nothing of the spirit of Hellenism as understood by Murray in Socrates or Plato, because the religion of Socrates was part of the dark flower of the mystery religions that eventually triumphed in the form of Christianity.

Nussbaum, Martha. *The Fragility of Goodness.* New York: Cambridge University Press, 1986.

This is a deep and difficult book, but also very creative. Nussbaum examines what she considers the moral problem at the heart of Greek tragedy. She understands tragedy as a conflict between equally valid but irreconcilable claims (pp. 134, 153). The result is a tragic choice that involves doing wrong no matter what one chooses, with disastrous results. In this way, tragedy highlights the fact that the good human life depends on contingent circumstances beyond human control. How can human beings deal with contingency? On the whole, she thinks that there have been two "strategies for the defeat of luck" (pp. 9, 20). The first one is associated with Plato, and involves an inhuman ascetic withdrawal from the world to a solitary life in communion with the immutable and unchanging. The second is associated with Aristotle and the tragic poets. Instead of withdrawing into a solitary and ascetic life, the second solution accepts the contingent in human life. It regards human life not as the solitary control over the soul, but as a vulnerable plant that is both active and receptive. She celebrates a life lived among friends and loved ones in a community, where truth is arrived at by dialogue that reaches a considerable degree of consensus—not the solitary pursuit of truth in communion with the immutable and transcendent. In other words, the truth is anthropocentric, but not relativistic (pp. 11, 20). At the same time, Nussbaum believes that Plato is not as opposed to the tragic poets as he appears in his middle dialogues. Instead, she thinks that he questions the inhumanity of the position he once held. In the *Symposium* he gives voice to the ideas of the tragic poets (Ch. 6). She thinks that the conflict between Socrates and Alcibiades is a tragic conflict between reason, as represented by Socrates, and *eros*, as represented by Alcibiades. She also believes that Alcibiades sided with the democrats in Athens, while Socrates sided with the oligarchs. In her view, the city could have been saved if only the two had been reconciled. Shut out, Alcibiades destroys the Herms in an orgy of violence, and the city is doomed (p. 199). As a result of this tragic clash, Plato recanted his earlier denunciation of the tragic poets in the *Phaedrus* (Ch. 7). I share Nussbaum's sympathetic view of the tragic poets, although I have a different understanding of tragedy (Section 6.1). I am not convinced that in the *Symposium* Socrates represents reason. I think he represents a cold asceticism, which is a very different matter, for reasons as I explain in Section 4.2. I think that Alcibiades sided with the democrats only when it suited him, but otherwise he was a Socratic and an oligarch through and through (Sections 1.1 and 1.4).

Nietzsche, Friedrich. *The Birth of Tragedy and The Genealogy of Morals*. Translated by Francis Golfing. New York: Doubleday & Co., 1956.

Nietzsche was right in thinking that Socrates spelled the death knell of tragedy by insisting on cosmic justice. In that sense, he was a pre-cursor of Christianity. I agree that the similarities between Socrates and Jesus are significant (Section 3.8). I find that Nietzsche's view of Socrates hovers between great insight and the endorsement of Plato's legend. I object to Nietzsche's philosophical reaction to the tragic reality of existence and support the views of Albert Camus (Section 6.4).

Ostwald, Martin. *Autonomia: Its Genesis and Early History.* American Philological Association: Scholars Press, 1982.

Oswald argues that autonomy was used primarily to refer to a smaller state existing in the shadow of a larger power, when the latter's policy was noninterference in the internal affairs of the smaller state. It was also a status granted to the smaller power by the whim or pleasure of the greater power or *hegemon*. There is no doubt that autonomy was far superior to domination by the larger power, but it was not as good as freedom. The latter is something that one earns for oneself and does not depend on the largess of another. So, when Xerxes offered the Greeks a peace treaty consisting of return of all their lands, autonomy for their cities, and the rebuilding of all the temples he destroyed, the offer amounted to a demand for capitulation, especially since Xerxes was still in Thrace (p. 15). Ostwald points out that in the foundation of the Delian League, no mention was made of autonomy for the member states. It follows that Greek states had more freedom under Xerxes than as members of the Delian League under Athens, which might explain why some of them were not anti-Persian and were not easily recruited to the Pan-Hellenic cause. This state of affairs was rectified in the Second Athenian Confederacy of 377 B.C.E., which guaranteed the autonomy of the member states and defined that autonomy in ways that made it clear that Athens had learned from the mistakes made in the era of the Delian League (p. 48).

Otto, Walter F. *The Homeric Gods: The Spiritual Significance of Greek Religion.* London: Thames and Hudson, 1954, translated from the German by Moses Hadas.

This book succeeds in capturing the naturalistic spirit of Homeric religion. For Otto, the Olympians represent a masculine religion of sky and light, which he juxtaposes to the feminine, earthy, and dark religion that preceded it. The validity of the latter was not totally extinguished, but its harshness was moderated. Moreover, the manliness of the warriors is invariably accompanied with a feminine quality that takes the edge off their masculinity, and accounts for the nobility of their manhood, which might otherwise become merely harsh or heartless cruelty. This explains why the great warriors generally have a goddess that is close at hand. Otto suggests that it is easier for these manly men to accept the assistance of a goddess than a god, with whom they might be more inclined to compete.

What Otto means by the spirituality of Greek religion is not oneness with the divine, but an awareness of divine presence as manifest in the splendor of the world. Apollo, the iconic Greek God, represented insight, moderation, and order. He preferred clarity, form, and distance, not enthusiasm, intemperance, intoxication, and proximity (p. 78). He is not only opposed to "Dionysiac exuberance," but also to the Christian emphasis on the "eternal worth of the individual." Instead, Apollo directs man's attention away from "his ego and the profound inwardness of his individual soul," to the eternal and unchangeable, which "transcends the personal" (p. 78). For Otto, the Olympians had "no thought of initiating man into supernatural mysteries or revealing to him the secret character of their divinity. It is not heaven but himself that man must study, and this does not imply examination of conscience or confession of sin" (p. 241). In the Olympian religion, the divine is not revealed in miracles, absolute justice, or infinite love, but in the "splendor of clarity, the intelligent sway of order and moderation" (p. 79). The admonition "Know thyself" refers to knowing the "limitations of humanity," and realizing how far removed mankind is from "the majesty of the eternal gods" (p. 241). My defense of Homer against the Socratic assault in Section 5 is more prosaic, but it does not contradict Otto's analysis.

Parker, Robert. *Athenian Religion: A History*. New York: Oxford University Press, 1996.

Parker rightly undermines the distinction between the religious and the political interpretations of the prosecution of Socrates. On the political view, he was tried and convicted for having been the teacher of Alcibiades and Critias—two men who did the most to harm Athens. On this view, Socrates was convicted because he taught subversives. On the religious view, Socrates was condemned because he represented the paradigmatic "impious intellectual or Sophist" (p. 201). The latter combined atheism with natural philosophy and moral relativism. In this interpretation, Aristophanes' *Clouds* is very important, since it depicts Socrates as the embodiment of the "moral malaise" that brought Athens down. The upshot of Parker's discussion is to undermine the distinction between the religious and the political accounts of the trial.

Parker rightly thinks that the religious innovations of Socrates could not have been a threat to the city—namely, his personal *daimonion*, and his insistence that the gods were benevolent and cared about justice. These views "would never, surely, have caused him to be singled out as a target for attack" (p. 203), because "impieties of thought" (201) alone, were not relevant. Indeed, "the Athenians very rarely moved against verbal impiety," because a "wide variety of opinions about the gods could be comfortably accommodated in a religion that lacked dogma and revelation" (pp. 209–210). Hippon, who had very radical views on religion, went totally unmolested (p. 210). Diagoras, the Melian poet, was outlawed from Athens with a price on his head for mocking the Eleusinian Mysteries in 415/4 (p. 208).

In light of his observations, Parker's conclusion is strange. Instead of thinking that polytheism, with its plurality of gods, and its absence of scriptures or revelation, made the ancient Greeks more tolerant than the monotheists that came after them, Parker concludes that their tolerance was due to their failure to "live up to intolerant principles" (p. 210).

Plutarch. *Lives*. 4 Vols. Translated by Aubrey Stewart and George Long. London: G. Bell and Sons, Ltd., 1910. "Life of Alkibiades," Vol. I.

Plutarch provides several stories that reveal the egoism and cruelty of Alcibiades, who treated his admirers (except Socrates) with contempt. There is the story of Anytus who invited him to a party. He refused the invitation; then he got drunk with some other fellows and made his way to Anytus' house and ordered his servants to take away half the gold and silver goblets. The guests were appalled, but Anytus shrugged it off. Apparently, Alcibiades had a big dog; he paid 70 minae for it, but for some reason cut off its tail, so everyone felt sorry for the dog and horrified at the cruelty of Alcibiades.

Rohde, Erwin. *Psyche: The Cult of Souls and Belief in Immortality among the Greeks.* New York: Harcourt, Brace, & Co., Inc., 1925.

Illustrates how the Orphics took over the cult of Dionysus and reinvented it to suit their religious beliefs. The *Theogony* of Hesiod is also co-opted. Likewise, Homer's Zeus is transformed into the Orphic Zeus who devours the World-God and becomes the whole universe: "Zeus the Beginning, Zeus the Middle, in Zeus all things are completed" (p. 339). He regards the Eleusinian Mysteries to be very different from Orphism (p. 221) and solidly within the Greek pantheon in being a harvest cult of Demeter with no faith in the immortality of the soul, even though the cult promised the participants a privileged life in this world and after death in Hades (p. 219). The Mysteries were considered "secret," however the secret was not a dogma that could be let out (p. 222). The mystery was a dramatic performance or religious pantomime, which was probably a representation of the rape of Korê-Persephone, the wondering of her mother (Demeter) and the final reunion of the two goddesses. It is easy to see how this could have been lampooned by Alcibiades and his crowd in the profanation of the Mysteries that led to their prosecution for impiety, and cast a cloud on Socrates.

Sachs, David. "A Fallacy in Plato's *Republic*," *The Philosophical Review*, Vol. 72, No. 2 (April 1963), pp. 141–158.

Sachs reveals the fallacy in Plato's conception of justice. He shows that it is possible to be just in the peculiarly Platonic sense of the term while being unjust in the ordinary sense of treating others unfairly. In Section 3.7, I argue that if the argument fails on the theoretical level, it also fails on the practical level as a defense of Socrates. Just because Socrates, or even his students, were capable of self-mastery, it does not follow that they treated others fairly.

Snell, Bruno. *The Discovery of the Mind: The Greek Origins of European Thought.* New York: Harper & Row, 1960.

Snell argues that Greek tragedy represents the discovery of the mind, understood as the inner self with its inner conflicts and deliberations. He claims that in Homer, individuals make decisions in response to external stimuli; but in the tragedies we see something very different.

Stone, I. F. *The Trial of Socrates.* Toronto: Little, Brown & Co., 1988.

This book is invaluable. It should be read by all philosophers and political theorists, because it presents the unvarnished facts about Socrates that are generally ignored, in order to inspire reverence and subservience when appealing to the spurious argument from authority, to which scholars remain depressingly vulnerable. Unlike Dodds in *The Greeks and the Irrational,* Stone does not think that the age of Greek enlightenment was also a witch hunt against philosophers, sophists, and free thinkers. His argument against Dodds is as compelling as it is conclusive (pp. 231–247). Stone regards the case of Socrates to be an exception in an otherwise tolerant society, which was nothing short of the school of Hellas, where thinkers flocked. The thesis of Stone's book is that the conviction of Socrates was a crime of Athens against her own democracy and her own devotion to freedom of thought and speech. He tells us that his goal in writing the book is not to excuse what Athens did, but merely to "mitigate the city's crime" and "remove some of the stigma" left by the trial on democracy and on Athens (p. xi).

Nevertheless, Stone does not depart from the traditional view of the trial as the conviction of an innocent man. He regards Socrates as a wrongheaded enemy of Athenian democracy, who was convicted merely for his ideas, and his exercise of the

Athenian freedom to express them. Despite his brilliance and his investigative talents, Stone stops short of drawing the conclusions that his evidence calls for. He finds nothing that connects Socrates with the crimes of his radical oligarchic students. He accepts at face value Xenophon's claim that Critias hated Socrates and even passed a law during his reign of terror to stop Socrates from teaching, lest he whip up the youth against the tyranny of the Thirty. He interprets the refusal to obey the demand to convict Leon of Salamis as an act of civil disobedience by Socrates against Critias and the Thirty. I see it quite differently (Sections 1.2, 1.6, 3.2, and 3.3). Stone assumes that Socrates was as opposed to the regime of the Thirty as he was to the democracy. He is convinced that Socrates was neutral regarding the conflict between the democratic and the oligarchic parties in Athens. Stone concludes by arguing that Socrates could have successfully defended himself if only he had appealed to the importance of freedom of thought and speech, since these were Athenian values—the feature that made Athens what is was and lifted it above all other cities. I find this argument unconvincing (Section 3.9). See also my discussion of F. M. Burnyeat's review of Stone's book in this Bibliography.

Taylor, A. E. *Varia Socratica*. Oxford: James Parker & Co. 1911.

This is a collection of essays that includes "The Impiety of Socrates." In that essay, Taylor argues that Socrates was indeed guilty of impiety (p. 9). In the context of the Greek city-state, piety was displayed by honoring the gods in accordance with the cults authorized by the state (p. 7). By the same token, impiety was not a matter unbelief or atheism; nor was it a matter of having false beliefs about the gods that contradict the myths of Homer and Hesiod, since the latter were not doctrines, dogmas, or articles of faith. The real source of the difficulty is that Socrates was closely connected to the Pythagorean communities of northern and central Greece (p. 20). The secret religious practices of these communities were not authorized by the state, and may involve conduct that is contrary to Athenian interests. It follows that impiety is "also high treason" (p. 16). Taylor uses evidence from Plato's *Phaedo* and *Gorgias* to show that Socrates did indeed share orphic beliefs, which were not authorized by the state. See discussion in Section 2.7.

———. *Socrates.* New York: Doubleday, 1953.

Taylor provides an excellent biography of the early as well as the late Socrates. He thinks that the early dialogues of Plato are a reliable source of information on the historical Socrates. Plato's account of the trial and death of Socrates could not have been fabricated, since many people who were present at the trial and/or the death of Socrates would be reading it. Taylor also thinks that there is nothing in Xenophon that contradicts what Plato tells us about Socrates (pp. 22, 25, 30, 34). Yet, he is aware that if Xenophon's picture of Socrates was accurate, and Socrates was pious in the traditional sense, he would never have been prosecuted (p. 24). So, Taylor concludes that Xenophon conceals the more original aspects of Socrates' ideas and personality, which are revealed by Plato. Taylor is fully cognizant of the historical and political events that led up to the trial and conviction of Socrates. Nevertheless, he thinks that all the evidence against Socrates was circumstantial. Taylor regards the association of Socrates with Alcibiades, Critias, and Charmides as a "misfortune" (pp. 100, 115). Taylor denies that Socrates was the educator of Alcibiades or Critias for the reasons Plato provides in the *Apology*—namely that he had no pupils (pp. 111, 113). Taylor thinks that the heart of the animus against Socrates came from his Orphic religious views (pp.125-6). Even though Taylor makes a connection between religious mysticism and eroticism, he insists on the sexual purity of Socrates (p. 49), and notes that he was not accused of homosexuality, which Taylor believes (against all evidence to the contrary) would have been "an effective weapon in the hands of his accusers" (p. 49, note 3). In any case, Taylor thinks that it is his religious views that led Socrates to be extremely critical of the Athenian democracy and its democratic leaders on the ground that they did nothing to improve the souls of their subjects; in which case, their souls would continue to be entrapped in the prison of the body. Taylor recognizes that the religious mission of Socrates was also a political one, which required the proper regime to be achieved—a regime that was antithetical to the democratic one. As a result, he concludes that the real charge against him was "*incivisme*, disloyalty to the spirit of Athenian life" (p. 90). Surprisingly, none of Taylor's insights led him to suspect that Socrates' intellectual influence inspired or incited the conduct of Alcibiades, Critias, or Charmides. In contrast to Taylor, I argue in Section 4 that Plato's *Symposium* provides ample evidence of the powerful intellectual influence that Socrates had on his friends and associates. In contrast to Taylor, I show that there is a clear connection between the early and the late dialogues, and that the ideas of Plato in the late dialogues are the logical consequence of the Socratic ideas presented in the early dialogues.

Taylor, Charles. *Hegel and Modern Society*. New York: Cambridge University Press, 1979.

Following Hegel, Taylor romanticizes the pre-Socratic Greeks. He thinks that they were at one with nature and with their society. The idea that they were at one with nature cannot begin to account for their tragic perspective on human existence. The idea that they were at one with their society assumes that they identified the good with the ethos of their society, and were therefore not capable of taking a critical attitude that transcends the norms of their society. Such extravagant assumptions infantalize "the Greeks," and make them less interesting than they deserve.

Veyne, Paul. *Did the Greeks Believe in their Myths? An essay on the constitutive imagination* (1983). Translated by Paula Wissing. Chicago: University of Chicago Press: 1988.

This is a disturbingly postmodern work. Veyne's answer to the question is that of course the Greeks believed their myths because there is no truth apart from the myths of any society. See my discussion of Veyne in Section 7.5.

Vlastos, Gregory. *Socrates: Ironist and Moral Philosopher*. New York: Cornell University Press, 1991.

Vlastos claims that the greatness of Socrates is having made the "care of the soul" the business of everyone. Even if this was indeed the case, and that the "care of the soul" is to be understood in the universalistic spirit that transcends class and social status, as Vlastos maintains, then it must, at the very least, be pointed out that Euripides has a greater claim for having challenged this aristocratic sentiment unambiguously, and without the political and theological baggage that Socrates brought to the fore. For example, in *Electra* (415 BCE), Euripides makes the simple peasant the noblest of all the men in the play. In that play, Orestes recognizes this when he says, "There's no clear sign to tell the quality of a man," and that "wealth is a false standard" (372ff).

Vlastos, Gregory. "The Historical Socrates and Athenian Democracy." *Political Theory*, Vol. 11, No. 4 (Nov., 1983), pp. 495–516.

Vlastos argues that the Socrates of Xenophon is an oligarch in the classic sense of the term because he distinguishes between the "beautiful people" and the "necessary people" (i.e., the working classes). In this classic oligarchic view, only the former are entitled to rule the city. In contrast, the Socrates of Plato is not an oligarch but a democrat who prefers the constitution of Athens above all other constitutions, as indicated in Plato's *Crito*, where his loyalty to the Athenian *Laws* is supposedly the reason he refuses to escape, and maintains that the injustice towards him was not a function of the democratic constitution, but of the people who accused him. I reject these claims for reasons I provide in Sections 1.4, 1.5, 1.6, and 3.5. Vlastos acknowledges that the Socrates of Plato subscribed to a "royal art," which is a moral project intended to improve the souls of everyone in the city, including aliens, women, and slaves. In my view, the "care of the soul" is a quasi-theocratic political vision with all the authoritarianism, perversity, and oppression characteristic of theocratic efforts to save the soul (Section 4).

Waterfield, Robin. *Why Socrates Died: Dispelling the Myths.* New York: W. W. Norton & Co., 2009.

This historical account of the democratic politics of Athens captures not only the factual elements, but also something of its spirit (Ch. 2). The thesis is that Socrates was a scapegoat who was killed for being a teacher of subversive ideas—ideas that were by no means confined to him—ideas that involved the radical questioning of the religious and political status quo; ideas that were the source of the social upheavals of fifth century Athens (pp. 201ff). The fact that his students included Critias and Alcibiades also made him a target. However, Waterfield does not think that the ideas of Socrates had anything to do with either the depravity or extremism of his students. On the contrary, he regards Socrates as a man of great virtue; he simply did not succeed in training his acolytes to lead the sort of moral and political revolution that he thought Athens required. He went willingly to his death as a scapegoat for Athens, as if he were the voluntary victim of the Thargelia—the annual ceremony in which Athenians rid themselves of the pollution that was the source of the displeasure of the gods by chasing some criminals out of the city and flogging them. This is an example of the conventional view that I challenge in this book.

Watmough, J. R. *Orphism*. New York: Cambridge University Press, 1934.

Watmough regards Orphism as the sublimation of the religion of Dionysus. He thinks that Protestantism had the same effect on Catholicism (p. 63). He writes: "The religious consciousness, bursting its too narrow confines, seems at once to soar upward and to plunge downward; and the onlooker is puzzled, and perhaps repelled, by the strange spectacle of a cult both more spiritual and less civilized than any within the range of established observance."

Weil, Simon. "The Iliad or the Poem of Force." *An Anthology*. Edited and introduced by Siân Miles. London: Virago Press, 1986.

Weil recognizes that the poem is an effort to bring home the harshness of human existence. Men and women alike, even when they are born to wealth and privilege, "yield to a harsh necessity." Men are tormented by the constant threat of violent death, and women live in continual dread of slavery. In contrast to Jasper Griffin's view that the Greeks won because they deserved to win and the Trojans lost because they deserved to lose, Weil rightly observes that there were no winners in the epic.

Winspear, Alban D. and Silverberg, Tom. *Who Was Socrates?* New Jersey: The Cordon Company, 1939.

This book has been a source of inspiration to me, since it tries to make sense of the case for the prosecution. The thesis of the book is that there is a correlation between social forces and intellectual ones. According to Winspear and Silverberg, the religious skepticism of the natural scientists and the ethical relativism of the Sophists were part of an intellectual revolution that questioned the established aristocratic order. When Aristophanes wrote the *Clouds* in 423 Socrates was part of this intellectual skepticism, which was allied with democratic politics (p. 85). In contrast, the opponents of these skeptical trends were allied with the "ancient constitution," which is a code word for the old aristocratic order. Aristophanes was a conservative who found the skeptical intellectual trends threatening to the old order; mocking these new intellectual trends was intended as biting social satire. Socrates must have been well known enough at the time to be the butt of the jokes. However, when Plato wrote the *Symposium*, which is set in 416 or 415, Plato presents Socrates and Aristophanes as being on very friendly terms. Winspear and Silverberg surmise that the ideas of Socrates underwent a radical intellectual transformation, which Plato tells us about in the *Phaedo* (See my discussion in Section 2.6). Abandoning the skepticism of the Sophists, he allied himself with the Pythagoreans. This intellectual shift went hand in hand with a political shift away from the democratic to the aristocratic faction in Athenian politics. Winspear and Silverberg reject the claims of Socratic apologists that Socrates was above the political fray. Unlike those who believe that the charge of impiety was simply a cover for the political case against Socrates, Winspear and Silverberg agree with A. E. Taylor that the religious charge amounted to "subverting the state religion and bringing in Pythagorean divinities" (p. 79).

Winspear, Alban Dewes. *The Genesis of Plato's Thought*. New York: The Dryden Press, 1940.

A study of Plato's thought in light of the history and politics of his time. It is refreshingly free from the aura of serene reverence that books on Plato often exude. In his own words, he has tried to protect researchers from "the loving distortions of discipleship" (p. v).

Wood. Ellen Meiksins, and Neal. "Socrates and Democracy: A Reply to Gregory Vlastos." *Political Theory*, Vol. 14, No. 1(February, 1986), pp. 55–82.

This is a definitive critique of Gregory Vlastos, "The Historical Socrates and Athenian Democracy," described in this Bibliography. They rightly argue that the idea that Plato's Socrates is democratic is preposterous. The Woods think that the trial of Socrates may have been unjust, but "the suspicions aroused among the Athenian people by Socrates' close associations" (pp. 71–2) were completely reasonable. They suspect that Plato's sentiments in the *Seventh Letter* (324d) are likely to have been true for Socrates. Namely, that Socrates supported the regime of the Thirty, then was shocked by its violent crimes, and refused to participate in them. In the final analysis, I reject this seemingly plausible reading on the ground that, if it were true, then Socrates would have shown some remorse during his trial for what he unwittingly inspired (Section 3.3).

White, Mary. "Greek Tyranny." *Phoenix*, Vol. 9 (1955), pp. 1–8.

Argues that "the earliest tyrants in Athens were not demagogues for the simple reason that there was no *demos* upon whose shoulders they could rise." Instead, the earliest tyrants were the successful champions of the middle class against the restrictive aristocracies of birth. The resentment of the middle classes was connected to the development of the hoplite phalanx, which required training, discipline and effective co-operation. As the phalanx replaced the aristocratic cavalry in warfare, the hoplites, who were also the rising middle class, resented the aristocratic monopoly on political power. The earliest tyrants championed the middle class. Their triumph over the aristocracies set the stage for the eventual development of democracy. In other words, the early Greek tyrannies were *sui generis* and must be studied in the context of their time. In its earliest use, the term *tyrannos* denoted absolute or royal power—human or divine. Zeus was *tyrannos*; Oedipus was *tyrannos*. It was used to refer to Oriental kings and satraps as well as to Greek rulers. It was used to refer to all one-man rule regardless of its character. It did not acquire its derogatory meaning as despotic power based on fraud and violence until the fifth century when the tyrants had been driven out of Athens, and Athenian democracy won its glorious victories over the Persians. At that point, tyranny was contrasted with democracy and all forms of one-man rule were reviled—the Persian monarchy and the Greek tyrants alike. This revulsion was illustrated by the honor paid to Harmodios and Aristogeiton, as the tyrannicides whose statues stood in the Agora, and who were celebrated by a song saying that they slew the tyrant and gave equality and law to Athens (by killing Hipparchos, the brother of the ruling tyrant, they accelerated the fall of the tyranny). In the famous Persian debate on political theory (*Histories* 3.80–82), Herodotus allows the champion of democracy to use tyranny pejoratively by contrasting it with freedom, even though Herodotus did not necessarily use the term pejoratively. Thucydides is more consistent in using *tyrannos* to refer to an illegal and despotic form of government. White claims that the difference between the two historians mirrors the difference in usage between the Ionian (Herodotus) and the Attic (Thucydides) use of the term. It is worth noting that Socrates served his city as a hoplite.

Williams, Bernard. *Shame and Necessity*. Berkeley: University of California Press, 1993.

> I am deeply indebted to this outstanding work. Williams provides a critique of the "progressive" approach to moral thought in general and Greek ideas in particular. The progressive view assumes that the history of ethical concepts from the ancient

world to the modern one can be understood as a story of development, progress, greater depth, sophistication, and complexity. In this view, the ancient or archaic Greeks (i.e., the Homeric Greeks) are akin to children, in comparison to our own moral sensibilities. Williams rejects this progressive trajectory not only on the ground that it does not allow us to understand the archaic Greeks, but also because it provides us with a false picture of ourselves. In his view, a less patronizing attitude would address serious shortcomings in the modern (i.e., Kantian) understanding of morality. At the heart of the matter is the distinction between a shame culture and a guilt culture. Williams agrees with A.W. H. Adkins (*Merit and Responsibility*) and others that Greek culture was primarily a shame culture. However, far from thinking that shame and guilt are two very distinct ways of looking at morality, Williams thinks that there is considerable overlap between them.

The upshot of Williams's book is that we should not congratulate ourselves too much for our moral superiority in comparison to the archaic Greeks. We are more like Aristotle—the man who not only accepted slavery, but defended it! In contrast, the ancient Greeks regarded slavery as horrible and unnatural. Aristotle, being the Socratic that he was, was unwilling to accept the unjust structure of the world. Williams observes that the racialized character of American slavery makes it akin to the Aristotelian notion of slavery as a "necessary identity" (i.e., people whose physical appearance alone determines their social position as slaves). According to Williams, there is a Christianized Aristotelianism that thrives in the modern world with its preoccupation with "necessary identities," or social identities sanctioned by nature. This is particularly true where the sexes are concerned. It is not merely a feature of religious communities; it thrives in the pseudoscientific guise of sociobiology. Even though the latter has replaced Aristotelian teleology with natural selection, it still espouses "necessary identities," not as a result of teleology, but as a result of natural selection. Williams concedes that modern liberalism has been an enemy of "necessary identities." It has set itself the task of framing institutions of social justice that mitigate the effects of chance and necessity on the lives of individuals. However, Williams thinks that liberalism accepts whatever cannot be mitigated. In other words, it accepts the deep injustice in the structure of the world, a world in which the flourishing and worthwhile lives of some are bought at the expense of the toil, oppression, and suffering of others.

Williams concludes (and I wish he was right) that we are living in an age "beyond Christianity" and even beyond its Kantian and Hegelian legacies. He thinks that we are closer to pre-Socratic Greeks than any other age. We know that history is not moving towards a grand purpose. We know that there is no Leibnizian cost-benefit analysis to prove that all the suffering will be worthwhile in the end. He thinks we are ready to acknowledge the "hideous costs of many human achievements that we value, including this reflective sense itself." In short, he thinks that we are ready to acknowledge that "we are not made for the world and the world was not made for us." I share Williams' critique of moral autonomy, which I apply to Socrates (Section 6.3).

Wilson, Emily. *The Death of Socrates: Hero, Villain, Chatterbox, Saint.* London: Profile Books, 2007.

This book is an impressive account of the many ways in which Socrates has been regarded in the history of the West, starting with his fellow Athenians, antiquity, Christianity, the Middle Ages, the Renaissance, the Enlightenment, the Romantic Age, and the age of totalitarianism.

Xenophon (pseudo). *The Constitution of the Athenians.* Trans. by J. L. Marr and P. J. Rhodes. Oxford: Oxbow Books, 2008.

This work is known by modern scholars as *The Old Oligarch* and its authorship is uncertain. It is a political pamphlet that reads like a tirade against democracy and in favor of the rule of the "better people." Marr and Rhodes think that the importance of the Old Oligarch is that it represents the "instinctive, old-fashioned class prejudice" of certain upper-class Athenians, which came to the fore after the Athenian defeat in Sicily in 413 and culminated in the oligarchic coups that overthrew of the democratic constitution in 411 and 404 BCE. They suspect that the author might have been a student of the Sophist Antiphon, who was believed to be the master-mind of the oligarchic revolution of 411. However, they do not believe that this attitude was a general characteristic of the upper classes as a whole. The vast majority of the wealthy elite was loyal to the democratic constitution and took advantage of the opportunities it provided to pursue successful political careers—Cimon, Pericles, Nicias, and even Thucydides played significant roles as elected generals and important leaders in the assembly. Nevertheless, there was "hard-core antidemocratic irreconcilables," whose opportunity came after the disaster in Sicily in 413 (p. 20). I believe that Socrates belonged to that hard-core of antidemocratic irreconcilables (Sections 1.4, 1.5, and 1.6).

INDEX

A
Accusation of Socrates, by Polycrates, 2, 89
Achilles, 84, 136, 138–139, 143, 153, 156, 159, 162, 180, 182, 184–185
Adkins, A. W. H., 160–162, 170n120
Aeschines, 2, 92, 110, 128n44
Aeschylus, *Persians*, 142
Agamemnon, 67n65, 144, 153–154, 156, 157, 159, 160, 162, 172, 177
Alcibiades, 2–9, 11, 12, 14–19, 23, 25, 33n85, 40, 43, 44, 71–73, 82, 87, 88, 93, 94, 107–111, 114, 127n31, 151, 160, 178, 187, 200, 201
Amnesty, 11–13, 20
Amputations, 26, 83, 95, 99n56
Antigone, by Sophocles, 78, 175, 177
Anytus, 1, 12, 56
Aphrodite, 61, 134, 152, 153, 155, 157
Apollo, 4, 46, 108, 117, 134, 139, 150
Arginusae, generals at, 76–77
Aristocracy, 20, 22, 83
Aristotle
  hubris, 151, 152

Poetics, 171
Asceticism, 42, 59, 111, 136–137, 172
Atheism, 24, 40, 55–57, 134, 206
Athena, 11, 49, 54, 58, 134, 144, 145, 150
Athenian Empire, 4, 142
Athenian Stranger, 21, 118–119, 123
Athens, 2–10, 12–17, 19–25, 27, 36, 37, 40, 42, 43, 49, 60, 62, 72–79, 85, 92–96, 104, 105, 110, 119, 121, 125, 142, 151, 160, 163, 175, 178, 179, 188, 205
Attica, 4, 42
Authoritarianism, 21, 90, 94, 103, 180, 197, 200–202, 205
Autonomy, 173, 180
  See also Moral autonomy

B
Barbarians, 142
Bible, 131, 141, 190–192
Body
  as prison of the soul, 210
  as tomb of the soul, 137
Brickhouse, Thomas C., 63n7, 67n84
Burke, Edmund, 15
Burnet, John, 74, 97n9, 197
Burnyeat, F. M., 67n62

C

Candy-makers, 18, 83
Care of the soul, 16, 23, 32n78, 82, 86, 104, 105, 114, 116, 117, 119, 120, 123–126, 201, 202
Carthage, 5
Catholic Church, 90, 122, 130n104, 202
Cavalry, 16
Charmides, 2, 8–11, 19, 26, 30n35, 71–75, 82, 87, 88, 93, 94, 96, 109, 110, 114, 124, 160, 178, 187, 201, 213
Christianity, 35, 41, 42, 88, 89, 131, 149, 179, 188, 189, 191, 196n61, 197, 199, 203–205, 210
Christianized Platonism, 90, 201
Christians, 1, 5, 35, 42, 62, 89, 90, 137, 139–141, 157, 158, 190–192, 198, 199, 204, 206, 210, 212
Civil religion, 2, 36–42
Cleon, 5
Clouds, by Aristophanes, 56, 81
Condorcet, Marquis de, 90
Conservatives, 15, 57, 166n40, 210
Constitutions, 7, 9, 13, 22, 23, 34n104, 38, 77, 83, 98n30
Cosmic justice, 5, 61, 143–149, 163, 173, 190–192, 196n61, 199
Courage, 50, 74, 77, 88, 106, 113, 127n31, 128n62, 134, 139, 140, 155, 160, 166n40, 172, 174, 177, 189
Crime, 1, 11, 23, 26, 35, 55, 59, 73, 88, 89, 91, 93–96, 122, 131, 151, 168n88, 173, 190–192, 213
Crime fiction, 190–192
Critias, 2, 8–12, 19, 23–27, 30n47, 71–75, 82, 84, 87, 88, 92–94, 96, 99n56, 110, 114, 124, 160, 178, 187, 201, 213

Croton, in Southern Italy, 61
Cyclops, 146, 147

D

Death, 1, 2, 5, 9, 12, 19, 21, 25, 28n2, 36, 39, 59–61, 66n59, 75, 78, 79, 80, 89, 91, 103, 105, 106, 111, 112, 121, 122, 132–134, 136, 138–140, 144, 146, 148, 150, 151, 156, 160–163, 172–178, 181, 184, 185, 190, 204–206, 209, 210
Delian League, 142, 239, 248
Deluded crank, 186
Demeter, 43–44, 134
Democracy, 3, 5–17, 19–23, 26–27, 31n61, 32n79, 43, 57, 62, 73, 74, 77, 79, 83, 91–95, 106, 120, 121, 214
Diagoras, of Melos, 44
Dionysus, 58, 124
Dodds, E. R., 41, 92, 93, 153, 192
Dogmas, 1, 38, 40, 122, 123, 133, 163, 205–206, 210
Dualism, 59, 137–142, 163

E

Eleusinian Mysteries, 43
Empire, 4, 6, 7, 30n34, 90, 119, 140, 142
Enlightenment, 41, 90, 92, 179, 197, 203–206
Euben, Peter, 98n30, 194n42
Euripides, 34n112, 61, 67n65, 126n14, 142, 143, 155, 156, 208
Euthyphro, 35, 36, 44–49, 52–53, 66n56, 74, 105, 106, 149
Evil
 gratuitous, 26, 93, 158
 necessary evil, 26, 84, 99n56

F

Fear, 4, 6, 7, 10, 12, 20, 24, 41, 80–81, 93, 120, 123, 134, 149, 173–175, 181, 183, 203
Finley, M. I., 65n35, 130n126
Fisher, N. R. E., 151
Foot, Philippa, 81
Foucault, Michel, 206, 209–211
Freedom, 7, 22, 30n34, 38, 78, 91, 93, 94, 106, 114, 119, 121, 153, 197, 199, 202, 204, 206, 207, 212
Freedom of religion, 38
Freud, 174, 200, 225–226

G

Gadfly, 27, 82
Geneva, 62
Gods, 1, 4, 5, 24, 25, 35–43, 45–55, 57, 58, 60, 63n2, 73, 84, 91, 93, 104, 107, 109, 120, 122, 123, 131–137, 139, 141, 143–146, 148–158, 162–164, 173, 175, 181, 182, 187, 191, 198, 200–203, 208–210
  moralization of, 51, 63n7
Guilt, 1, 2, 35, 40, 45, 46, 60, 71, 72, 77, 80, 87, 109, 148, 151, 153–159, 163, 174, 175, 178, 179, 182, 183, 185–187, 190, 192, 197–200
Gyges, 115, 132

H

Hades, 43–44, 58, 60, 134, 184
Hamilton, Edith, 99n47, 214n2
Harm, 37, 51, 52, 72, 80, 84, 94, 136, 150, 157, 182, 187
Harrison, Jane, 236–237
Hecabe, 138, 155–156
Hecabe, by Euripides, 155
Hector, 136, 138–139, 159, 162, 163
Hegel, G. W. F., 176–180, 197, 199
Heidegger, Martin, 96
Helen, of Troy, 155
Hellenism, 142, 205, 218, 245, 246
Hera, 134, 137, 139, 153
Heracles, 49, 100n67, 153–154, 174, 181, 182, 184
Heresy, 1, 36, 39–40
Hermae, 42–44, 57
  See also Herms
Herms, 42
Herodotus, 37, 39, 142, 157, 175
Heroic, 3, 27, 115, 138, 177, 184, 185, 188
Hesiod, 51, 58, 64n12, 149
Homer
  gods of, 25, 45, 47, 134, 137, 146, 149, 209
  Iliad, 135, 141–143, 148, 156, 161, 190
  Odyssey, 54, 136, 143, 150
  warrior ethos, 159 (*see also* Manly virtues)
Hubris, 5, 8, 25, 46, 54–55, 61, 79, 84, 149–153, 187, 197, 202–203, 213
  See also hybris
Hybris, 66n60, 167n81, 168n90

I

Immortality, 24, 25, 89, 111, 133, 163, 205, 209
Imperialistic hawks, 5
Impiety, 1, 2, 8, 11, 35, 36, 38–44, 47, 49, 55–57, 60, 73–74, 80, 122
Incantations, 58, 59
Incitement, 73, 93, 94
Indulgences, 59, 133

Iphigenia, 164, 230, 234, 240
Islamic Imam, 96

J
Jesus, 53, 84, 88–90, 92, 105, 106, 153, 163, 170n122
Jihad, 54, 62, 199, 210
Job, *in Bible*, 190
Jurors, 31n61, 80
Justice, 4, 5, 10, 11, 17, 18, 37, 47–55, 60, 61, 77, 78, 81, 87–90, 106, 112, 113, 115, 131, 132, 143–150, 160–163, 172–176, 181–183, 185, 187, 190–192, 199, 207, 208, 211, 213

K
Kaufmann, Walter, 155, 173
Kierkegaard, 25
Knowledge is power, 196n60

L
Leon of Salamis, 74–76
Leto, 150
Lies
 lie in the soul, 132, 153, 155, 159, 199
 of Homer, 132, 133
 of Plato, 56, 153
Lloyd-Jones, Hugh, 146, 148
Lycon, 1

M
Machiavelli, N., 84, 99n56
MacIntyre, Alasdair, 176, 177, 184
Manly Virtues, 132, 159–163
McPherran, Mark L., 63n7

Mecca, 199
Medical analogy, 82–84, 86, 95
Megara, 11, 28n11, 33n96
Meletus, 1, 12, 28n2, 55, 56, 94
Melians, 49–50
Memorabilia, by Xenophon, 72, 73, 82, 93
Menelaus, 138, 146, 147, 155, 156, 211
Mill, J. S., 91, 94
Monarchy, 22, 83
Monument, for Critias, 26–27
Moral autonomy, 173, 180
Morality, 24, 45, 47, 49, 52, 53, 57–59, 88, 92, 106, 113, 122, 142, 143, 146, 148, 152, 153, 163, 178–180, 182, 183, 185, 187, 188, 198, 202, 203
 morality of shame vs. guilt, 182
Moralization of the gods, 51, 63n7
Myth, 25, 50, 57, 59, 89, 115, 132–134, 136, 149, 150, 153, 189, 199, 204, 206–211
 true and false myths, 132

N
Nemesis, 150, 173
New Testament, 62
Nietzsche, Friedrich, 157, 160, 173, 187–190, 195n58, 200, 206–209, 211
Nihilism, 197, 205–211
Noble lies, 177
Nussbaum, Martha, 193n16

O
Odysseus, 49, 54, 136, 144–147, 159, 167n72, 182–184
Odyssey, by Homer, 54, 136, 143

Oedipus, 174–177
Old Oligarch, 13–18, 20, 26, 32n79, 33n85, 72, 120
Old Testament, 61
Oligarchic coup, 404 BCE, 92, 160
Oligarchic coup, 411 BCE, 9, 13, 92
Oligarchic radicals, 13–21, 23, 42, 93
  See also Old Oligarch
Oligarchy, 7, 13, 19, 20, 22, 26, 32n79, 75, 83, 119–120
Orphism, 57–62, 133
Ostracism, 223, 224
Otto, Walter, 46, 143

P
Parable of the ship, 82, 84, 85, 86
Paris, in Iliad, 148
Parker, Robert, 63n9, 64n22
Pederasty, 109, 110
Pericles, 3–5, 14, 17–19, 29, 39–41, 72, 113, 114, 201, 236, 245, 263
Peloponnesian War, 2, 3, 5, 7, 8, 19, 20, 40, 60, 142
Perictione, 9
Persephone, 43, 44
Persia, 7, 20, 21, 218, 223, 239
Persians, by Aeschylus, 142
Phalanx, 259
Philistines, 62, 141
Philoctetes, by Sophocles, 173, 180, 181
Philosophy, as practice of dying, 60, 136
Physicians of the soul, 119, 133, 201
  See also Medical analogy
Piety, 35, 36, 38, 44–49, 51–55, 57, 61, 74, 113, 120, 150, 152, 197, 199, 202–203, 210
Plague, 3–5, 19, 125, 174, 197
Plato
  Alcibiades I, 59, 73

Apology, 47, 55, 75, 81, 126, 185
Charmides, 9, 71, 74, 82, 96
  and Critias, 74, 82, 96, 124
  critique of Homer, 131–170
  critique of tragic poets, 62
Crito, 77, 78
  early and late dialogues, 103, 104
Euthyphro, 35, 36, 44–47
Gorgias, 57, 84
Laws, 21, 52, 103, 115, 116, 120, 123, 125, 202
  legend of Socrates, 91, 187, 213
Lesser Hippias, 194n33
  lie in the soul, 132, 153, 199
  medical analogy, 82–84
Meno, 41, 114
  parable of the ship, 82, 84, 85
Phaedo, 19, 56, 111
Phaedrus, 44, 200
Protagoras, 2, 18, 104, 112, 113, 118
Republic, 20–22, 45, 81, 87, 114, 115, 116, 133, 136, 141, 153, 181, 185
  royal art, 114
Seventh Letter, 95, 125
  and Socrates, 21–23
  Socratic paradox, 104
Statesman, 21–22, 83, 84
Symposium, 2, 15, 44, 56, 73, 104
  thought experiment, 185, 186
Timaeus, 2, 198
  world soul, 187
Pluralism, 212
Plutarch, 12, 40
Political obligation, 77–79
Polycrates, 2, 82, 89
Popper, Karl, 91, 103
Poseidon, 134, 146, 147, 150
Postmodernism, 205, 206, 209, 211
Priam, in Iliad, 155
Priestly cast, 69n123

Priests, 38, 90, 149
Prometheus, 50–51
Propaganda, 115, 123
Protagoras, 2, 18, 19, 40, 41, 50, 104, 106, 110, 112–114, 116–118
Psychic intervention, 153, 157, 158, 224, 226
Punishment, 4, 25, 42, 59–61, 77, 89, 112, 137, 146, 147, 149, 152, 155, 157–158, 162, 163, 173, 183, 191, 205
Purges, 26, 83, 84, 93, 124

Q
Queen Elizabeth II, 38

R
Radicalizing influence, ix
Remorse, 76, 94, 95, 177
Responsibility, 19, 54, 55, 94, 95, 132, 153–159, 175, 199, 200
Revolutionaries, 2, 7, 152, 209, 210
Rohde, Erwin, 65n43
Rome, 1, 197

S
Sachs, David, 87
Sacrifices, 11, 36, 38, 39, 42, 49, 52, 53, 91–92, 122, 135, 137, 140, 143, 161, 163, 164
Sailing, *see parable of the ship*
Sarpedon, in *Iliad*, 161
Scriptures, 1, 38, 163
Sicilian Expedition, 5, 6, 43
Silverberg, Tom, 68n95, 100n69
Sisyphus, 24, 25, 151
Smith, Nicholas D., 28n2, 63n2, 63n7, 67n84, 99n43

Snell, Bruno, 169n95
Socrates
and Achilles, 84, 136, 159, 185
and Alcibiades, 2, 8, 9, 11, 16, 19, 25, 40, 72, 73, 82, 88, 94, 107–111, 178, 187
atheism of, 55–57
charges against, 12, 45
and Critias, 23–27
divinely inspired, 51, 55, 80, 86, 116, 180, 200
as gadfly of Athens, 27
and Heidegger, 96
impiety of, 57, 60
and Jesus, 88–90
as just man, 52, 173, 180
Orphism of, 57–62
on piety, 35, 53
and Plato, 21–23
religion of, 25, 44, 60, 122, 124, 136, 141, 205
trances of, 55, 107, 190, 200
trial of, 8, 12, 44, 77, 92, 93
Socratic paradox, 104–107, 112, 114, 125, 200
Sophocles, 78, 143, 173–175, 177, 180–187
Spartans, 3, 4, 7–11, 13, 17, 20, 25–26, 28n11, 49–50, 78, 94, 117, 118, 122, 123
Statesmanship, 15, 16, 86, 112–114
Stone, I. F., 20, 40, 47, 75, 92, 93
Syracuse, 5, 6, 18, 23, 42, 124, 125

T
Tartarus, 58–60
Taylor, A. E., 12, 33n96, 57, 60, 61, 75, 81, 87, 91
Thebes, 11, 19, 20, 174–175, 177
Theramenes, 10, 75
Thirty Tyrants, 8–11

Thrasybulus, 10, 12
Thucydides, 3–5, 7, 8, 18, 40, 43, 44, 79
Titans, 58
Tragedy, 5, 172–178, 181, 184, 187–192
Tragic poets, 62, 123, 132, 143, 171–196, 211
Triremes, 6, 14
Trojan Women, by Euripides, 143, 155
Tyranny, 10, 20, 21, 79, 83, 84, 90, 91, 122, 177, 203, 210, 213

U
Unexamined life, 95

V
Veyne, Paul, 207–209, 211
Virtue, 4, 47, 49, 71, 80, 82, 88, 92, 94, 104–107, 109, 111–115, 118, 119, 122, 123–125, 133, 145, 146, 149, 176, 177, 184, 191, 193n16, 194n22, 196n60, 198, 200, 202, 221, 227, 231, 240, 241, 257
Vlastos, Gregory, 41, 74, 81, 88, 91–93, 104–106, 197

W
Warrior ethos, 159, 161
  See also Manly virtues
Watmough, J. R., 65n47, 69n123
Wealth, 4, 13, 15, 16, 20, 43, 114, 115, 119–120, 145–146, 151, 152
Weil, Simon, 167n76
Williams, Bernard, 98n28, 154, 165n13, 173, 183, 185, 186, 211
Winspear, Alban D., 147
Witch-hunts, 92
Wood, Ellen Meiksins, 75, 98n30
Wood, Neal, 75, 98n30

X
Xenophon, 2, 8, 13, 14, 20, 40, 71–74, 76, 79, 82, 87, 89, 93, 94, 103, 113

Z
Zeus, 46, 50–52, 56, 58, 81, 106, 134, 135, 137, 139, 143–147, 150, 156–157
Zulus, 140, 141

The manufacturer's authorised representative in the EU is Springer Nature Customer Service Centre GmbH, Europaplatz 3, 69115 Heidelberg, Germany. If you have any concerns regarding our products, please contact ProductSafety@springernature.com

Printed and bound by CPI Group (UK) Ltd, Croydon, CR0 4YY
23/03/2026
02076736-0011